VENGEANCE IS OURS

The Church In Dominion

by

Albert James Dager

Sword
Publishers
Redmond, Washington

All Scripture quotations are taken from the King James Version of the Bible, unless otherwise indicated.

First Printing   July, 1990

Cover illustration & design: Heiko Vogler

VENGEANCE IS OURS: The Church In Dominion

Copyright © 1990 Albert James Dager

Sword Publishers
P.O. Box 290
Redmond, WA 98073-0290
(206) 391-7315

Library of Congress Catalog Card Number 90-090253
Trade edition ISBN 0-9626632-0-4

Dedicated first to the King of kings and Lord of lords, true God and Savior of the world.

And to Jean, my wife and faithful companion in ministry.

With special thanks to my father who taught me early the values of honesty and diligence, and my mother whose undying faith in me was more than I deserved.

Thanks also to the many friends who have helped in so many ways. I had intended to acknowledge by name those who contributed research material, editing skills, and financial assistance, but after some prayer I realized that a book such as this could have adverse repercussions on those involved in its production. Therefore, I came to the conclusion that I would be acting more responsibly for their welfare by not mentioning them. Knowing their spiritual maturity, I am also aware that recognition isn't important to them; their ministry is to the Lord, not for their own benefit. But they all know my personal gratitude and heart of love for their kind assistance.

Contents

===
===

Introduction

Christians everywhere are in a life-and-death struggle for their Faith. In some countries that struggle is manifested through physical persecution: imprisonment, torture, death. In Western nations—particularly in the United States—Christians are relatively free to pursue their beliefs (as long as they don't step on the wrong toes). Here the struggle is not so much perceived through physical reprisals, as it is through the world's values encroaching upon individual believers as well as upon entire churches.

For the most part, the churches in the West have become stagnated; they've either fallen into a dead formalism, or adopted a fervent religious spirit, both of which are impotent in the face of life's tribulations and the world's evils. Some are nothing more than showcases for pastors whose self-serving charisma keeps their congregations feeding black holes of financial ambition. The spiritual sustenance given in return is little more than abusive admonition to get in step with the pastor's current vision. Because so many of the leaders are void of understanding, their congregations lack spiritual discernment.

In addition, Christians are lulled into conformity to the world's values through constant exposure to television, movies, music and other mass communications media. For these reasons the holiness to which the Lord has called His people is little evident in most who call themselves Christians.

Faced with a world mired in ever-increasing evil, those churches that still adhere to God's truth have found themselves in conflict with political and social systems that threaten the fabric of family life and flaunt in God's face humanity's basest sins: abortion, homosexuality, crime, drug abuse, rebellion, ugliness of every sort characteristic of the unregenerate human soul. In its weakened condition, it seems as if the Church is doomed to a scant existence through the lives of a faithful few who refuse to bow their knees to the Baal of human philosophy and worldly pleasure.

But there is a new militancy stirring in the breasts of many in reaction to these evils. Crys of "enough is enough!" resound from pulpits and in the Christian media. Spiritual warfare seminars are attracting tens of thousands who desire to learn how to "take back from Satan what he has stolen." A call for vengeance upon God's enemies and a restructuring of society under godly principles is being heard in ever-widening circles. It's as if the proverbial sleeping giant is becoming aroused to once and for all throw off the fetters of lilliputian spirits that have kept the Church in bondage.

Many are working to bring about the day when, not only throughout the United States, but throughout the world, the Church will reign in righteousness, and will cause every knee to bow and every tongue to confess that Jesus Christ is Lord to the glory of God (Philippians 2:10). Every enemy that has shaken his fist at the Creator will find himself either destroyed from off the face of the earth, or in submission to the rule of His saints.

Some Questions Raised

The vengeance sought by those demanding righteousness in society has raised questions: Is it the Church's responsibility to take control of society and reconstruct it in accordance with God's Law? Shouldn't the Church content itself with preaching the Gospel and suffering at the hands of the ungodly? On the other hand, why should we allow evil to flourish in our midst without taking measures to ensure that it will not overtake any area of life in which we have influence? Is it not God's mandate to the Church that we do everything possible to conform society to His rule?

Regardless on which side of these issues Christians find themselves, one thing is certain: until we do reign over the kingdoms of this earth, we are called to be witnesses of Jesus Christ to all the nations. We are to demonstrate His Kingdom in our own lives in order to bring the Kingdom into the lives of those we touch.

As much as we desire to see righteousness prevail on earth, we cannot fulfill the Great Commission if we continue to allow ourselves to be influenced by the world's philosophies, even when couched in Christian jargon and preached from the pulpits of our churches. The day of accountability has come for the Church to be the Church. And there will no longer be any excuse for being spectator Christians, warming the pews of false teachers who tickle our ears with flights of fancy.

A Challenge To Test The Spirits

Into every Christian's life come genuine challenges to our intellectual honesty and, more importantly, to our commitment to God's truth. Such challenges are all the greater when we realize that persons whom we've held in high regard are inadvertently or even knowingly leading us astray. The greatest challenge facing the Church today is the discernment to know who is preaching the truth and who is preaching mere half truths which will lead people down the path of spiritual enslavement.

It isn't difficult to accept the truth about aberrant teachings and dangerous practices of non-Christian cults; Christian bookstores are replete with publications on cult belief systems and activities. But the same bookstores sell publications which, though not associated with specific cults, contain false teachings under the guise of "deep truths" and "new revelations." Many such teachings are gaining acceptance among a growing number of Christians, and are increasingly finding expression in the Christian media.

Because this book strikes at false teachings ascending within the Church, it has been with a great deal of pain and personal soul-searching that it was written. Certainly it will have an impact upon those propagating these false teachings, as well as upon those who learn from them. Certainly it will cause loyalties to be broken.

So be it. If loyalty to anyone takes precedence over loyalty to God and His truth as revealed in Scripture, then that loyalty must be broken. Jesus taught this very thing when He said, "He that loveth father or mother more than me is not worthy of me; and he that loveth son or daughter more than me is not worthy of me" (Matthew 10:37). In Luke 14:26, He goes even further by saying that if we love even *our own lives* more than we love Him we are not worthy of Him. If we are expected to hold allegiance to Jesus, even above allegiance to our families and our very own lives, how much more should we be loyal to Him above teachers, no matter how they impress us with their knowledge and eloquent oratory.

Some Serious Considerations

Though the message this book brings may be difficult for some to receive, I implore all who read it to pray that God will help you receive whatever truths He has for you herein; whatever may be of my own human reasoning I pray will fall by the wayside. I pray also for His protection from the enemy who would distort these words in the reader's mind and misrepresent my motive for bringing them to light.

This book was written with full awareness of my own vulnerability. I admit that the things I have witnessed from some whose teachings I question, have caused me to wonder whether they may not be from God. It is a fearful thing to think that I might in all sincerity cast aspersion upon true men of God whose work I may not understand. But I am convinced that what I present is the truth, offered with a heavy heart for those who, by necessity, must be named for their errors.

While I recognize that most will reject what I've stated, I urge the reader to lay aside prejudices and personal preferences for teachers and teachings. Receive this message in the spirit in which it is written: not as an attempt to sow discord among the brethren (of this I am sure to be accused), but as a humble attempt to shed the light of God's truth upon the darkness caused by teachings contrary to His Word.

The Church Will Not Be Defeated

As you read this book you may at first think that I am painting a picture of a defeated Church rather than a Church that will one day rule the earth. But I believe the real test of God's grace to sustain the Church is more evident in the midst of internal trouble than when all is going smoothly.

Historically, things have seldom gone smoothly for the true Church, although ecclesiastical systems which claimed apostolic authority did flourish. But these do not represent the true Church. The true Church, comprised of individual souls united by the indwelling presence of the Holy Spirit, has throughout history been persecuted by the dominant ecclesiastical systems. Outwardly the true Church has appeared defeated; but the power of God has always preserved a remnant of the faithful. No matter what Satan or men try to do to destroy the Church, whether through the introduction of damnable heresies, false teachings, persecutions, or compromise, the true Body of Christ will triumph in standing firm for God's truth.

One of the Church's greatest protections is the ability to discern truth from error. This can only be done by testing every teaching to see if it is in conformity to the spirit of the Word as well as to the letter of the Word. By the spirit of the Word I mean the Scriptures rightly divided according to the overall revelation of God, not just taken out of context to conform to one's religious biases.

I therefore encourage all who read this book to put it to the test. But no less do I encourage them to put to the test those teachings with which it deals. Let God judge men's hearts; that is not my intention. But each of us is responsible to judge what we are asked to believe.

PART I - PARADISE LOST

1
The Conflict Of The Ages

The spiritual battle for men's souls resides upon this single truth: that God is supreme and His creation must be subject to Him. In his rebellion against God, Satan ("Lucifer") originated the scheme to establish oneself as an equal to God (Isaiah 14:12-15). That was the nature of his temptation of Eve: ". . . ye shall be as gods, knowing good and evil" (Genesis 3:5). Satan's lie has three primary facets: man *is* God, or is *a* god, and man can become *like* God by acquiring certain knowledge needed to unlock the secrets of the universe. The essence of virtually all religious philosophy is the exaltation of the human spirit as a means to establish man as god over his own destiny.

Scripture chronicles man's attempts at godhood: the rebelliousness that led to the Flood and, afterwards, the Tower of Babel; the sorcery and witchcraft that dominated not only pagan cultures but even God's called-out people, Israel; and the heresies that were already at work within the Church during the time of the apostles and that continue today. Jewish Cabbalism, thought by some to be a phenomenon of the Middle Ages, is really a synthesis of apostate Judaism with the Egyptian mystery religion learned by the Israelites while in captivity. The resulting paganism in Israel was the cause of the revolts against God's prophets, who were sent to correct Israel and to turn her back to God's truth.

When the Church was established, the same spirit of rebellion was immediately at work to destroy the simplicity and purity of the Gospel; heretics led many into errors which either demeaned the person of Christ or exalted the position of the believer, or both. One such early heresy was gnosticism, which promised a form of salvation through acquisition of secret knowledge.

The Roots of Humanism

During the Church's early years, the Gnostics blended the ancient pagan mystery teachings with Christian teachings, thus devising esoteric interpretations of the Scriptures that remain with us today. Over the centuries, these polluted interpretations have resulted in many pseudo-Christian religious movements that pervert God's Word in order to justify the exaltation of humanity to the status of godhood.

Out of these arose deism, a philosophy of natural religion based on human reason rather than on revelation, and claiming that God has nothing to do with His creation; He just sort of wound up the universe and is letting it run down on its own. Deism, in one form or another, is the basic philosophy of most of the secret societies (Freemasonry, Rosicrucianism, Illuminism, etc.) whose hidden agenda was, and remains, the establishment of a moral, one-world society based on human reason and personal freedom.

Through these secret societies, kings have been dethroned and replaced by various socialistic and democratic governments. This was for a very good reason in terms of the secret powers' designs: kings and sovereign states stand in the way of a world society.

Because they lack the vested interest a sovereign ruler has in protecting his personal domain, democracies can more easily be enfolded into a world society. This is especially the case if wars of sufficient destructive force can be fomented to persuade the masses that the only answer to peace and safety lies in a world federation of states.

Western Civilization has largely been shaped by the esoteric philosophies of the secret societies working through the influence of members in strategic political positions. With the advance of mass communications technology in these last days, they have molded the thinking of the masses in a manner that has resulted in much outwardly perceived good, but in much inward evil.

Outwardly, the secret societies have helped formulate a sense of high purpose for man through the development of the arts and sciences. Inwardly, they have distorted the Gospel by introducing into society and into the churches esoteric philosophies that make man responsible for his own salvation. Today we know one product of deism by the name humanism.

Three Humanistic Views

Over the centuries, the basic humanism behind all of man's philosophies has essentially taken three forms: secular humanism, cosmic humanism, and Christian humanism ("Christian" in the philosophic sense of the word).

Secular humanism denies the reality of a personal God; man is seen as the highest order of intelligence in the universe, the product of billions of years of evolution. Most do not believe in an afterlife.

Cosmic humanism forms the basis of the New Age movement and related religious expressions, particularly Eastern mysticism.

It says that man is evolving toward a state of higher consciousness that will result in the attainment of godhood. Cosmic humanism is expressed through two basic philosophies: pantheism (everything is God and God is everything, and polytheism (there are many gods, the likes of which we will all eventually become).

Christian humanism recognizes the inherent values of Scripture, while denying its total inerrancy. Many even deny the basic tenets of the true Christian faith. It masquerades as Christianity by espousing biblical ethics while adopting a pluralistic attitude toward other forms of religious expression. Some forms of Christian humanism might accept the idea of a transcendent God, while others believe that God is within all people. Still others teach that God is both transcendent and immanent, similar to the beliefs of some forms of Eastern mysticism. Out of Christian humanism comes a wide spectrum of psuedo-Christian thought from liberation theology to modern ecumenism to positive thinking. These comprise what is called "new wave theology," and all are primarily concerned with the preservation of civilization, and the existing world system under a moralistic system of laws. The primary differences lie in the understanding of what constitutes morality.

Two Faces of Christian Humanism

The more liberal Christian humanists see man as intrinsically good, and regard references to man's sin nature as detrimental to a positive self-image. They are not necessarily opposed to the Gospel as long as it works for the individual's temporal good; but they regard any philosophy as equally acceptable.

Christian humanists are principally responsible for introducing psychology into the Church, specifically techniques such as inner healing, holistic health practices, and various forms of psychological counseling. Many adherents to these practices, however, are not aware of their underlying philosophy. They perceive only the surface good that they believe can be accomplished.

Another expression of Christian humanism is that which is found among Bible believers—those who hold strongly to most of the essential tenets of the Faith. They have been influenced by liberalism to the degree that they have accepted the validity of psychology and positive self-imaging. Many have also adopted a form of cosmic humanism, believing that they are capable of achieving the same anointing of Christhood that Jesus had. Their beliefs are predicated upon a new gnosticism which appears so very Christian as to deceive even the elect if possible. Through close examination, however, they are found in an error so serious that it threatens the stability of the churches in which these people fellowship and, in some cases hold positions of leadership.

In all forms of humanism we find one fundamental concept: man is (or one day will become) God, or "a god." Scripture, however, tells us that we are merely creations of a personal, transcendent, sovereign God to Whom we are to be subject. Man was created to guard the earth and to protect it from Satan, who seeks to turn man's affections away from God and inward toward Self.

The Challenge Before Us

This, then, is the conflict of the ages as revealed in Scripture. We who are Christ's are called to be His witnesses and to proclaim the Gospel of His Kingdom to the world. And we are to demonstrate the Kingdom by living in obedience to the laws of the Kingdom: God's Word. In this way, we become the salt of the earth and a light to a world suffering in the darkness of its own wisdom. This is the challenge that is set before the Church today as never before.

God, by His patience toward sinners, has allowed the world to come to the place where it is ripe for judgment. But before He judges the world, He will judge His Church (I Peter 4:17).

Are we living in obedience to His Word, or are we living in conformity to the wisdom of the world? Are we suffering under the attacks of the enemy, or are we engaged in proper spiritual warfare, resisting the evil principalities whence have come all the deceptions that have polluted the Church for two thousand years?

The issues with which we deal in this book will challenge the Church to question everything that is taught in the name of Jesus. We are to be like the nobel Bereans who tested the words of the apostles by the Scriptures. By rightly dividing the Word of Truth, we will be able to wage spiritual warfare not in our own strength or wisdom, but through surrender to God's strength and wisdom.

At times we may think that the course He has chosen for us demonstrates weakness and defeat; but this is only if we see God's plan in human terms. For it is in our weakness that His strength is manifested; it is in our defeat that His victory shines forth. Such are His ways, which are not our ways; such are His thoughts which are higher than our thoughts. Yet in spite of apparent weakness—in spite of perceived defeats—Satan and his minions will not prevail against the Church. Through it all will come forth a glorious Church that will rule with Christ in His Kingdom.

2
The Quest Temporal

Scripture tells us that when Adam sinned he incurred upon the human race the curse of death; and not only upon the human race, but upon the earth over which he held dominion. That curse upon man had two basic aspects: death upon everything that lived in the creation, and hard labor as a means to keep man alive.

Because man was given dominion over the earth, death (the wages of man's sin) is the lot of all who are of the earth, whether man, beast, or vegetation. It seems paradoxical that, in order to have life in this present age, it is necessary for death to occur. But without death, the human race would have burgeoned the earth with untold billions of people a scant thousand years after Adam was created. In man's unregenerate state, the misery the world is experiencing today would be compounded manifold.

Thus, man was not allowed access to the tree of life, lest he eat of it and live forever in his fallen state (Genesis 3:22). And just as death is necessary for man because of his sin nature, hard labor is necessary to keep him from finding too much time to devise evil.

Much as a child cannot understand the discipline he receives from His parents, man cannot understand the discipline of the Adamic curse. From God's perspective, the curse is not for man's harm, but for man's ultimate good. God inaugurated the curse out of His desire to redeem man from his sinful state. The only alternative was to destroy man altogether.

In spite of God's grace, it eventually did become necessary at one point to destroy everyone except for a single righteous man and his family. Out of Noah, then, has come the entire human race that exists today. But also out of Noah came the first concerted attempt to unite man in rebellion against God: the Tower of Babel.

Ever since God thwarted that attempt and scattered mankind over the earth, Satan has purposed to reunite mankind against

God. To achieve that goal, he knows that it is necessary to bring mankind back into unity on two levels: government for physical constraint, and religion for spiritual constraint. Part of his plans rest upon the ability to deceive man into thinking that he holds within himself the answer to overcoming the Adamic curse.

Man's Answers

Throughout the centuries, many philosophers have arisen to offer solutions to the human condition. But their approach has been anthropocentric rather than theocentric; they see man, rather than God, as the solution. In fact, they see man as a god himself, merely lacking in the knowledge needed to bring about a utopian society devoid of suffering.

The problem is, however, that man, in his fallen condition, cannot attain that knowledge without help from a source higher than himself. And there is a source of knowledge that has been all too eager to help man achieve his desire for a perfect society.

Satan and his emissaries, masquerading as angels of light, have guided man's steady increase in knowledge, first through the ancient mystery schools open to a privileged few initiates, then in later history through the universities open to anyone who desires to attain the knowledge needed to set his own course in life.

This, then, has been the end to which man, with the aid of Satan and his minions, has devised his sciences: to overcome the curse of death, and to make his life easier in order to be able to do whatever seems right in his own eyes.

Rejecting God's Word that defines his problem as sin, man has chosen to believe that his problems stem from external conditions rather than internal. If his science can alter those external conditions he will be able to achieve his full potential and attain the godhood that has eluded him since Satan's promise in the garden.

The arts and sciences have been man's greatest achievements toward those ends. And in these fields those who spearhead new innovations in the exaltation of the human spirit earn the greatest accolades. The wisdom of man is worshiped in the temples of museums, art galleries, and schools of higher learning.

But there is another temple to which mankind flocks because, in spite of his great achievements, he knows in his innermost being that he lacks something vital. His conscience tells him there is a God to whom he must answer. His self-love tells him that that god is within himself. Thus, the temple to which mankind flocks is the temple of Self, ministered to by the priests of the world's religions.

3
The Quest Spiritual

K arl Marx said, "Religion is the opiate of the people." He was right.

Every religion devised by man has dulled his spiritual senses to the reality that he is utterly lost and devoid of any good by which he can save himself from an eternity of torment or, at best, oblivion.

Religion has the unique ability to appease man's conscience while leaving him condemned by that very conscience. It's a sad fact that the majority of mankind is wrong in almost all its important choices, particularly those that impact his concepts of God, eternity, and man's eternal destiny.

The religious traditions which sprang from the ancient pagan mysteries have had as their goal the uniting of mankind under a single ethic: a world governmental and religious system that would ensure the survival of the human race and eliminate the fear of war, poverty, sickness, and all elements that comprise God's curse upon mankind. It is man's goal, therefore, to establish an ethical society based on reason and morality gleaned from religious ideals.

Theosophy

Throughout history the ancient mystery religions have taken many forms, from paganism and witchcraft to humanism and secular psychology. Today they may be classified under the general name of "theosophy," the blending of science and religion to create a universal brotherhood of man under a one-world state wherein an ethical society will flourish.

The term, "theosophy" (lit., "Divine Wisdom," or "Wisdom of the Gods")[1] has several synonyms, some of the more common being "the Esoteric Philosophy," "the Wisdom-Religion," "the

Secret Doctrine," "the Ancient Wisdom," and "the Esoteric Tradition."[2]

Though modern theosophy makes certain teachings of the ancient mystery religions available to the masses, these are only the exoteric teachings. The deeper esoteric mysteries are reserved for those initiated through secret rites and sworn to secrecy under penalty of death. The exoteric teachings are the foundation for the New Age movement—today's vulgar expression of the "higher" mysteries permitted for the masses,.

Those exoteric teachings have also found their way into the Church under a form of "Christian theosophy," also known as New Thought. This is important to Satan's plans to destroy the effectiveness of the Church. He has put it in the minds of men infected by his delusion to, in turn, infect the Church with sufficient error as to make it usable for his purposes.

To the esotericists (theosophists, deists, etc.) bent upon uniting mankind, Christianity is anathema, and its adherents must be converted to accept all religious expressions as valid. Since the Church alone has the spiritual power to resist this deception Satan *must* make it believe his lies. When the churches are sufficiently corrupted or neutralized, Satan will have a clear path toward uniting the world against Jesus Christ.

Unity In Diversity

Disregard of biblical truth is essential to bringing Christianity into unity with all religions. Particularly, if Satan can get the Church to believe that there are other gods besides the one true God (even "lesser" gods such as man himself), he'll have weakened its resolve to challenge the religious unification of the human race.

It isn't important to Satan that everyone believe the same thing or belong to the same religious institution. All that's necessary is that the Gospel be diluted sufficiently so as to render it ineffective.

Unity in diversity is the goal toward which the world's religions are working. In some churches, unity in diversity is still more narrowly defined, but the purpose is to join in fellowship everyone who names Jesus as Lord regardless of doctrine.

This disregard for doctrine, and subsequent acceptance of every aberration that goes by the name of Christian, is necessary for the eventual unification of all religious thought. Therefore, opposition to deception in the Church is being stifled under the pretense that those who expose deceivers are sowing discord among the brethren and hindering unity. A result of this tactic is that many Christians have been discouraged from judging error in the Church for fear of hindering the unity sought by religious leaders.

4
Theosophic Inroads
& Doctrines Redefined

Satan's lies have found fertile ground in the Church not only because many Christians lack proper knowledge, but because we lack the necessary humility that can protect us against deception. Those who seek their own wills above the will of God are easy prey for deceivers who exalt men and/or the Church to the status of godhood. The Church has accepted Satan's lies characterized by one or more of the following teachings:

- men are gods;
- men may become gods;
- men may become like God;
- faith is a "law" or "force" that may be activated by anyone, whether a disciple of Jesus or not;
- the ability to perform miracles, signs, and wonders is latent within all—we need only learn how to activate the spiritual laws upon which faith is based;
- God is bound by these spiritual laws and must respond to anyone—even His enemies—if they exercise knowledge of them;
- Jesus is our "elder brother" who mastered the spiritual laws of nature; He is our example to do the same;
- men may attain immortality by becoming perfected spiritually;

- the visible Kingdom of God will be established on earth when a sufficient number of people have been perfected, or at least are living in accordance with biblical morality.

Many who teach these things would deny they are theosophists; they think of themselves as orthodox Christians who have received special revelations from God. But whether they adhere to theosophical doctrines consciously, or are merely pawns in the conflict of the ages, is immaterial. A child playing with matches needn't have knowledge of thermodynamics to cause damage.

It is evident from the recent emergence of these aberrant teachings within the Church that—through schooling or personal association—theosophy is having an impact upon many of today's prominent teachers. Some, though sincere in their profession of faith in Jesus, may themselves be victims of esotericists who knew how to use biblical and Christian terminology to gain their confidence, or they may have learned from others who were themselves victims.

Theosophists have made special efforts to merge their teachings with the basic tenets of the Christian faith. This has resulted in some rather interesting esoteric interpretations of Scripture. By cleverly twisting the meanings of major Christian doctrines—the deity of Christ, His Virgin Birth, His sacrifice for sin, the resurrection of Christ and of His people, His coming again—those doctrines can be made to fit perfectly into the theosophical model of religion. But unless openly stated, their aberrant interpretations of these basic doctrines will escape the average Christian and deceive him into placing his trust where he ought not.

Consider Carefully

As we look at these doctrines from the standpoint of esotericism as opposed to Scripture, I urge the reader to consider carefully what is stated, as it is critical to understanding how deception can enter the Church. The affirmation of basic doctrines cleverly redefined demonstrates how esotericists use biblical terminology to convince Christians that they are brethren.

Those who would subvert the Faith will not challenge the essential doctrines outright until they've established a beachhead of confidence. Only after they feel secure in the confidence of their listeners will they begin to gradually turn those listeners' affections from the truth to aberrant interpretations. Yet it is not these interpretations with which I am primarily concerned (any mature Christian would unequivocally reject them), but the inroads into the Church of other teachings based on these interpretations.

Though there are few in the Church who would agree with these interpretations, many have bought the rest of the package and have opened the door to damnable heresies. These, then, are offered as a warning to learn as much as possible what someone believes before accepting him as a brother in Christ.

THE DEITY OF CHRIST

Theosophists would agree that Jesus is divine. But then, they would say, so are all men, if not actually, at least potentially. It is therefore not inconsistent for theosophists to speak of Jesus as "Son of God" and similar "Christian-sounding" phrases implying His deity. Nevertheless, whereas Christians believe that the transcendent Word of God became man exclusively in the person of Jesus of Nazareth, theosophists believe that a man named Jesus became a god by mastering the laws of nature through faith. As John H. Dewey, the leading apostle of Christian theosophy during the turn of the twentieth century stated:

> The law of FAITH as announced by Jesus and exemplified in his life, is the supreme law and method of all divine realization for man.[1] (Dewey's emphasis)

To most theosophists, Jesus was merely one man who displayed an exceptional expression of the divine nature. Among others are Buddha, Confucius, Mohammed, and Mohandas Gandhi. To some, however, Jesus was unique in His expression of the divine nature. They would say that no one has ever attained His status of spiritual enlightenment. However, they also believe that all men have the *potential* to reach that same degree of spiritual enlightenment; i.e., to be equal with Jesus. Some even say that, theoretically at least, we have the potential to be greater than He by further mastering the spiritual laws of nature to do good for mankind.

To them, Jesus' uniqueness lies not in His person as the Word of God incarnate, but in His particular anointing as "the Christ" to bring enlightenment and truth for His time in history, just as Buddha and Mohammed did for their eras. Jesus, it is said, had Christ "formed" in him. Though it is believed that there are exceptional "Christs" for different ages of man's evolutionary journey, it is taught that we may all have Christ formed in us, thus expressing in our own lives the "Christ principle." Theosophists, therefore, have no problem with calling Jesus the "Son of God":

> That he was fully and absolutely human, the veritable "Son of man," no sane mind will deny. That he was also fully and

absolutely divine, the veritable "Son of God," we with equal positiveness claim and affirm.[2]

On the basis of this statement, Dewey might easily have been accepted into Christian fellowship. But further study of his beliefs reveals that he qualifies his remarks:

> This incarnation of the Divine in Jesus, however, but reveals and demonstrates the innate capacity of our common humanity as the offspring of God, for receiving into its unfolding life the full Spirit of the Father, and becoming divine, as illustrated in the life of our great Exemplar [Jesus].[3]

> The manifestation of God in one man [Jesus], demonstrates the possibility of a like demonstration in all men.[4]

Were these teachings confined to the inner sanctums of the Masonic, Rosicrucian, and Mormon temples—were they bandied about only among theosophists seated around their tables of discussion—they would pose no genuine threat to the Church. But we are now hearing from prominent teachers in the Christian media that man was created with a divine nature which was lost due to the introduction of sin. By being born again by the Spirit of God we lose our sin nature and regain our divine nature.[5]

There is no such teaching in Scripture. Rather, it is based upon a theosophic interpretation of II Peter 1:4 which, properly understood, tells us no more than that the believer in Jesus is a partaker of the divine nature through the indwelling of the Holy Spirit. But it is the divine nature of the Holy Spirit, not ourselves, to which Peter was referring.

The quality of divinity belongs only to God, the Creator of the heavens and the earth. As the Word of God incarnate, Jesus is divine, as is the Holy Spirit through whom God accomplishes His purposes. The First Commandment of God is, "I am the Lord thy God. . . . Thou shalt have no other gods before me" (Exodus 20:2-3). Some may beg the question by stating that the word "before" qualifies the statement to mean only that our Creator God must come first before other gods, including ourselves. But the context is that we are to have no other gods, period. No one else is to be venerated to any degree.

God has stated that there are no legitimate gods besides Himself (Deuteronomy 4:35). Therefore, whenever the Scriptures speak of other gods, they are speaking of false gods: demons, idols, or men who attempt to take upon themselves the attributes of divinity. Yet many in the Church today have bought the lie that they themselves are "little gods," and perfectly legitimate ones at that.

John Dewey's New Thought approach to Jesus is reflected also in the idea that we should think of ourselves as equal to God in the same manner that Jesus, as His only begotten Son, was equal to God. In the Church, we find a similar reasoning in this dialogue between Kenneth Copeland, and Paul and Jan Crouch, founders of the Trinity Broadcasting Network.

In addressing the teaching that we are gods, on a segment of the *Praise The Lord* program, Paul Crouch asked Copeland, "Are you a god—small 'g'"? Copeland, looking very self-assured, opened his Bible and, after building an elaborate but illogical case to affirm himself as a god, read from Philippians 2:5:

> **Ken Copeland:** Let me ask you this. Will you do anything the Bible tells you to do?
>
> **Paul Crouch:** Yes sir!
>
> **Copeland:** If you understand its command you'll make an effort to do it won't you?
>
> **Paul and Jan Crouch:** Yes.
>
> **Copeland:** Alright. Let's see what it tells us to do. In Philippians, chapter two, verse five, "Let this mind"—it won't just come on you automatically, and if you walk in traditions you'll not do this—"Let this mind be in you, which was also in Christ Jesus: Who, being in the form of God, thought it not robbery to be equal with God." Now, He says, "Now you ought to think that way!"
>
> **Jan:** And we do.
>
> **Copeland:** "Made himself of no reputation, and took upon him the form of a servant, and was made in the likeness of men: [And] being found in fashion as a man, he humbled himself, and became obedient unto death, even the death of the cross. Wherefore God also hath highly exalted him, and given him a name which is above every name."
>
> Now what happened here? He said Jesus came, took of Himself no reputation. *But* His attitude was, "I don't call it robbery to be called equal with God; I'm not robbing God to say that I'm His Son."
>
> **Paul:** Hmmmm.
>
> **Copeland:** God's happy over this. I'm not making Him mad to say I'm His son. I don't know why you're upset about it.
>
> **Paul:** It was His idea in the first place.
>
> **Copeland:** Yeah, man! God wanted sons. Wasn't no use in Him sending Jesus if He didn't want some more.
>
> **Gloria Copeland:** Just like Him.
>
> **Paul:** Uh huh, uh huh, uh huh.

Ken Copeland: He could have left me the sorry turkey I was back there before I got saved, man. If that's what He wanted. But He didn't. And He paid the ultimate price to get you and me. Why? To leave me the way I was?

Paul: No.

Copeland: "Just as I am, just as I am, without one plea." Well, thank God He didn't leave me just as I was. Amen? So He said, "You let this mind be in you."

Paul: "Who thought it not robbery."

Copeland: "Who thought it not robbery to be called equal with God."

Paul: Oooooo! You're going to really get 'em mad now! [laughter]

Copeland: Naw, I won't! They ain't listenin'. [laughter]

Paul: Yeah, I think they are!

Copeland: Well, I'll bet you they're not; most of them aren't. A guy that listens to what we're saying, with spiritual ears, you figure out where we're coming from, you see?

Now wait a minute; we ain't quite finished with this. You gotta finish this off. Because you can't just read a Scripture for them and say, "Well that's it."

It says that God exalted Him. First Peter, five, the fifth verse: "Likewise you younger, submit yourselves unto the elder. Yea, all of you be subject one to another, and be clothed with humility: for God resisteth the proud, and giveth grace to the humble. Humble yourselves therefore under the mighty hand of God, that he may exalt you in due time." How? By casting all your care on Him.[6]

Prior to this exchange Copeland quoted Psalm 82 in an attempt to prove that born again believers are gods. Yet God's words in Psalm 82 to the judges (*elohim*) of Israel were words of chastisement to rebellious men, not born again believers. To use this Scripture is to say that all men are gods, even those in rebellion. To keep it in context, it applies only to the judges of Israel. We see, then, that He was calling them *elohim* because it was their responsibility to represent Him in exercising judgment upon His people.

Likewise, in John 10:34, Jesus was addressing rebellious judges of Israel, making them see their error in calling Him a blasphemer because He said, "I and the Father are one." He was using sarcasm in reminding them that they should not be upset if He calls Himself the Son of God while they believed that they themselves were gods. He knew that they did not rightly divide the Scriptures, but had been tainted by the same esoteric philosophies that have tainted today's "god-men." In essence, Jesus was saying, "If you think of yourselves as gods, why are you upset with me for saying that I am the Son of God?"

A Little Logic

Now, a bit of logic is in order: Most who subscribe to the idea that they are gods, tell us that godhood applies to born-again believers, not just to anyone. Yet they use as their proof text Scriptures that address as "gods" fallen men who are in rebellion against God. The men Jesus addressed in that instance were not born again, nor were the judges of Israel that were addressed in Psalm 82:6. Those who teach that we are gods have identified themselves with the rebellious judges of Israel and the hypocritical teachers of the Law in Jesus' day.

Even if we were to allow that God has ordained man as a lesser god, it is unconscionably blasphemous to insist that we are equal to God Almighty or to Jesus, who is the only-begotten of the Father—true God in the flesh. Copeland, however, twists these verses to make it appear as if the Jews wanted to stone Jesus merely because He called God His Father, rather than because He implied that He is God. He then built a case to justify thinking of ourselves as equal with God because we are God's sons. Those who disagree he accused of having an anti-Christ spirit, which he defined as an "anti-anointed-one spirit" (he being an "anointed one").

Copeland's first error is in equating the believer with Jesus, just as theosophists do. He then uses that equation as the basis to teach that God is pleased if we think of ourselves as equal with Him. And if we think of ourselves as equal with Him we will be displaying humility which, in turn, qualifies us for exaltation!

We are not sons of God in the same sense that Jesus is. He was begotten by the Father through the Holy Spirit. We are adopted by God's grace which is evidence of His mercy upon us.

A careful reading of Philippians 2:5-8 shows clearly that to have the mind of Christ is not to think of ourselves as equal with God, but rather to exhibit the same humility that Jesus did in His obedience. That He "thought it not robbery to be equal with God" is a parenthetical statement, which is clearly evident in the context of the Scripture.

The On-going Incarnation

Copeland is not the only one to espouse this teaching. Earl Paulk, pastor of Chapel Hill Harvester Church in Atlanta, Georgia, and a leading figure in the charismatic movement, is another of many today who are teaching what is called "the on-going incarnation of God." The Church, says Paulk, "is the essence of God; His on-going incarnation in the world."[7] The idea is that, yes, Jesus is Christ, but so is the Church, as the "Body of Christ." This is not dissimilar to theosophist John Dewey's understanding of divine incarnation:

It will be conceded by every candid thinker, that whatever attributes of divinity became manifest in Jesus the acknowledged son of Mary, found organic expression in and through functions that were wholly and strictly human. No other understanding of the "Divine Incarnation" is possible. And what is this, but the practical demonstration in a living example of the claim put forth by Christ himself, that man is the child of god, with an inherent ability to become perfect even as his Father in heaven is perfect?[8]

The incarnation of God is unique to Jesus. While the believer has dwelling within him the Holy Spirit, only in Jesus does the fullness of the Godhead dwell bodily (Colossians 2:9). He is by nature God; we are by nature mere men in whom God was pleased to place His Spirit for His purposes.

Anti-Christ Redefined

Earl Paulk labels "antichrist" those who do not recognize his teaching on the alleged on-going incarnation:

The greatest test of the spirit of the antichrist is its attitude toward the church. The attitude isn't directed toward Jesus. Jesus is not personally a threat to any community unless there is a living, thriving church functioning in that community. Therefore, the spirit of the antichrist refuses to recognize that God is here in the flesh.

Consider some of the popular entertainers who make fun of the Church today. Study their lives. They do not attack Jesus Christ, nor do they talk about the Jesus who lived by the shores of Galilee. Instead they attack Oral Roberts, Kenneth Copeland and Jim Bakker. They attack the Church of Jesus Christ and its representatives. Mockery and criticism are the means by which the spirit of the antichrist operates most successfully.[9]

If we are to examine the lives of today's popular entertainers, let us first examine the lives of the popular "entertainers" in the Church who espouse error and make a sham of the Faith before the world. In view of the lifestyles of so many prominent people in the Church, is it any wonder that the world ridicules them?

Yet Paulk states that to ridicule these men demonstrates the spirit of anti-Christ. This charge is based on the belief that *they* are now Christ in the world. This means that our salvation is based on their Christhood as well as Jesus'.

To equate ourselves with Jesus is to demean His person. And that plays directly into the hands of Satan. For it is Jesus who must be exalted in order for the believer to receive the truth from God. To exalt ourselves closes the door to understanding His Word and leaves us open to further deception. If we are to be exalted, let God exalt us in His own time and in His own way; those who would exalt themselves He will abase.

Forming Christ In Us

A parallel teaching to the on-going incarnation that is gaining ascendency in the Church is that we must have Christ formed in us just as Jesus had Christ formed in Him. And this from no less a prominent voice than James Robison:

> God wants us to see Jesus as merely the big brother in a huge family of brothers and sisters who are like Him.
> If we know this, as Paul says we should, then we recognize God's hand in everything that happens. Instead of crumbling under the pressures of unpleasant circumstances, we realize that God is simply forming Christ in us.[10]

God does not want us to think of Jesus as "merely" our big brother. He wants us to see Jesus as our Lord and Master. The "big brother" idea is pure New Thought. He is the firstborn of many brethren through the Resurrection, but not "merely" our big brother. Such New Thought statements about Jesus bring Him down to our level or raise us up to His. There is no concept of sacredness toward our Savior in such remarks. But besides this, after quoting Luke 2:11, 40, 46, 51-52, and Hebrews 5-8, Robison tells us they show how Jesus had the Christ-life formed in Him:

> Notice God's formative pattern. First came the light, in the form of wisdom and knowledge from God. Then came the experiences, first in the home where Jesus was subject to human parents and later in the carpenter shop and the world community. Learning what it meant to be ruled by God through His daily experiences in life—the things He suffered—Jesus had the Christ-life formed in Him.[11]

What Robison is stating here is pure New Thought; it is not biblical. I'm not saying he is consciously aware of the origins of this teaching, but he states that this is a truth of which the Church has not had more than a fleeting glimpse, and that God had revealed it to him only in recent months before he wrote these words:

> As I consider the implications of what God is telling us with statements like this [Galatians 2:20, and Colossians 3:4], my mind almost explodes. I do not believe the Church until this time has ever received more than fleeting glimpses of this overwhelming truth. In recent months God has shown me a few fragments that I have been able to receive.[12]

While we are to be conformed to the image of Christ by maturing in the Faith, by nature we are mere humans who are privileged to have God's Spirit indwelling us. God's Spirit is distinct from our spirit. God's Spirit is not distinct from Jesus' Spirit. He is the Word of God made flesh. This is why the Holy Spirit is often referred to as the Spirit of Christ or the Spirit of God. Jesus did not have the Christ-life formed in Him. He *is* Christ. The person and the office are inseparable; they were inseparable even at His birth. The angels announced His entrance into the world with the words, "For today in the city of David there has been born for you a Savior, who *is* Christ the Lord" (Luke 2:40). They did not say Jesus would *become* Christ the Lord.

Robison even quotes that Scripture, but misapplies it to show us that it was Jesus' growing in wisdom and stature that formed the Christ-life in Him. But the anointing or office of Christ is not the same as His wisdom and stature. He was Christ no matter what degree of wisdom or stature He enjoyed during his growth from babe to manhood. He was Christ even while his mind and body were maturing. He had the Christ-life then, and only He ever had the Christ-life as part of His nature.

Robison's teaching did not originate in God's Word or in the Church. It originated in theosophy.

THE VIRGIN BIRTH

Theosophy generally denies the doctrine of the Virgin Birth of Jesus. However, in order to gain the confidence of Christians, theosophists spiritualize what the Scriptures state is applicable to the physical: Jesus was born of a virgin by the power of the Holy Spirit. By spiritualizing this truth they can say they believe in the Virgin Birth. But their definition would be qualified:

> [Jesus' virgin birth] was originally a highly mystical and philosophical teaching, which became in time a theologic dogma and legend. ... It is a mystical or symbolic tenet referring to the birth of the Christ in man from the virgin-part of one's being, i.e., from the spiritual or highest portions of man's constitution. It also has a cosmical significance — the Virgin-Mother of Space giving birth through her Child, the Cosmic Logos, to her multitudes of children of various kinds. There are thus two aspects of this mystical or symbolical doctrine: there is, first, the Cosmical Virgin, and, second, there is the mystical "virgin-birth" of an initiate. An initiate is one "reborn," or, as the saying goes, "born a second time." He is not born of course in initiation from a physical father and mother, for his body is born in the usual manner; but in initiation, the "new man," the inner man, the Christ-man, is born *from himself* because of his

bringing out or unfolding into active manifestation the divinity within him and overenlightening him; and his "Virgin-Mother" is that part of himself which is the root of his being, the spiritual soul in its spotless and unstained purity. From the Virgin or Spiritual Soul is born the human Christ or the human Buddha, without admixture of extrinsic elements of any kind, and without other means than the man's own yearnings and strivings to become the god within himself.

The Christian Church has interpreted these very mystical doctrines physically and thus has largely lost the far nobler and really profound symbolic sense.[13] (Author's emphasis)

So one may say he believes in the Virgin Birth of Christ, but hold an entirely different view from that of the Scriptures—in this case applying an occult analogy to them.

The ploy of esotericism is increasingly evident in the Church through the penchant of some teachers to cloud the simple truth of the Gospel with teachings that impress the unlearned as "new revelations." This is evidence of a new gnosticism based on salvation through knowledge.

Essential to the gradual erosion of the Scriptural truth of Jesus' actual Virgin Birth is the teaching that we are equal with Him. For if He was not born of a virgin, then He cannot be God incarnate in any sense apart from a theosophical interpretation. Many in the Church have bought the first lie by believing they are equal with Jesus, which will lead to other lies that attack the Faith.

Paul warned of such deceivers entering the Body of Christ:

> But I fear, lest by any means, as the serpent beguiled Eve through his subtilty, so your minds should be corrupted from the simplicity that is in Christ.
>
> For if he that cometh preacheth another Jesus, whom we have not preached, or if ye receive another spirit, which ye have not received, or another gospel, which ye have not accepted, ye might well bear with him. (II Corinthians 11:3-4)

In light of today's deceptions, we would be wise to ensure that the meanings teachers apply to the doctrines of the Church are clearly stated, and are backed by the whole counsel of God's Word.

ATONEMENT

Jesus' death as atonement for sin is also given by esotericists an entirely different meaning from that stated in Scripture. True Christians believe that Jesus' blood cleanses us from sin, provided we come to God in true faith. Only Jesus could pay the price for our sins; no one else's suffering or death has any merit with God.

The esotericist, however, holds a different view, while giving the impression that he believes in the Atonement. Theosophist G. de Purucker states,

> If a man loves another greatly, can he not save his friend from future sorrow by taking upon himself his friend's karman [consequences of actions destined to follow from reincarnation to reincarnation]? The question is purely academic in a way, because when the last word is said, the karman of the friend is the friend himself, and therefore the answer in general is comprised of an emphatic negative; nevertheless, there is a possibility, not indeed of taking upon oneself the friend's karman, but of shouldering by means of a powerful will and a high intelligence directed to that end, a certain portion, be it large or small, of the consequences which in the normal course of Nature, with heavy and perhaps crushing effect, would fall upon the friend. The secret in such a situation lies in allying one's own life intimately with the life of the one whose heavy karman it is thus hoped to aid in carrying or exhausting. . . .
>
> In those cases where such noble and altruistic action be taken for the benefit of all that lives or for the results which it is hoped will benefit a large portion of mankind, it is a Buddha-like thing to do, it is a Christ-like thing.[14]

So the esoteric view of atonement does allow for Jesus' sacrifice, but only up to a point; anyone can bear the consequences of another's sins through altruistic acts of piety. Theosophists say they accept Jesus' death as atonement, but their doctrine is faulty, and they can mislead Christians who lack understanding into thinking they are hearing from a brother in Christ. The efficacious sacrifice of Jesus is actually denied by all schools of esotericism:

> This doctrine of vicarious substitution, both in form and spirit, is diametrically opposed to the positive teaching of Jesus, which makes righteousness itself salvation, obedience to the righteous law of God in the doing of the Father's will in the personal and social life. . . .
>
> These authoritative words of the Christ, with the whole Sermon on the Mount, from which they are taken, and the full tenor of all his teaching most unmistakably emphasize the *doing* of the Father's will, and unity with him in a righteous life, as the only salvation possible or desirable for mankind, while not a precept or parable of his can be brought to sustain in the slightest degree this doctrine of substitution; as though it were possible for the absolute justice and goodness of the All-Father to demand or accept the punishment of the innocent for the guilty, or could impute the righteousness of the sinless to the

sinner, or accept any as righteous who are not really so. But as righteousness of life is secured only through personal obedience to the law of right, no man can become righteous before God, except by his own act of obedience. If this were possible in the economy of God, then the very idea of justice would be a delusion and a sham, and the thought and talk of a changeless moral order a pitiable and unmeaning farce.

Surely salvation from sin in this life, by lifting man above the power of temptation, as promised by the Christ, and exemplified in his own life, would prevent all consequences of sin in this world or any other. And this is the only salvation worthy of the name.

How is this to be accomplished but by the perfection of human life itself, through the unfolding and bringing forth of the divine or spiritual nature in that life.[15] (de Puruker's emphasis)

This is exactly the belief of many in the Church today whose beliefs have been influenced by Manifest Sons of God theology.

At-one-ment

By manipulating the word "atonement," esotericists have devised the doctrine of "at-one-ment," which states that those who master their physical nature become "at one" with the "Divine":

The casting out of devils and reforming the vicious, the reclaiming of drunkards and restoration of the insane to soberness and reason, giving strength to the weak and courage to the lowly and disheartened, and working "not after the law of a carnal commandment but after the power of an endless life," for the universal emancipation, enlightenment and uplifting of mankind, become the easy and true work of life.

Man then becomes one in spirit and purpose with the Divine, and is led, governed and crowned with wisdom, sympathy and power. It is the Christ or God-anointed life; the true at-one-ment of man with God, the human with the Divine, Christianity as Christ taught and lived it.[16]

When man has thus learned to specifically direct the force of life in the control of the elements in his own organism, he may then accumulate power within himself to master and control the elements and forces of the world outside himself; but as this is to be acquired through cooperation with divine power, he can attain absolute control over himself and that which is below only by first becoming at-one with the Divine, which is within and above him.[17]

This esoteric view of "at-one-ment"—achieving godhood in order to control the elements of nature—is a major tenet of mind science religions. Though expressed in different terms, it has crept into the Church through the positive confession and positive thinking teachings which declare that faith is a "force" that God used to create the universe, and that anyone can use that force for his own benefit.[18] This teaching, too, puts man in the "god class."

THE RESURRECTION

The Resurrection of Jesus is a primary doctrine of the Christian Faith. For if He had not been resurrected we would still be in our sins (I Corinthians 15:12-26). The esotericist does not believe in resurrection, but in reincarnation—the evolutionary process by which souls are allegedly perfected by working out their karmic consequences from one lifetime to another. Yet the term, "resurrection," does find its way into esoteric philosophy, specifically in relation to reincarnation, and its use can be misleading:

> No sane man, it is to be supposed, today can or does believe that the physical body, as regards its physical elements—or rather when once its elements have been returned to earth—shall be gathered together again into one component and perfect whole at some future period which Christians call the Judgment Day; when the "last trump" shall be sounded, according to the quaint imagery of older times. . . . Yet back of this idea of the "resurrection of the body" there actually is a most beautiful truth or fact of Nature. This truth may be expressed in two forms; or, as the mathematicians say, it is expressible in both a general and in a special case.
>
> This special case involves a mystery—a teaching of the ancient Mysteries; but hinted at, it might be phrased thus: When a man has received his final degree of initiation he is said to be "raised" to Masterhood in the same physical body. This point need not be elaborated further here.
>
> The general case, however, is to be explained by the reassembling of the life-atoms in the manner described in preceding paragraphs. These life-atoms are man's own offspring, at least most of those which build man's constitution are; inbuilt into his body during the physical life which he leads on Earth, although they are not derivative from outside but spring forth from within himself. Therefore they are psycho-magnetically attracted back to the Reimbodying Ego on its return journey to the new earth-life, and the Reimbodying Ego can no more avoid or escape receiving these life-atoms again into itself than it can avoid or escape being itself. To it they are again drawn because out from it they formerly went. They too, these life-atoms, during the Reimbodying Ego's term of devachanic rest and

peace, have had their own wonderful adventures—adventures in the different spheres and on the different planes of the seven globes of the planetary chain; and thus when the "descending" individual or Reimbodying Ego reaches the grades of our physical plane, and the baby-body is finally born, its growth thereafter is assured by and through and because of the aforesaid magnetic attractions and repulsions, and by the body's receiving into it and expulsion from it of these its former life-atoms. These are continuously attracted to and built into the physical body, as it passes from babyhood into childhood into youth, and from youth into manhood—the very life-atoms which had made the Reimbodying Ego's physical body on Earth in the last earth-life. Thus it is that the body of the former earth-life is resurrected—is *arisen*.[19] (Author's emphasis)

But what does God's Word say?

> *It is appointed unto men once to die, but after this the judgment: So Christ was once offered to bear the sins of many; and unto them that look for him shall he appear the second time without sin unto salvation.* (Hebrews 9:27-28)

We will die only once. There is no reincarnation by which we may eventually attain spiritual perfection through our own works of righteousness. It is only the precious blood of Jesus that cleanses us from sin and provides for our salvation if we trust in Him.

Yet even the term, "resurrection," is used by esotericists to justify its inclusion in Scripture. They cannot deny it's there, so they apply to it a meaning more in keeping with their esoteric traditions. They also use it to gain the confidence of believers in order to sow seeds of destructive doctrines.

In the Church today, there is an indirect attack against the Resurrection through the ridiculing of the catching away of the saints—the so-called "rapture." How so? Because the Resurrection is the primary doctrine of which the rapture is a part.

While those who denigrate the rapture do not deny the Resurrection openly, there is little or no mention of it in their teachings. They teach instead that certain "overcomers" will become immortal by attaining spiritual perfection.

This is more critical to our salvation than some may realize. The Resurrection is a central doctrine of our Faith, and without it we have no hope for eternal life (I Corinthians 15:1-26). It is only immediately after the resurrection of the saints at the coming of Jesus that those who are alive in Him will become immortal. That is the real meaning of the "rapture," regardless of the events that transpire after.

THE SECOND COMING

When esotericists speak of the Second Coming of Christ, they are not speaking about the Second Coming of Jesus. Because the office of "Christ" is not considered by esotericists to be exclusive to Jesus, they do not affirm *His* Second Coming. Rather, they make vague mention of the "Coming of Christ," or even "Second Coming of Christ." They separate the "Christ *principle*" from Jesus and apply it to all who attain a certain level of spiritual enlightenment.

In a broad sense, they teach that the "Second Coming of Christ" will take place through the raising of humanity's consciousness to where a significant number will realize that *they* are the embodiment of the Second Coming in its fullness. This is a tenet of Manifest Sons of God theology which is finding renewed vigor among many charismatics in the Church.

AN ESOTERIC "STATEMENT OF FAITH"

Though holding erroneous interpretations of any or all the doctrines represented above, one may make a declaration of faith similar to this:

> I believe that Jesus is the Son of God, true God and true man, God incarnate, virgin born, that His death was an atonement for sins, that he has been resurrected, and that Christ is coming again.

On the basis of this confession, a person may gain the confidence of Christians and, once having done so, may easily fill their minds with other teachings that will gradually sway them away from the truths essential to their salvation.

The teachers with whom we deal in this writing may not be theosophists in the strict sense of the word, but there is sufficient evidence to suggest that they have been infected by New Thought philosophies, possibly by sitting under the teachings of wolves in sheep's clothing.

It's no secret that most theological seminaries today are in the hands of liberal theologians who question the veracity of the major tenets of the Faith, including the inerrancy of Scripture, the deity of Christ, the Virgin Birth, and the resurrection of the dead. Many others have bought into the mystical teachings of esoteric philosophy which equate the believer with Jesus.

We see, then, that a clear definition of terms is essential for a proper understanding of the theological stance held by those who teach the Body of Christ.

5
Dominion Theology

We have seen how man's philosophies are predicated upon two important suppositions: 1) man is God or "a god"; 2) his highest goal is to establish a society based on the universal brotherhood of man. Recognizing that societal order is important to the achievement of these goals, the leaders of the esoteric philosophies have established the need for a basic moral code upon which society can survive. This code is designed to give man as much personal freedom as possible and still keep him from sliding into anarchy.

The Scriptures are valuable to the shapers of the world society for two reasons: 1) they offer a strong moral ethic upon which an orderly society may be based; 2) they have the confidence of billions of people, even though the vast majority of those billions do not have true faith in Jesus Christ. However, because man's moral codes are not based exclusively on God's Word, they are subjective and dependent upon the particular philosophy to which one ascribes. Thus, we find a great diversity of opinion as to what constitutes true morality. But whatever subjective values the world's philosophies profess, even in opposition to one another, the desire of most people is a world where they can live at peace.

This desire is no less prevalent in the Church. And almost from its inception there have been those who have attempted to meld the basic philosophical values of the world with biblical ethics. Augustine's *City of God* described how the earth would flourish in righteousness under the guidance of the Church. This caught the imagination of the Roman Church, which saw its role as ruler over the temporal powers as a divine mandate.

Through the centuries, there have been many attempts to implement a theonomic form of civil government, the Holy Roman Empire being the most prominent. Under papal rule the "divine right of kings" was acknowledged as long as the king subjected himself to papal authority. Those kings who sought to throw off papal authority were deposed, or at the least excommunicated. Depending upon the degree to which the king's subjects were loyal to the papacy, kings were either forced into humble submission to the pope or managed to break his yoke.

The perceived mandate to rule the nations in the name of Christ has never been renounced by the papacy. The Reformation tore the heart out of its temporal power, but only for a time.

BACK TO ROME

The mandate to rule the nations in the name of Christ was the natural outgrowth of Gnostic influences in the early Church. The theosophic philosophies that had captured the minds of the Roman Church prelates, gave rise to the belief that, since Christ came to save the world, it must be through the Church that that salvation will be wrought. Jesus, after all, had been absent for three centuries; the rising tide of heathenism that threatened the Roman Empire, which was perceived as "Christian" after the supposed conversion of Constantine, caused concern. If something was going to be done about evil in the world, the Church would have to do it.

Constantine's declaration that the Roman Empire was to be Christianized naturally suggested in the minds of the Roman Church hierarchy that it must be God's intention to use the military might of the Roman Empire to spread the Faith throughout the world. But in Rome the Faith had already become corrupted through acquiescence to pagan philosophy.

Virtually all the early "Church Fathers" had been schooled in Greek and Roman philosophy. They believed that man has within himself a "divine spark" which must be awakened in order to bring him to perfection. Plato called this divine spark the "immortal principle." Historian Abraham Freisen states:

> This argument, that one had a divine spark within, came into Christian thought through the Church Fathers. These great thinkers of the early church, beginning with Justin Martyr and culminating in St. Augustine, had nearly all been Platonists before they became Christians. Because of certain similarities, they were attracted to Christianity as a higher form of the same truth that Plato had perceived. Augustine especially in his early years developed the Platonic view of the soul and integrated it into Christianity. Thus he could say, "The soul has within itself a hidden abyss, and the things of time and this world have no place therein, but only what is high above." It was in this hidden abyss of the soul that God resided. Therefore, one could find God only by turning inward.[1]

In the Introduction to *The Confessions of St. Augustine* (The Heritage Press) George N. Shuster confirms Freisen's observation:

> The ideas set forth in the *Enneads* of Plotinus were to remain deeply embedded in [Augustine's] mind. But the dominant concern of the time was with varying forms of what we should now term Theosophy. The countries bordering on rich Constantinople and learned Alexandria were hotbeds of mystical cults and symbolistic religions, several of which were then very influential. Augustine describes those which especially fascinated him, in particular the teaching of the Manichæns, who believed that the world is ruled by two Principles, one Good and the other Evil, and that the conflict between them cannot be resolved.[2]

Addressing Augustine's search for God, Shuster states:

> So also there stir in the human soul the desires which can find their fulfillment only in God. 'Our hearts,' [Augustine] says, 'are restless until they rest in Thee!'
> Yet how shall we know God? Augustine takes it for granted that the world is, and must therefore have been caused. The world is likewise beautiful, as mathematical patterns are, and must therefore have been designed. But the place to seek Him out is none the less in our 'own inward things.' What are these? Knowledge and the love of knowledge are inextricably bound together in man's spirit. He does not see what *is* in isolation. What *ought to be* is always conjoined. Down these twin roads that are nevertheless one he enters into contact with a Reality implicit in which is perfection. The more we know of it, the more we shall necessarily know of God, for in a sense it is God.
> ... When Othello says that if Desdemona has sinned 'chaos is come again,' he alludes to the unity of the cosmic and moral order and so reflects Augustinian thinking. This has special appeal for our own time because while he was not a 'mystic' in the generally accepted sense, Augustine recognized in the human person a stature and range of creative endeavor that the newer Platonists he so genuinely admired had not accorded to it. The ultimate certitudes were knowable, in his view, not through a vision of the 'Ideas' which hover far above the world of sense, but through full awareness of the Self. 'I cannot doubt that I doubt' was for him the first immovable stone on the road to knowledge of Reality.[3] (Shuster's emphasis)

The search for knowledge from within oneself is the basis for gnosticism, and characterizes one form of theosophic expression.

Because he believed that knowledge of Reality was locked up within Self, Augustine did not perceive God as transcendent alone, but immanent within the human soul:

> With such a view of the soul, it is not surprising that adherents from Plato to the Renaissance Humanists, from Augustine to the medieval mystics and Thomas Muentzer, can speak of the "deification of man." After all, man has within him a divine spark which, if ignited, can start a holy fire that can purify the individual. Augustine at one point spoke of "growing god-like." Pico della Mirandola, the fifteenth-century Renaissance Humanist, spoke of "being reborn into the higher forms, which are divine." Similarly, the medieval mystics and Thomas Muentzer also spoke of being deified, or reaching god-like perfection while yet in this life.
>
> The mystics, however, spoke of growing god-like with a difference. It was a difference that had to do with the role the Holy Spirit played in bringing about a "successful" conversion. By the latter they meant the ability to live the perfect Christian life. . . . Such a conversion could only take place if the rubble heaped upon the human soul had been cleared away, if the "garden of the soul" had been properly weeded, as Tauler put it. Then one had to turn away from all "creatures," all external things, and turn inward to one's soul where God resided. Now the work of the transformation could begin, now "the divine birth in the soul of man" could take place. Knowing the external written Word of God was not enough.[4]

Out of this revulsion for "external things" came the idea for cloistered monastic life lived under austere conditions. Ultimately, the belief that celibacy and asceticism are virtues which all who would aspire to religious life should maintain, resulted in Roman Catholic clergy being forbidden to marry, and in their requirement to takes vows of poverty and chastity. The Roman Catholic priesthood, then, set itself above the masses and instituted its own schools of initiation called monasteries and seminaries. The similarities of thought and form reveal that they learned the patterns for monastic life from the esoteric schools.

In time, the need to satiate the passion for knowledge required that Scripture be relegated to a lesser role in establishing Truth; it became necessary to equate the papal pronunciamentos as equal with Scripture, having supposedly come through divine inspiration. From this came the doctrine of Infallibility: whatever the pope speaks *ex cathedra*, while seated on the alleged throne of Peter, is to be believed as inspired sacred dogma; it cannot be challenged even if contrary to the Scriptures.

With the Reformation came enlightenment; it dawned on some Roman Catholic priests that Scripture alone holds the infallible Word of God. *Solo scriptura* became the rallying cry that sent shock waves through the Roman Catholic Church, and inflicted the Holy Roman Empire with what appeared to be a mortal wound.

Since the Reformation, the papacy has worked to bring all Christians back under its authority. Early attempts at counter-reformation worked to a small degree only; it became necessary to exert more force than arguments could achieve. The Inquisition and various other means to force perceived "heretics" back under papal control only drove the people further away and alienated kings who saw in the Reformation an opportunity to free themselves from papal control. Eventually, the Roman Catholic Church realized that the only thing that could possibly work would be subversion and discrediting of the Protestant movement. But it has taken time; almost 400 years have passed, and the patience of the Roman Catholic counter reformation is beginning to bear fruit.

Overtures For Papal Authority

Today's headlines give evidence that prominent leaders within many churches are looking to the pope as the single greatest hope for the unification of Christianity. It stands to reason that if the pope is a man of God, why should we continue to refuse his authority? For the sake of unity, why not accept his authority and present the united front necessary to achieve dominion over the nations, particularly in view of the present penchant among secular governments to seek the pope's blessing?

Although many Roman Catholics have undoubtedly been touched by the Holy Spirit and are coming into a greater understanding of what it means to have a personal relationship to God, Roman Catholicism itself has not changed. It is still as strong a political system as ever, ruled by a hierarchy whose intent has been from its inception to establish the pope as the Vicar of Christ on earth over all the nations.

Roman Catholicism is being given further credibility by Protestant leaders of every persuasion, many of whom may not be aware of the papal mandate for dominion. Paul Crouch, president of Trinity Broadcasting Network has declared that the word "Protestant" has been eliminated from his vocabulary,[5] and Catholic programming promoting the doctrines of Romanism are aired on a regular basis over his network. *Charisma and Christian Life* magazine now carries ads for Roman Catholic publications, as does *Christian Retailing*, a magazine for the Christian booksellers trade. Billy Graham has been declared a brother in Christ after visits to the pope.[6] Robert Schuller felt he could not build his

Crystal Cathedral until he got the pope's blessing on his plans.[7] Anglican Archbishop Joseph Runcie, in 1990, called for the unification of all Christianity under the pope's authority.[8] Harald Bredesen, along with other Christian leaders, worked hard for the privilege of presenting their "Prince of Peace" award to Pope John Paul II. Several Protestant leaders have referred to the pope as "the Holy Father," a title Scripture reserves for the Father in heaven.

In an article entitled, "A Pope for All Christians: What Will it Take?" Dr. Charles Dickson hints that the Catholic Church itself is hopeful for this unification:

> Christians are now talking openly about the office which Pope John Paul II himself called, "the greatest obstacle in the path of ecumenism." . . .
>
> Fortunately, time has a way of mellowing emotion; and now we are moving into the period of asking ourselves more rational and less emotional questions. What will it take to have a pope for *all* Christians? And, more basic than that, why do we need one anyway?
>
> To address the latter question first, most people are aware that the world's great religious traditions generally have a place of authority and position to which they look as a kind of geographic center of their faith. For Islam that center is Mecca; for Judaism, it is Jerusalem; and, of course, for Roman Catholics it is Rome. Protestants have no such center, because years of divisiveness have resulted in a multitude of factions.
>
> While in the past there was little concern and, at times, even exultation at this lack of centralization, thoughtful Protestant leaders are now beginning to question the wisdom of their situation. They wonder if there should not be a central authority to unite those who share a common faith. Should the historic papacy be recognized as the head of Christendom?
>
> The Protestant world is no longer closing its mind to such ideas.[9]

The Church is today committing the same sin of unbelief that the Israelites committed when they demanded to have a king. Their protection was God Himself, and they rejected Him in favor of having a man to whom they could look for protection. Those who desire to have a pope for all Christianity, are forgetting that the best means by which the truth can be preserved is *not* to have a centralized authority. God works in the hearts of individuals; the autonomous churches, though disagreeing in some areas, offer hope for those who see serious error and abuse in hierarchical structures. Once that protection is gone, Christians will be at the mercy of a super church whose seat of power is the Roman Empire.

The Empire Revived

History reveals that the fourth and last kingdom of Daniel's vision is the Roman Empire, which followed upon the Babylonian, Media-Persian, and Greek empires in that order. The Roman Empire is the last earthly government, and it was to devour the whole earth (Daniel 7:23). Nebuchadnezzar's dream coincided with Daniel's vision. The feet of the image in the dream were mixed with iron and clay—partly strong and partly weak (Daniel 2:1-45).

Today, the Roman Empire stretches throughout the entire earth. Everywhere democracies exist, they owe their jurisprudence and form of government to the Roman Empire's influence. With the dismantling of communism in Russia and the Eastern European countries, we are seeing removed the last vestiges of resistance against the Empire. With the polarization of the Eastern Orthodox churches due to the religious vacuum created by communism for over forty-five years, the Roman Catholic Church has before it the opportunity to capture back the Eastern empires that have eluded its grasp for centuries.

One of the major forces behind the scenes of what appeared to be sudden, spontaneous demands for democracy is the Roman Catholic Church. Beginning with Catholic Poland, the rest of the Eastern European nations have tumbled like dominoes; and the Roman Catholic Church, having polarized Protestantism, is receiving cooperation in bringing its own "gospel" to the people—a gospel which exalts the pope as a man of peace who can unify mankind.

We may rejoice at the release of millions from the grip of communist tyranny; we may rejoice that some will find salvation through the evangelistic efforts of true Christians; many souls will be saved in the process, according to God's plan. But we should not close our eyes to the reality of the Roman Catholic Church's financial power, coupled with acquiescing Protestants. The word-faith preachers are also exporting their heresies along with Bibles, creating a false sense of security for people who are going from the frying pan into the fire. All these factors will have a great influence in melding millions of souls into the Roman Empire.

In Nebuchadnezzar's dream, the feet of iron and clay represent those nations that comprised the Roman Empire at its fullest extent prior to its suffering its setback. The clay represents the rest of the nations that have been melded into the Empire not so much through military might, but through economic might. It was not the West's (i.e., the Roman Empire's) bombs that brought communism to its knees; it was communism's inability to compete in the international market and provide for its own people. The markets are controlled primarily by Western financial powers.

The Only Hope

Lacking the return of Jesus, the Church has no answer for the world's problems. The gospel it preaches—which for the most part is not the true Gospel, but an attempt to woo people through another gospel of easy-believism—has been largely rejected. As a result, the Church is increasingly abandoning hope that Jesus will return to put the world in order. Since Scofield Dispensationalism has been proven wrong in much of its eschatology, the Church is rapidly moving away from expecting Jesus' return. The reasoning is similar to that of the early Roman Catholic Church: if Jesus doesn't come back, then we must put the world system in order for Him. Augustine's *City of God* will become a reality through the spread of another gospel: a gospel predicated not upon the blood of Jesus for the salvation of souls, but upon the unification of the churches to bring the Kingdom of God to earth.

This gospel—a resurgence of the papal mandate for dominion —has gained momentum within mainstream Christianity. What we are witnessing in today's dominion theology is a resurrection of the Holy Roman Empire. And those who will not go along with the Plan will find themselves on the black lists of the established churches. Just as the Holy Roman Empire has for centuries persecuted our brethren—and has never apologized, or admitted wrongdoing—it is about to vent its wrath upon today's saints.

Mystery Babylon, that great city that sits on seven hills—that has diplomatic relations with virtually every nation on earth, and recognizes every government as valid except that of Israel—is about to be revealed in all its opulent wickedness:

> And there came one of the seven angels which had the seven vials, and talked with me, saying unto me, Come hither; I will shew unto thee the judgment of the great whore that sitteth upon many waters:
>
> With whom the kings of the earth have committed fornication, and the inhabitants of the earth have made drunk with the wine of her fornication.
>
> So he carried me away in the spirit into the wilderness: and I saw a woman sit upon a scarlet coloured beast, full of names of blasphemy, having seven heads and ten horns.
>
> And the woman was arrayed in purple and scarlet colour, and decked with gold and precious stones and pearls, having a golden cup in her hand full of abominations and filthiness of her fornication:
>
> And upon her forehead was a name written, MYSTERY BABYLON THE GREAT, THE MOTHER OF HARLOTS AND ABOMINATIONS OF THE EARTH.
>
> And I saw the woman drunken with the blood of the saints, and with the blood of the martyrs of Jesus: and when I saw her, I wondered with great admiration.

And the angel said unto me, Wherefore didst thou marvel? I will
tell thee the mystery of the woman, and of the beast that carrieth her,
which hath the seven heads and ten horns. . . .
And here is the mind which hath wisdom. The seven heads are
seven mountains on which the woman sitteth. . . .
And the woman which thou sawest is that great city, which
reigneth over the kings of the earth. (Revelation 17:1-7, 9, 18)

Roman Catholicism is not the ultimate conspiracy; it is, however, the major element working for the religious unification of
man. The political element is found in the secret societies' efforts
toward establishing a one-world government.

DOMINION TENETS

Dominion theology is not the product of an easily delineated
segment within the Church, but is propagated through a loose
network of autonomous sub-groups that emphasize different
aspects of a basic philosophy. There are some who, though not
holding a definitive dominion belief, expect the Church to experience a revival that will impact entire nations to where they will
become Christianized. Others have lesser expectations, believing
that at least some cities will be Christianized, somewhat like
Calvin's Geneva is said to have been.

Whether a particular dominion concept incorporates belief in
a worldwide theocracy or theonomic form of government, or in the
subjugation of individual, autonomous states or cities, depends
upon the particular brand of dominion theology to which one
adheres. Also, whether Jesus will return immediately after the
Church takes control, or after it has been in control for some time
up to and including the end of a vague Millennium, is likewise
dependent upon beliefs peculiar to each movement.

There are many teachings crucial to dominion theology which
we will be examining in future chapters. Some are stressed above
others within the framework of different movements, but they are
all in general agreement. At the least, they are willing to overlook
their differences at this time in order to impact the rest of the
Church in the hope of unifying it under their central doctrines.

It isn't important whether these teachers propagate the full
spectrum of dominion theology. What is of concern is that they
have adopted unscriptural beliefs that threaten the purity of the
Faith, and are preparing the churches to unify with Roman
Catholicism. They are also supporting one another in spreading
these doctrines throughout the Church via the mass communications media and special pastor's conferences.

Throughout the course of this study we will be examining the
various movements within the dominionist camp, as well as some

of their major proponents and teachings. But first it is important to give a general outline of dominion theology itself.

Taking Back The Kingdoms

A basic premise of dominion theology is that when Adam sinned, not only did man lose dominion over the earth, but God also lost control of the earth to Satan. Since that time, some say, God has been on the outside looking in, searching for a "covenant people" who will be His "extension" or "expression" in the earth to take dominion back from Satan. According to the dominionist interpretation, this is the meaning of the Great Commission.

Some teach that this is to be accomplished through certain "overcomers" who, by yielding themselves to the authority of latter-day apostles and prophets, will take control of the kingdoms of this world. These kingdoms are defined as the various social institutions, such as the "kingdom" of education, the "kingdom" of science, the "kingdom" of the arts, and so on. Most especially there is the "kingdom" of politics or government.

No Rapture

To the dominionists, the idea of the Lord returning to remove His saints from the earth smacks of defeatism. It is perceived as a pessimistic eschatology that is unacceptable to the dominion-oriented mindset. That mindset insists that the Church *will* be victorious, triumphing over all of God's enemies in order to present the earth to Jesus when, or if, He does eventually come back.

Some say they believe in the rapture, but they redefine it as a "feeling" of rapture, or excitement, when the Lord returns to receive the earth from the hands of His triumphant Church. In other words, every-one will be "caught up" emotionally. This is a misapplication of the term "caught up," which is an idiomatic expression peculiar to the English language. To be "caught up" in some exciting event is not the equivalent of the Greek *harpazo* as found in I Thessalonians 4:17, II Corinthians 12:2-4, and Revelation 12:5. This Greek word is used to describe the catching up bodily as in Acts 8:39 where Philip is "caught away" by the Holy Spirit to another locale.

Instead of believers being caught up, dominionists believe that it is the non-believers who will be caught up and destroyed, leaving only those who will live in harmony with the dominionist agenda.

No Hope For Israel

Since there will be no bodily catching away—or rapture—of the Church (at least, some say, until the Church has taken dominion in the face of adversity), there will be no restoration of the nation of Israel. Dominionists essentially deny that God has a future plan for Israel. They say that the Church is now Israel; there will be no seventieth week of Daniel for natural Israelites.

All of the prophecies regarding future Israel—both in the Old and New Testaments—are made to apply to the Church. The restoration of the dry bones in Ezekiel 37:1-11 is said to be the Church's restoration from out of Babylon (defined as denominationalism). This restoration will result in all believers possessing the same mind and goals delineated by the latter-day apostles and prophets who are beginning to make their appearance.

The error of dominion theology is in believing that the Church is now Israel because of faith. The Church is not Israel; we are *grafted into* Israel (Romans 11:7-27).

Scripture tells us that, generally, the eyes of the Jews have been blinded until the age of the Gentiles is completed, after which time they will believe in Jesus as their Messiah. This will happen when they see Him come for His Church; the whole nation will see Him whom they have pierced, and will mourn (Zechariah 12:10; John 19:37; Revelation 1:7).

This does not, however, absolve us of the need for witnessing to Jews now; on the contrary, as we see the day approaching, we must be all the more diligent in our evangelism to all segments of humanity including the Jews. It does no good to offer aid to Israel without also taking them the Gospel. Only let's take them the *true* Gospel.

Millennial Views

Another teaching of dominion theology in general is that the Great Tribulation is not a time when a personal anti-Christ and False Prophet will wage war against God's people, but rather a time of tribulation for the world brought about by God's judgment *through* His people. There is no personal anti-Christ; anti-Christ is a spirit of rejection against Church authority.

Since dominionists do not believe in a literal catching up of the Church to be with the Lord, most subscribe to a mid- or postmillennial position: Jesus will return after the Millennium has been completed, or at least after it has begun under the rule of the Church. Some are amillennialists, believing that Jesus will never come back personally, or that He already came back to His own generation; in the latter case, it is believed that we are already in the Millennium, and that the task of the Church is to complete the "mopping up" process of purifying the earth from evil elements.

Many premillennialists are beginning to buy into the dominion concept, but have not shed a sufficient amount of their

Dispensationalist tendencies to accept it fully. They would call themselves "premillennial dominionists," who believe that the rapture will occur after the Church has taken dominion to some extent, but before the millennial reign of Jesus is established.

Denials

Some of the most vocal dominionists even deny that they believe in dominion theology on the basis that they do not hold to every aberrant belief. But *any* belief that the Church or Christians have a *mandate* to gain authority over the temporal institutions of men, to *any* degree, is dominion theology.

Another reason for denial is simple dishonesty; some do not want those outside their circle of initiation to be alerted to their dominionist beliefs because they fear hindering the progress they have made through subtle inroads into the mainstream of Christianity. It is not beyond some to lie to conceal their hidden agenda.

Those on the fringes of dominionist thought who still believe in the rapture will one day have to come to grips with their beliefs and either fall completely into the dominion camp, or reject dominion theology altogether. What would be the point in taking dominion only to leave the earth to the ungodly when we are caught up to be with the Lord? They will come to see that, whether there will be a rapture event that leads to three-and-one-half years in heaven (or seven years, according to some), or one that lasts only moments, the very concept of a rapture does not fit into dominion theology.

The Church Failing

Dominionists perceive the Church as having thus far failed in fulfilling Jesus' commission to take dominion over the nations, because it has not understood what He meant when He told His disciples that they would be His witnesses throughout the whole earth. The dominionist interpretation of being a witness means to take dominion, bringing all things (individuals and governments) into obedience to Christ. In order to demonstrate the Kingdom of God, the Church must not only be united under specially anointed men and women, but must be prosperous, having taken control of a significant portion of the world's wealth. This belief is justified by quoting Psalm 24:1:

> The earth is the Lord's and the fulness thereof; the world, and they that dwell therein.

If the earth is the Lord's, and if we are joint heirs with Christ, then the earth is ours—now. Or so the reasoning goes. Not to take dominion is not to receive our inheritance.

Either the dominionists fail to see that if the earth is already the Lord's, then we do not need to make it His, or their intention is really to make it theirs.

Diverse Movements

Within the dominion camp are several movements whose teachings are similar over all, yet diverse in some ways. These movements, though to a greater or lesser degree disavowing association with each other, are sufficiently homogenous in their eschatological and theological stances that they can all be placed under the common banner of dominion theology. Some actually overlap one another. The more prominent of these movements are:

- Latter Rain
- Manifest Sons of God
- Identity
- Restoration
- Charismatic Renewal
- Shepherding-Discipleship
- Kingdom Message
- Positive Confession
- Reconstruction

Some movements are more extreme than others, and each is somewhat unique in its approach to the basic tenets of dominion theology. Not everyone within each movement is necessarily in agreement with each other, let alone with those in other movements. Still, each has teachings that are sufficiently aberrant that they warrant careful testing by Scripture. Each has a part in propagating all or a major number of dominionist teachings, though some individuals within some movements would deny that they are dominionists. Some are networking together for their common cause. Some teachings are quite bizarre, and reveal occultic influences.

Not everyone in these movements believe all dominionist teachings. For example, not all charismatics are dominionists. Yet while the adage "guilt by association" does not always hold true, a consistent pattern of support and fraternization are sufficient grounds to question whether or not one holds the views of those he supports and with whom he seeks unity.

Some Terminology

There is certain terminology peculiar to dominion theology, knowledge of which can alert us to the possibility that we are hearing from an adherent. A few occasions of word usage may prove nothing, of course, But a pattern of usage and dependence upon terminology peculiar to dominion theology is reason for concern and for further investigation into a teacher's beliefs.

The following terminology should cause concern even though much will be defended as scriptural by those who use them:

Anti-anointed one	Latter rain
Antichrist spirit	Manifested sons of God
At one	Many-membered man child
Birthing in the spirit	New breed
Bride company	New order
Christ principle	New Zion
Covenant people	On-going incarnation
Dominion	Overcomers
Ecclesias	Power
Elijah Company	Reconstruction
Feast of Tabernacles	Restoration
Five-fold ministries	Serpent's seed
Get this into your spirit	Signs and wonders
God-like faith	Sonship
Immortalization	Spoken word
Jezebel spirit	Tabernacle of David
Kingdom now	Theonomy
Kingdom principles	Unity
Kingdom theology	Unity in diversity

Two Major Streams

There are nuances to the philosophical approach to dominion, but the various movements can all be classified under two basic headings: 1) Reconstruction, which establishes an intellectual basis for dominion theology, and is basically non-charismatic; 2) what I call "Charismatic Dominionism" for lack of any term previously forthcoming.

The latter encompasses most of the factions apart from the Reconstruction movement and makes up the bulk of the dominionist community. Its common element is its adoption of major teachings from the Latter Rain Movement of the late forties and early fifties.

There are indications that Reconstruction and Charismatic Dominionism are finding common ground for unity in spite of some Reconstructionists' denunciation of charismatism.

PART II - CHARISMATIC DOMINIONISM

1
The Latter Rain

Some two decades before Pentecostalism found its way into the denominations as the Charismatic Renewal, it experienced a new surge of experience-oriented theology within its own ranks. It was from this neo-Pentecostal experience—what came to be called the "Latter Rain Movement"—that Charismatic Dominionism sprang. The more prominent leaders of that movement blended Pentecostal fervor with teachings that the Church was on the brink of a worldwide revival. That revival would result in a victorious Church without spot or wrinkle, and the saints (or a number of saints called "overcomers") would attain sinless perfection. Thus perfected, the Church would inherit the earth and rule over the nations with a rod of iron.

To understand Charismatic Dominionism one must know the history of the Latter Rain Movement and the teachings of those who formulated its theological and eschatological beliefs.

FRANKLIN HALL

In the fall of 1946, a "major fasting and prayer daily revival center" was established in San Diego, California. Under the leadership of Franklin Hall (assisted by Jack Walker, father of child evangelist "Little David" Walker), the teaching of fasting as a means of bringing about revival and the "restoration" of the Church spread through the Pentecostal world.[1]

Other ministers who helped establish the fasting and prayer center were Dr. Waltrip (husband of Kathryn Kuhlman), Stanley Comstock, Earl Ivy, Tommy Baird, Myrtle Page, and Franklin Hall's brothers, Delbert, Harold, and Virgil. (Delbert Hall and his wife, Florence, were pastors.)[2]

The Summer 1985 issue of Franklin Hall's newsletter, *Miracle Word*, reveals some of the early history of his work:

> A fasting chain came about. Several were on major fasts around the clock. Many were fasting for not only days but

weeks at a time. One lady, Sister Mary Sommerville, fasted without food for eighty-three days. She was so strong on this notable fast that she ran and danced all over the place, being drunk on both the inner and outer filling of the precious Holy Spirit.[3]

Hall claims more than one thousand converts during the first year of the center's existence, with scores being healed of diseases through fasting and prayer. Alleged appearances of the Holy Ghost in fire and smoke are also related in Hall's newsletter:

> Once or twice the Fire department was briefed by folk seeing the Holy Smoke and Fire through the windows upstairs. They came running up the steps with the hoses to put out the fire. Some of the firemen, seeing that it was not a natural fire, sat down in the large revival center hall and worshipped the Lord getting saved.[4]

Spreading the Word

Hall sold some assets and borrowed against his home to finance the printing of "millions of pieces of literature" to send to people all over the world.[5] He attributes what was perceived as the great healing revival of the late forties and early fifties to this outreach.

During this time (1946) Franklin Hall wrote his book, *Atomic Power With God Through Fasting and Prayer*, which was to have a significant impact upon both Pentecostalism and the neo-Pentecostalism that was just emerging. Gordon Lindsay's publication, *Voice of Healing*, helped spread Hall's fasting message, as did Thomas and Evelyn Wyatt's worldwide radio broadcasts.

Hall's newsletter records how other well-known preachers of his day received his message:

> Rev. Walter Frederick, former Assembly superintendent in Canada, sent Brother Hall's literature to every Pentecostal preacher in Canada.... A few of the others (not too well-known then) ministers who had major fasting experiences by our writings in the 1946, 1947 to 1950 fasting era and who also became famous are:
>
> Wm. Freeman, Gordon Lindsay, A.A. Allen, O.L. Jaggers, Gayle Jackson, Oral Roberts, David Nunn, Wm. Branham, W.V. Grant, Wm. Hagen, Dale Hanson, [and] Tommy Hicks.[6]

Hall's writings on fasting and diet for spiritual restoration might be seen as the beginnings of today's "Christian holism."

Occult Influences

As evidence of God's favor upon those who fast, Hall claimed that even the prayers of pagans will be answered by God if they are accompanied by fasting:

> Many, if not all, the American Indian tribes sought revelation of the Great Spirit through Prayer and Fasting. When they had famines, food shortages, lack of rain, etc., the Great Spirit was sought through prayer and fasting, and their prayers were answered.[7]

Hall uses this as an example of how fasting is necessary to have our prayers answered. In fact, he states that "without fasting, prayer becomes ineffectual."[8] If we analyze Hall's claims, we must come to the conclusion that those who pray to demons will have their prayers answered if they fast, but Christians will not have their prayers answered if they don't fast. At the least, it seems, they would be hindered greatly.

In effect, this idea negates grace and makes one's relationship to God dependent upon works. By giving credit for answered prayer offered to the demon gods of pagan religions, Hall displayed a mindset characteristic of occult science.

The occult influence on Hall's career is evident in later writings. His book, *The Return of Immortality*, suggests that Christians can become immortal through stages of spiritual growth, and through experiences with what he calls, "UFO's, UHO's, and the UIO gravitational and levitation control."[9] His teachings on attaining immortality in this life through psycho-spiritual exercises and righteous living were the foundation upon which others who followed him based *their* immortalization theories.

Immortalization

Hall's main point in his immortalization theory is that "the sleeping, so called, unfoundationally built church" must awaken to "a real cause and calling, that when God's word is completely acted upon and complied with, will result in bringing about the real gushers and torrents of the long, past due, RAIN OF RIGHTEOUSNESS. A rain of IMMORTALITY UPON THE EARTH that so many prophets have written about and portrayed in their prophecies."[10] (Hall's emphasis)

Hall's premise is not based on God's promise of immortality after the resurrection, but on the idea that those who apply Hall's teachings will become immortal while in their present flesh-and-blood bodies:

Permanent, lasting Freedoms from all sickness, harmful, accident things and defeat will come about. Freedom from the imprisonment of all gravitational forces will also be brought upon the whole man.

This study teaches one the power and secrets of space flight. Space floatation [sic] and hovering ability. It gives the Bible formula for weightlessness, the "raising up" power of those who come to Immortality (Jn. 6 chapter and Rom. 2:7).[11]

Hall gives "evidence" of his already having attained a degree of immortality which allegedly affects everything that comes in contact with his body:

Brother Hall's light colored jacket is seven years old and has never been pressed or cleaned or aireated [sic] in 7 years, since new, yet it has been worn repeatedly in many overseas countries and regularly in all crusades everywhere (excepting one). It has been on more than 200 airlines in travels. It has no spots, stains, discoloration or body odors anywhere on it or inside it — similar to the children of Israel's clothes under the Glory, Immortality Cloud of Fire Power.[12]

What Hall calls the "Immortality blessings" are alleged to be more successfully attained through open-eyed prayer. "Coming with closed eyes," he states, "destroys faith."[13]

He claims that there is an "Immortal Substance" that comes upon those who feed upon it "from within Christ's now body"— the "FIRE — IMMORTAL — PACKED — BODY"[14] (Hall's emphasis).

What Hall means by these esoteric references is difficult to ascertain. But an "Immortal Substance" is claimed to be seen on those who attend his meetings, as a fine gold and silver, sparkling material that emanates from sometimes visible "Immortal Heavenly Objects" (IHO's), "Unusual Heavenly Objects" (UHO's), and "Unidentified Flying Objects" (UFO's).[15]

The sparkling shining FINE GOLD and SILVER are seen upon their SKIN, brought about through the faith-power of impartation. The polished brass, the beryl stone appearances are even now manifested today.[16] (Hall's emphasis)

Hall invites the reader of his book to witness these phenomena by attending "the International Holy Ghost and Fire Seminars of Brother and Sister Franklin Hall" at his Arizona headquarters. This sparkling material Hall calls, "The shiny metal like, Jesus' substance."[17]

Astrological Influences

While Hall has many good things to say about fasting from a health standpoint, when it comes to spiritual matters he often transcends scriptural parameters and delves into the occult. The book upon which many "faith healers" of the Latter Rain Movement publicly acknowledged their dependence, *Atomic Power With God Through Fasting and Prayer*, is evidence:

> In the zodiacal sign, "Scorpio," which is the eighth sign of the Zodiac, we have a picture of a scorpion with its stinger lifted ready to strike. This is the sign of death, and is supposed to govern the sex area. Just before this sign in the heavens, there is a sign of the Judge, Jesus, who is the giver of LIFE. Jesus proceeds toward death and pulls the STING OUT OF DEATH. "O, death, where is thy sting? O, grave, where is thy victory?"[18] (Hall's emphasis)

Hall's penchant for a form of "Christian astrology" is evidenced further in his statement that, "in 1848 A.D. the Aquarian Age was introduced to the world."[19] Those familiar with the New Age Movement will recognize the Aquarian Age as the "Golden Age" of enlightenment when mankind will allegedly take a quantum leap in his evolutionary progress to immortalization.

Strange Sayings

Hall's writings are replete with strange statements difficult to decipher. The following, though a bit lengthy and poorly written, are examples:

> So much has been said about the travels of the astronauts, about conquering space and even going to Venus or Mars, about the power behind the saucers. The overcoming saints, however, are hundreds of years ahead of our scientists. These heaven projected saints will be so clothed and covered with the Immortality, supernatural, ZOOMING sparkling Substance, that it will be no more trouble at all for them to take off.
>
> Where will they go?
>
> They will fly right into the Glory Cloud residence of our Lord and Savior, Heaven in Him. Into His Cloud Fire Body. (Rev. 12:5)
>
> What distance will they go?
>
> The distance, at first, may not be very far away, however, as the 8th church from out of the 7 churches of revelation, called the "overcomers," become more and more adjusted and acclimated to Holy Ghost space flight, great distances will be taken, will seem like no distance at all.

Jesus taught a small, but precious group of His followers—those who were able to bear it, that gravity would be completely loosed from them, in the last days, when they learned how to train their appetites into a different channel. We must learn to labor for the meat that endures unto everlasting (IMMORTAL) *life*. The meat that draws us away from gravity holding things. Jn. 6:27.

The "not-perisheth" menu is the menu of Immortality weight releasing power. The "endureth unto everlasting life" menu.

. . . The quickening power of the Holy Ghost brings about Immortality REVERSE ENERGY EMPOWERMENT.[20] (Hall's emphasis)

Gravity-freed, great people will run up walls, not break rank, and if they fall on a sword, the Immortality power from Jesus' body, on them, will protect them. It appears that, they also can walk or run upside down. See Joel 2:3-11[21]

In an ad for another of his books, *Formula for Raising the Dead*, Hall cautions the potential purchaser, "This volume is only for very advanced Holy Ghost people. Do not order unless you are open to an apostolic teaching and have read four other books by Bro. Franklin Hall."[22]

Although much of what Hall teaches today was not part of his original work, the heavy flavor of occultism in his teachings was evident as far back as 1946 and should have provided sufficient warning. Yet many prominent teachers credit the empowerment for their ministries (especially alleged healing ministries) on Hall's *Atomic Power With God Through Fasting and Prayer*.

In 1956 Hall founded his Deliverance Foundation; by 1970 it claimed thirty-two affiliated churches totalling two-thousand members. He attributes the loss of fervor for the neo-Pentecostal revival to lack of fasting and to "spiritual coasting" by its leaders.[23]

WILLIAM BRANHAM

Inscribed on a pyramid-shaped tombstone in a Jeffersonville, Indiana, cemetery, are the names of the seven churches of the Book of Revelation. "Ephesian" at the base represents the beginning of the Church Age; "Laodicean" near the top represents the end of the Church Age. On the opposite face are the names of seven men whose impact on the Church throughout its history has been significant.

Were the two faces of the pyramid juxtaposed one over the other, we would see the names of the churches superimposed over the men's names in the following order:

Ephesian—Paul
Smyrnean—Ireneaus
Pergamean—Martin
Thyatirean—Columba
Sardisean—Luther
Philadelphian—Wesley
Laodicean—Branham

Among many proponents of Charismatic Dominionism these men are considered apostles to the various stages of Church history. To a significant number, William Branham was the greatest apostle and prophet for the Church's final age.

Franklin Hall's Influence

In 1948, Branham, a Baptist preacher turned Pentecostal, was greatly influenced by Franklin Hall's teachings, especially through Hall's *Atomic Power With God Through Fasting and Prayer*.

Branham gained notoriety for his teachings on what he called "God's Seventh Church Age," which is supposedly the final move of God before the manifestation of His Kingdom throughout the earth. He based this belief primarily on Joel 2:23 and Revelation 1:20-3:32, the latter recording Jesus' messages to the seven churches in Asia Minor.

Branham claimed that the angels (messengers) to the churches were men who appeared at various times throughout Church history bringing new revelations that led the Church into progressive stages of sanctification. As his tombstone indicates, Branham was thought to be the angel to the Church of Laodicea—the end-time Church.

In his teachings on Joel 2:23, Branham defined the "latter rain" as the neo-Pentecostalism of his day. He taught that God's promise to restore what the locust, cankerworm, caterpillar, and palmerworm had eaten, would be the "restoration" of the Church out of denominationalism, which he equated with the Mark of the Beast.

Although denying he was a believer in the oneness doctrine, Branham had his own form of oneness teaching that defined God as one person who manifested Himself as three different "attributes": the Father, the Son, and the Holy Spirit, rather than three Persons comprising one Godhead.[24] He believed that the doctrine of the Trinity was the "Babylonian Foundation" of the denominations.[25]

Branham believed that the Word of God was given in three forms: the Zodiac, the Egyptian pyramids, and the written Scriptures.[26] The Zodiac theory was not new, having been put forth by Joseph A. Seiss in his 1884 book, *The Gospel in the Stars*. Almost a decade later, in 1893, E.W. Bullinger's book, *The Witness of the Stars*, was published, and gave impetus to the theory that has carried on to the present time. Of late, this theory has been revived through the teachings of D. James Kennedy, William Banks and Marilyn Hickey.

The idea that the Great Pyramid of Giza in Egypt was constructed by Enoch as a memorial to God is at least as old as the Zodiac theory, and is popular with the Dawn Bible Students, an offshoot of the Jehovah's Witnesses.

The Serpent's Seed

It was said of Branham that he had a simplicity and apparent humility which attracted many followers. Gordon Lindsay, founder of Christ for the Nations, told of how Branham impressed audiences with his "utter and complete consecration."[27] Yet in spite of this alleged humility and consecration, he had great difficulty controlling a strident, hateful attitude toward women. His words, transcribed from a sermon, reveal his struggle with that attitude:

> But I remember when my father's still up there running, I had to be out there with water and stuff, see young ladies that wasn't over seventeen, eighteen years, up there with a man my age now, drunk. And they'd have to sober them up and give them black coffee, to get them home to cook their husband's supper. Oh, something like that, I said, . . . This was my remark then, *"They're not worth a good clean bullet to kill them with it!"* That's right. And I hated women. That's right. And I just have to watch every move now, to keep from still thinking the same thing.[28] (Branham's emphasis)

Somehow, Branham overlooked his father's role in contributing to these girls' delinquency, and focused his anger on them. This anger toward women contributed to the development of Branham's bizarre "Serpent Seed" teaching. Based on a twisted interpretation of Genesis 3:13, Branham taught that when Eve said, "The serpent beguiled me, and I did eat," she meant that the serpent had seduced her sexually. Out of this bestial affair was born Cain. Since that time evil has passed from generation to generation through women, who keep the seed of the serpent alive;[29] therefore, because of their enticements, women are responsible for the evil in the world.

The Serpent's Seed teaching indicates that Branham didn't take the Scriptures literally where they state plainly that Cain was the product of Adam and Eve's union:

> *And Adam knew Eve his wife; and she conceived and bare Cain*
> (Genesis 4:1).

Branham preached a rigid moral code that lambasted women for their manner of dress, and may have been responsible for his "revelation" that allowed for divorce.[30]

Supernatural Manifestations

From the time of his infancy it was perceived by his parents that William's life had upon it the touch of the supernatural. Born in 1909 in a mountain cabin near Berksville, Kentucky, William Marrion Branham's childhood was spent in extreme poverty. His father was only eighteen years old, and his mother fifteen, when he came into the world weighing a scant five pounds—the first of nine boys and one girl.[31]

The following account may be legend or fact, but it was a major part of Branham's testimony: On the day of his birth, after being washed, he was placed in his mother's arms by the midwife who then went to a window to open the shutter. (There was no glass in the Branham house in those days.) As dawn broke, sending a few rays of light into the room, there was seen a circular halo about a foot in diameter above the bed where little William lay in his mother's arms.[32]

Thousands of people have supposedly seen this recurring halo, which is ostensibly revealed in a photograph taken in Houston, Texas, during a January 1950 campaign.

When he was three years of age, Branham first experienced what he called "the Voice." At age seven the Voice commanded him, "Don't you never drink, smoke, or defile your body in any way. There'll be work for you to do when you get older."[33]

The Voice accompanied Branham throughout his lifetime, and eventually made itself known as an "angel" that directed him in virtually every aspect of his personal life.[34] While conducting healing services Branham would often fall into a trance during which his angel would work through him. Asked once if the healings were done by the Holy Spirit, Branham replied, "No, my angel does it."[35]

Branham was one of the foremost proponents of the theory of healing and of imparting the Holy Spirit through the laying on of hands. He claimed to feel heat in his hand as he touched affected parts, and appeared to exhibit a remarkable clairvoyance in knowing intimate details of the lives of people he had never seen before. No doubt this was due either to the angel's possession of his mind, or to trickery similar to that of which W.V. Grant, Jr. and Peter Popoff were exposed by illusionist James Randi.[36]

Difficulties With The Brethren

Branham's unorthodox methods of healing and allegedly imparting the Holy Spirit by the laying on of his hands came under severe criticism by the Pentecostal Assemblies of Canada. These practices became major sources of controversy between the Latter Rain Movement and the established Pentecostal denominations who held to their belief that one must tarry in prayer for the gift of the Holy Spirit.

In spite of his bizarre healing methods and aberrant doctrines, Branham enjoyed remarkable popularity among Pentecostals, and was warmly received by such notables as Oral Roberts, W.V. Grant, A.A. Allen, Gordon Lindsay, O.L. Jaggers, George Warnock, Demos Shakarian (founder of the Full Gospel Business Men's Fellowship International), and the man from whom Branham gleaned many of his beliefs, Franklin Hall.

Although many Pentecostals were willing to overlook Branham's aberrant teachings and embrace him as an apostle and prophet, his popularity declined in the late 1950s after his numerous bold proclamations of "thus saith the Lord." This manner of attempting to establish his doctrines as equal with the Word of God caused many Pentecostal churches to become reluctant in allowing him to speak.

No one conversant with American Church history during the mid-twentieth century will deny that William Branham had a tremendous effect on the neo-Pentecostalism of his time. From all accounts, he seemed to exhibit remarkable healing powers which no doubt gave credibility to his teachings.

Branham was welcomed by many Pentecostal churches and parachurch organizations such as the Full Gospel Business Men's Fellowship International. For years he was a frequent speaker at FGBMFI's regional and national conventions. This organization in particular provided his most reliable financial support. In 1961, the editor of FGBMFI's magazine, *Voice*, wrote, "In Bible Days, there were men of God who were Prophets and Seers. But in all the Sacred Records, none of these had a greater ministry than that of William Branham."[37]

It should be acknowledged that often what Branham taught as a guest speaker for other organizations differed from what he taught at his own church, Branham Tabernacle. There he felt freer to disclose his more aberrant teachings. Yet toward the end of his career his public espousal of strange doctrines and insistence that his teachings were directly from God became even more controversial and he was used less frequently by the FGBMFI For several ensuing years, however, his speaking engagements were underwritten by local chapters.

Eulogies

Branham's life ended abruptly while on a trip to Arizona. His car was hit head-on by one driven by a drunken driver, and for six days he lay in a coma. On Christmas Eve, 1965, he passed away.

The entire Pentecostal world was shaken by the tragedy. "A number of old friends—among them Oral Roberts, Demos Shakarian, and T.L. Osborn—telephoned their concern."[38] Demos Shakarian wrote:

> Rev. Branham often made the statement that the only Fellowship to which he belonged was FGBMFI. Often, when called upon to speak at various conventions and chapter meetings, he has traveled long distances to keep those engagements. His spirit of service was an inspiration.[39]

Many of Branham's followers believed that he had truly come in the spirit of Elijah; some believed him to be God, born of a virgin.[40] They fully expected him to rise from the dead and come back to them at the end of three days.

To date, William Branham's body is still in the grave. But his occult methodology of healing was picked up by hundreds of pastors and teachers upon whom he had lain his hands, and who have traded on it to a greater or lesser degree.

THE SHARON BRETHREN

In the fall of 1947, two former pastors for the Pentecostal Assemblies of Canada, George Hawtin and Percy G. Hunt, joined in an independent ministry with Herrick Holt, pastor of the North Battleford, Saskatchewan, Church of the Foursquare Gospel. That ministry—Sharon Orphanage and Schools, which Holt had originally started in a large residence in North Battleford—had come to occupy about one thousand acres of farmland some ten miles outside the city limits.

With Hawtin and Hunt came seventy students from Bethel Bible Institute. Both taught at Bethel before Hawtin was asked to resign for lack of cooperation, and Hunt resigned out of sympathy. George Hawtin's brother-in-law, Milford Kirkpatrick, and Ernest Hawtin, George's brother, soon joined in ministry at Sharon.[41]

Herrick Holt had been preaching that God was going to be doing a "new thing" in accordance with the prophecy of Isaiah 43:18-19:

> *Remember ye not the former things, neither consider the things of old. Behold I will do a new thing;*
> *Now it shall spring forth; shall ye not know it? I will even make a way in the wilderness, and rivers in the desert.*

Of great influence upon the work at Sharon were the teachings of William Branham. At one of his campaigns, several of the school's brethren had Branham lay his hands on them for the impartation of spiritual power. With renewed fervor, the brethren took Branham's teachings back to Sharon, unaware that the power (or belief in some power) bestowed upon them by Branham would make their ministry the focal point of the Latter Rain Movement for several years to come.[42]

Another influence—on the Hawtin brothers in particular—was J.E. Stile's book, *The Gift of the Holy Spirit*, which asserted that if one were truly repentant, and believed on the Lord Jesus Christ, all that was necessary for him to receive the Holy Spirit was for another believer to lay hands on him.[43]

Franklin Hall's teachings also influenced the Sharon brethren greatly. Wrote Ernest Hawtin:

> The truth of fasting was one great contributing factor to the revival. One year before this we had read Franklin Hall's book, entitled, "Atomic Power With God Through Fasting and Prayer." We immediately began to practise [sic] fasting. Previously we had not understood the possibility of long fasts. The revival would never have been possible without the restoration of this great truth through our good brother Hall.[44]

On February 11, 1948, a young woman at the Bible school prophesied that a great revival was about to break out. The next day, according to Ern Hawtin, the Holy Spirit fell with great power:

> Day after day the Glory and Power of God came among us. Great repentance, humbling, fasting and prayer prevailed in everyone.[45]

News of the events at North Battleford spread, and soon people were coming from everywhere in hope of receiving spiritual power. They believed that the long drought was over for Pentecostals, whose use of the gifts had declined since the advent of Pentecostalism at the turn of the century.[46]

A striking characteristic of the Sharon revival was the effort to avoid the establishment of another denomination as had happened during the earlier Pentecostal movement. George Hawtin was especially adamant about this and labored to instruct those who were touched by his ministry not to fall into that trap. He felt that the unity of the Church was essential to bring about its restoration, and he therefore encouraged the establishment of autonomous, local congregations.

It became a hallmark of the Latter Rain Movement that innumerable independent churches sprang up with no denominational affiliation. This did not set well with the Pentecostal denominations who lost many members to this "new thing."

A major point of controversy between the North Battleford brethren and some Pentecostal denominations was the teaching by the former that there are present-day apostles and prophets for the Church.[47] And though George Hawtin wrote in the June 1948 issue of *The Sharon Star* (the school's newsletter) that "no church exercises or has any right to exercise authority or jurisdiction over another church, its pastors or members," the traveling presbytery from Sharon, of which he was a part, did indeed exercise authority over other congregations through personal directive prophecy.[48]

In spite of the Sharon group's insistence upon autonomy, they eventually became sectarian to the extreme, holding to the notions that no teaching was valid unless it originated with them, no fellowship was to be engaged in with anyone outside theirs, and that *they alone* were the purveyors of God's truth. If anyone would be an overcomer, it must be through obedience to their authority.

Even some who were endorsed as apostles and prophets by the Sharon group eventually became disillusioned and broke ties with them. Among these was Reg Layzell who wrote:

> At the first camp meeting you were made a member of the Body of Christ by the Spirit of God. And even if you said you were not in the Body you still were. No man could put you in or take you out. Now the error: they claim you are only put in by them and can be put out [only] by them.[49]

A significant event in the history of Sharon Orphanage and Schools was its July 7-18, 1948, camp meeting, to which thousands of people from Canada and the United States flocked, hoping to receive something special from God. Residents from at least twenty states attended, and the great Latter Rain Movement burst upon the world.

From that time, the movement spread rapidly and Sharon Orphanage and Schools soon became only one of many centers of teaching for the Latter Rain Movement.

In his thesis on this movement, Richard Riss, an advocate of the Latter Rain teachings, states:

> It should be noted however, that prior to the revival, these practices [laying on of hands and acceptance of apostles and prophets] were already commonplace in some places, including Elim Bible Institute, which was at that time in Hornell, N.Y., and

which, until the revival, had not had contact with North Battleford.[50]

It should also be noted . . . that prophecy was a major distinguishing mark of the Latter Rain Movement, whereas, in the case of the healing evangelists, healing was more prominent, and in the case of the early pentecostal revival, tongues had prominence.[51]

Although it was the Sharon brethren that gave real impetus to these teachings, Elim Bible Institute was a center for neo-Pentecostalism for years prior to the outbreak of the Latter Rain Movement. Elim Bible Institute has continued even to this day with its influence, basing much of its teachings on Latter Rain doctrine, while the Sharon group has largely been relegated to obscurity. But there can be no denying that Sharon Orphanage and Schools gave such great impetus to the teachings of the Latter Rain Movement that it's influence is still being felt in the Church.

GEORGE WARNOCK

Among those present at the Sharon camp meeting in July 1948 was George Warnock who at one time had been personal secretary to Ern Baxter, an associate with William Branham's healing ministry.[52] During the course of the meetings at Sharon, one of the teachers, James Watt, made a passing remark that the third of Israel's feasts, the Feast of Tabernacles, was yet to be fulfilled.[53] This struck Warnock and he began to associate it with the end-time ministry of the Church, and the idea of restoration.

In the fall of 1949 Warnock took up residence at Sharon, "assisting in the office work, and helping in the Bible School and in the local church."[54] In 1951 he wrote his book, *The Feast of Tabernacles*, in which he laid out a specific doctrine for the Latter Rain Movement. He taught that the Church was about to usher in the completion of God's feasts through perfection of the saints and their dominion over the earth.

Essentially, this Latter Rain teaching implies that the three great annual feasts of the Lord in Israel's worship (Passover, Pentecost, and Tabernacles) typify the whole Church Age, beginning with the death of Jesus on the cross, and consummating in "the manifestation of the Sons of God"—the "overcomers" who will become perfected and step into immortality in order to establish the Kingdom of God on earth.[55]

According to Warnock, this will be accomplished through the restoration of the Church in unity and, once that restoration is realized, the saints will "eat the Lord's Supper in reality."[56]

BILL BRITTON

At the annual Sunday school convention of the Assemblies of God in 1949, held in Springfield, Missouri, Bill Britton, a 39-year-old pastor, heard about the Latter Rain Movement and decided to become a part of it. As a result, Britton became an avid proponent of the "deeper life" and "sonship" messages. His focus was on the teaching that the "man child" of Revelation 12 is the true, overcoming Church of the New Order, and that Christians who do not receive this revelation are of the old order of denominationalism or "Babylon."

To enter into sonship was to attain the full degree of the manifestation of the sons of God through a maturing process in character, spiritual ministries, and gifts. The extension of this teaching was that Jesus became the Christ through the maturation process, and that all believers can attain that same maturity and enter into immortality.

He also taught that Satan was not a fallen angel, but was created as an evil being by God, with a specific purpose. This same theme was put forth by Identity preacher J. Preston Eby in his writing entitled "The Serpent."

Britton founded the House of Prayer in Springfield, Missouri, which published *Voice of the Watchman*, a prophetic newsletter espousing Latter Rain and Manifest Sons of God doctrine. He had a wide-reaching effect among Pentecostals until his death in 1985.

ORAL ROBERTS

A product of the Latter Rain Movement, Oral Roberts followed in the wake of William Branham, but focused his energies on attempts to minister healing. Today, he is considered America's premier healing evangelist.[57] The *Dictionary of Pentecostal and Charismatic Movements* credits Roberts with wide-reaching influence upon neo-Pentecostalism and today's charismatic movement:

> Roberts' success in healing evangelism thrust him to the leadership of a generation of dynamic revivalists who took the message of divine healing around the world after 1947. His ecumenical crusades were instrumental in the revitalization of Pentecostalism in the post-World War II era. He was also influential in the formation of the Full Gospel Business Men's Fellowship International in 1951 as well as a leading figure in laying the foundation for the modern charismatic movement. . . . By 1980 a Gallup Poll revealed that Roberts' name was recognized by a phenomenal 84 percent of the American public, and historian Vinson Synan observed that Roberts was considered the most prominent Pentecostal in the world.[58]

DEMOS SHAKARIAN

Another Latter Rain adherent and avid follower of William Branham was Demos Shakarian, a prosperous dairy farmer from the Downey, California area. In 1951, Shakarian told Oral Roberts that he felt God was leading him to start a fellowship for businessmen. As a result, the first meeting of the Full Gospel Business Men's Fellowship International was held in Clifton's Cafeteria in Los Angeles, with Roberts as its first guest speaker. Since then the organization has grown to encompass chapters all over the United States and in many foreign countries.

The major thrust of FGBMFI has been to bring the Pentecostal experience to those outside the Pentecostal churches. Meetings focus on evangelism and the baptism in the Holy Spirit as perceived by neo-Pentecostalism, which must be accompanied by the evidence of speaking in tongues. Evangelization is considered of primary importance to FGBMFI. Through Roberts and various other guest speakers over the past decades, FGBMFI has been one of the most influential groups to come out of the Latter Rain Movement and touch virtually every prominent leader in the Charismatic Renewal.

CONTINUING INFLUENCES

Out of the Latter Rain Movement came many teachers whose impact is still being felt today. Some of the most influential are relatively unknown. Many are strong leaders of smaller churches and ministries. Some of the more well-known have focused on specific areas of ministry and have been relatively silent about the full extent of their Latter Rain beliefs.

Besides the teachings of Hall, Branham, Warnock, Britton and the Sharon Brethren, many other Latter Rain teachings have been retained through the influences of various men and women who are still active in groups that spun off from that movement.

2

Today's Movements

Although the Latter Rain Movement has had lasting effects upon Pentecostalism in general, its effects upon the major denominations was minimal after the mid-fifties. This was due in part to the role the Assemblies of God played in confronting the Latter Rain extremes. Yet in spite of their efforts to stem the influences of the Latter Rain Movement, that denomination, as well as others, lost many pastors and members due to their opposition.

Today, the doctrines of the Latter Rain Movement are experiencing a resurgence due to the charismatic movement and its influences in the Christian media. Although by all appearances the name has died out, the Latter Rain Movement has resurfaced under other names, and is held together by a network of teachers and organizations whose roots are in the healing ministries that grew out of the William Branham and Franklin Hall experiences.

These form the basis for several movements through which men are seeking to establish the Kingdom of God on earth before Jesus returns. They are not always in agreement on the methods to attain that end; nor are they necessarily in agreement as to the philosophical direction that should be taken to accomplish their purpose. However, one area in which most if not all are in agreement is that the Church must be united in a dominion mindset.

Some branches of the dominion theology movement are more militant in their stance, and/or more zealous in the propagation of their particular brand of dominion theology. The more prominent of these movements work together, often without conscious collaboration, to establish the dominion mindset within the Church. Some have even attained cult status among many Christians. Whether one ascribes to the radical element or the passive—or rests somewhere between the two—is not as important as the overall threat to the Church that these movements present through their aberrant teachings.

Yet in spite of these dangers, I'm convinced that there are many sincere Christians who have become involved in these movements because they are alarmed at the increase of sin and perverse attitudes in society. They long for a world with a more sane and moral social structure, and are easily led to believe that if Christians can only take control, God's righteousness will reign on earth. How His righteousness will be implemented—whether by legislation, coercion, example, or by a miraculous move of the Holy Spirit upon the hearts of mankind—is not fully agreed upon even among the leaders in the dominion movements.

Nevertheless, close scrutiny reveals that all hold certain elements in common, making it difficult to discern one from the other. For example, some Manifest Sons of God teachings are indistinguishable from some of the teachings of Restorationism. We are more concerned, therefore, with the teachings themselves, and the men who promote them, than we are with the various movements, which basically comprise a networking system of individuals and groups. Yet it's important to this study that we briefly outline these movements and deal with some of their peculiarities.

IDENTITY

The Identity movement teaches that the Anglo-Saxon race and their kin (Scandinavians, Irish, Welsh, Scots, etc.) are the lost tribes of Israel, who are destined as God's chosen people to rule the world. The full name of Identity is "Anglo-Israel-Identity Movement."[1]

It is believed that, as God's chosen people whose king (or queen) sits on the throne of David (allegedly the British throne), and whose lineage can be traced back through the Jewish patriarchs to Abraham, the Anglo-Saxon race has special favor with God.[2]

"Israel-America" (comprised of Anglo and related descendants in the United States)[3] has a special anointing to lead the nations in establishing God's rule throughout the world.

The nation of Israel that exists today in the Middle East is considered a pretender to the name of Israel, being allegedly comprised of certain Asian peoples known as "Kazars;" biblical prophecies relating to God's dealings with Israel in the last days are believed to have been fulfilled in the Anglo-Saxon race. Daniel's seventieth week has come and gone, as has anti-Christ, and now we are to look forward to the establishment of Yahweh's Kingdom on earth. This is to be administered through the Anglo-Saxon Christians who have come to recognize their unique destiny.

Anti-Semitism

Though Identity is overtly anti-Semitic, its proponents claim that those who are against them are the true anti-Semites. Identity holds in common with most dominionists the rejection of the nation of Israel on the basis that the Church is now spiritual Israel and has inherited the promises given to Abraham, Isaac, and Jacob. But there is a deeper reason for the antagonism toward Israel exhibited by Identity and other dominionists. They realize that should national Israel remain established, the belief that God is going to save a remnant of Jews to be a witness for Jesus in the last days would be validated. Hence, the Church will have to be taken out of the world before Jesus sets His feet upon the earth, and before God's wrath is poured out upon rebellious mankind (Matthew 24; Mark 13; Revelation 6 & 7). If this is true, then the dominion theory falls apart, and the Kingdom of God will not be established over the nations until after Jesus returns with His saints to destroy the anti-Christ's kingdom.

While those who do not subscribe to the dominionists' agenda agree that Jews—as are all men—are lost until they come by faith to recognize Jesus as their Messiah, they also recognize that *natural* Israel (as opposed to today's *national* Israel) does have a purpose in God's plan for the last days, and that they will be grafted back into His Kingdom.

Whites Only

Identity's hatred is not limited to Jews. Blacks and other non-whites are looked upon as inferior beings who may be allowed to enjoy the benefits of the kingdom as long as they remain subject to their Anglo-Saxon superiors. They cannot hold positions of significant authority, however, because the promises to Israel belong only to the "true" Israelites—the Anglo-Saxon believers. America is the new "Zion"—God's city, from where Identity's "Israel" will one day rule the nations. In order to purify the nation, Identity desires that all blacks be sent back to Africa.

The snag in Identity's plans for America is the tremendous influx of non-white immigrants whom they see as parasitical and detrimental to the establishment of God's white-dominated society. As a closely-knit cult, Identity does not generally proselytize anyone other than whites with their version of the Gospel.

As a side note, there is a black counter movement to Identity known as the Yahweh Sect. This cult believes that American blacks are the true descendants of the biblical tribe of Judah, and that they are living in the land of the "white devil."[4] They also believe that their destiny is to rule the earth in the name of Yahweh. Both

Identity and the Yahweh Sect practice paramilitarism with a view toward enforcing their rule through armed conflict.

In view of Identity's racial policy it isn't surprising that radical racist groups such as the Ku Klux Klan and neo-Nazis have infiltrated their ranks.[5] All their errors aside, these groups are zealously moralistic and wish to see the rest of mankind living according to their standards.

Salvation By Race

This isn't to say, of course, that they themselves even live by Scripture. To borrow a clever phrase, their ideology is more akin to salvation by race than to salvation by grace. Although Identity's members consider themselves Christians, they welcome Aryan pagans into fellowship while mounting hate campaigns against Christian Jews, blacks, and other non-whites.

Not all Identity people are overtly racist, but their philosophy reflects a dangerous mindset that threatens to exacerbate an already tense situation between the races. Their paramilitarism and rebellion against any constituted authority by which they feel their ideology threatened combine to create a volatile situation that could someday erupt into full-scale racial warfare.

Even older than the Latter Rain Movement, Identity found fertile ground to propagate its own brand of dominion theology among the neo-Pentecostals of the mid-twentieth century. Seeing the opportunity to cloak itself with the respectability of the Church, Identity has aligned with the charismatic movement, and today presents the Anglo-Israel-Identity Movement as "just as much a result of the work of the Holy Spirit as the Charismatic renewal."[6]

Not all who adhere to Anglo-Israelism (a.k.a. British-Israelism) are part of Identity. But on the basis of little more than conjecture and hearsay, British-Israelism has found credibility in the eyes of many otherwise sensible Christians. Yet even if true, the very nature of British-Israelism and the strife it engenders is contrary to the warning of Scripture that we not engage in endless disputes about genealogies (I Timothy 1:4; Titus 3:9).

Notwithstanding that God still has a plan to graft back into His nation a remnant from among those who are Israelites in the flesh, true Israel consists of all who have come to God by faith in Jesus Christ, whether Jew or Gentile (Romans 2:28-29). To God, no one has any standing except by His grace. In Christ there is neither Jew nor Greek, bond nor free, male nor female, but we are all one in Him (Galatians 3:26-29). As Jesus said, God is able to turn stones into children of Abraham (Matthew 4:9), so who is anyone to boast of his ancestry—especially an ancestry built on little more than fanciful conjecture?

MANIFEST SONS OF GOD

Today's Charismatic Dominionism is largely an outgrowth of the Manifest Sons of God, a generic name that applies to several sects birthed through the Latter Rain Movement. Manifest Sons teachings contain all the elements of classical dominion theory: perfection, immortalization, restoration of the Church, restoration of the offices of apostles and prophets, absolute authoritarianism, extreme shepherding-discipleship, attainment of godhood—you name it, the Manifest Sons of God have it.

Central to Manifest Sons of God doctrine is the belief that sonship to God comes through higher revelation. The Christian life, it is believed, is fragmented into stages of maturity: the first step is that of servant of God; the next is that of friend of God; following this is to become a son of God and, ultimately, gods ourselves.

The Scriptures demonstrate that we are concurrently three of these: servants (Galatians 3:10), friends (John 15:14-15), and sons (I John 3:1). There is nothing in Scripture to support the idea that Paul, or any apostle or prophet, ever put aside his servanthood to attain sonship (several epistles begin with the salutation by the apostle identifying himself as a servant of God). Nor is there any evidence that Paul or any of the other apostles believed that they would ever take the final step and become gods themselves.

Two major sects to which the Manifest Sons of God title applied were The Walk and the Body of Christ. The Walk came out of the Latter Rain Movement under the "apostleship" of John Robert Stevens, a William Branham disciple whose Church of the Living Word in Redondo Beach, California, operated for a number of years as the headquarters for the movement. Out of The Walk, grew many small churches.

The Body of Christ

The Body of Christ sect was the brain-child of Sam Fife, a Baptist minister who claimed to receive revelations from God concerning the restoration of the Church through his apostleship. Although Fife's movement had no specific name (every church group had its own name) they came to be known as the Body of Christ because of their reference to themselves as such, believing that they were the true Church. It was a generic name that, over the years, stuck to Fife's movement.

The Body of Christ started in the early sixties as a home meeting with people from a local Baptist church in Miami, shortly after Fife began receiving his revelations. Believing that he was to father a chosen prophet, Fife left his wife for a time to live with another woman. This resulted in loss of his pastorate with the Baptist Church.

As the movement grew, Fife's followers left their homes and moved to wilderness farms operated by the Body of Christ sect. Eventually these farms were scattered over the United States, Canada, South America, and various other parts of the world. In order to implement his program, Fife anointed several apostles to oversee the various outreaches.

Fife believed that he would never die, even if his plane were to crash; if he did die he would be resurrected within three days. Since his demise, of course, he knows better.

Besides John Robert Stevens and Sam Fife, there were many apostles that came out of the Manifest Sons of God, such as George Warnock, Francis Frangipane, Royal Cronquist, and Bill Britton. Some still survive and are working within other churches to spread their doctrines.

Basic Tenets

An essential ingredient of Manifest Sons of God teachings is a peculiar interpretation of Romans 8:19-23:

> For the earnest expectation of the creature waiteth for the manifestation of the sons of God.
> For the creature was made subject to vanity, not willingly, but by reason of him who hath subjected the same in hope,
> Because the creature itself also shall be delivered from the bondage of corruption into the glorious liberty of the children of God.
>
> For we know that the whole creation groaneth and travaileth in pain together until now.
> And not only they, but ourselves also, which have the firstfruits of the Spirit, even we ourselves groan within ourselves, waiting for the adoption, to wit, the redemption of our body.

A doctrine crucial to the Manifest Sons of God is that perfection (sinless living) will result in immortalization. Those who overcome death will qualify as worthy to rule in the Kingdom of God.

Whether Jesus will return at the beginning, during, or after the Millennium is open to conjecture. Some who have been infected by the Manifest Sons of God teachings even believe He will not return physically, but rather that Christ and the Church are becoming one in nature and essence, and that the Church, as the "on-going incarnation of God," *is* Christ on earth.

There are even those who, like Sam Fife, believe that they have already attained a state of perfection and, as a result, will never die. They have reached a higher degree of spiritual evolution, so to speak.

For all the elaborate surmisings with which these people have deluded themselves, a careful reading of Romans 8:19-23 shows that the "manifestation of the sons of God"—the redemption of our bodies—cannot be properly understood apart from I Corinthians 15:51-52, which states that we shall all be changed "in a moment, in a twinkling of an eye, at the last trump: for the trumpet shall sound, and the dead shall be raised incorruptible, and we shall be changed." These verses, with I Thessalonians 4:15-17, make it clear that the "manifestation of the sons of God"—immortality—will take place *after* the resurrection of the dead at the coming of Christ for His Church:

> *For this we say unto you by the word of the Lord, that we which are alive and remain unto the coming of the Lord shall not prevent [go before] them which are asleep.*
>
> *For the Lord himself shall descend from heaven with a shout, with the voice of the archangel, and with the trump of God: and the dead in Christ shall rise first:*
>
> *Then we which are alive and remain shall be caught up together with them in the clouds to meet the Lord in the air: and so shall we ever be with the Lord.*

Almost all the teachings of the Charismatic Dominionists can be traced to the Manifest Sons of God. And not only do they spring from the Manifest Sons of God, they must ultimately return to the "pure" Manifest Sons of God doctrine: man need not die; by taking hold of secret knowledge he can become like God.

Scandals

The Manifest Sons of God movement suffered massive dissipation as the result of many scandals that arose out of the extreme cult status it had attained within the various sects. Nevertheless, its devotees, fervent in their beliefs, dispersed to spread its doctrines to other churches. Some of its followers have since become pastors themselves, and are leading their flocks down the same path toward "godhood" as did Stevens and Fife.

Because association with the Manifest Sons of God movement proved to be a source of embarrassment, there are few today who would admit they are Manifest Sons of God devotees. Much as a communist would deny his affiliation with the party because he doesn't carry a membership card, Manifest Sons of God adherents deny they are what they are. Many prefer to identify themselves with the Kingdom Message, whose tenets, not surprisingly, are nearly identical to those of the Manifest Sons of God. The test, however, is what one teaches and believes, not whether he is an "official" pastor or member of a Manifest Sons of God church.

Whether or not the Manifest Sons of God will ever make a comeback as an organized segment within the Christian community only the Lord knows. But their influence has been more far-reaching through undercover proselytizing than it would have been had there been no breakup. They continue to affect more and more Christians who are sufficiently naive to think they can become immortal by acting spiritual. The grandiose promise of ruling the world as implementers of God's judgment holds special appeal for the prideful, "god-conscious" persons who perceive authority as rulership rather than servanthood.

KINGDOM MESSAGE

The Kingdom Message teachings are almost identical to those of the Manifest Sons of God movement. Its leaders deny they are Manifest Sons of God, so rather than buck heads with them it's easier to classify them under another name which they themselves have adopted: the Kingdom Message.

The emphasis of this revised Manifest Sons of God movement is on a "Kingdom Now" theology which states that the Kingdom of God is a present reality in the earth, and is only waiting for the manifestation of the sons of God to demonstrate the Kingdom by taking their authority over the kingdoms of the earth. This will take place before Jesus can return.

The Kingdom Message is a half-truth. The Kingdom of God is a present reality in the earth today, but the manifestation of the sons of God will not take place until after the resurrection. The Kingdom will not be manifested over the nations before then.

Another major teaching borrowed from the Manifest Sons of God is that those Christians who will attain positions of authority over the kingdoms of the earth are the "many-membered man child." They will personify the fulfillment of Revelation 12:1-5:

> And there appeared a great wonder in heaven; a woman clothed with the sun, and the moon under her feet, and upon her head a crown of twelve stars. . . .
> And she brought forth a man child, who was to rule all nations with a rod of iron.

In the Kingdom Message the rapture is a non-entity and open to ridicule. There is also a strong emphasis on shepherding-discipleship under the authority of latter-day apostles and prophets.

RESTORATION

The Restoration teachings focus on the belief that the Church has not functioned as God planned since the first century. Therefore it must be "restored" to its original purpose of achieving dominion. This involves restoration of the offices of apostles and prophets, restoration of the "Tabernacle of David" (signified by the restoration of worship and praise), and the restoration of power (signs and wonders).

Similar to the Manifest Sons of God, Restoration believes in immortalization through perfection. Thus its emphasis is on purifying the Church through repentance and holy living.

Certainly no one can find fault with repentance and holy living. But at the heart of Restoration is the goal of establishing the visible Kingdom of God on earth in the physical absence of Jesus. Holy living, forgiveness, and unity of the Body of Christ are essential to the attainment of that purpose. In other words, at the heart of repentance and holy living is not a humble dying to self, but the desire to see God move more quickly in establishing the Church in dominion over the nations.

Restorationists would deny this, but their messages in literature and speech betray dominion as the underlying motive for desiring holiness and unity. Yet I would not for a moment doubt that there is a genuine love for God and the brethren in Christ in the hearts of many who are following the Restoration movement. One day the eyes of those whose hearts are right will be opened to the truth. In the meantime, the Restoration preachers are realizing tremendous gains in their constituencies.

False Piety

Restoration preachers appear to be among the humblest of God's servants, often crying, and confessing their own sins before the people and presenting themselves as examples of how Christians should examine their own hearts. One of the Scriptures most quoted by Restoration preachers is Matthew 7:1: "Judge not, that ye be not judged." In their view, it is especially imperative that people not judge teachers, regardless of doctrine. We are to let Jesus judge them.

They totally ignore the context of Matthew 7:1, which implies hypocritical judgment, not the judgment necessary to preserve the purity of the Faith. We are often exhorted by Scripture to judge not those outside the Body of Christ, but those inside the Body of Christ, including teachers (I Corinthians 5:12, 6:5; John 7:24).

A favorite cry of Restorationists—indeed of all dominionists—is, "Touch not God's anointed!" This, someone has correctly said, is "the last refuge of religious tyrants"—those who fear their teachings and lives will not stand the test of biblical scrutiny. Their clergy-laity mentality recoils at the truth that all of God's people are His anointed. And many are being "touched" to their detriment by these religious tyrants.

Restorationists point to David as the example of one who would not touch God's anointed even though God had given him Saul's throne. What they choose to ignore is that David gathered from Saul's kingdom an army of his own and even lent his support to the king of Babylon to war against Saul's army. What he wouldn't do was raise his own hand to kill Saul. Nor should we raise our hands to kill these false prophets. But God's Word gives us every right to raise up armies of detractors even from the midst of their own ranks. While it is imperative that we honor the positions of those in leadership in the Body of Christ, our first responsibility is to the truth of God's Word. Far better to be found "touching" a religious leader who is teaching error than to be found "touching" God's Word.

In Romans 14:10-13, one of the dominionists' favorite Scriptures about judging, we find that the context reveals we are not to judge a brother for what he eats or drinks. But we *are* to judge actions and teachings that lead others away from God's truth. Yet while those who propagate errors decry any judgment upon their ungodly teachings, they act contrary to those very same teachings by not only judging, but condemning those who judge those errors. This hypocrisy is rampant throughout all dominion movements.

The Tabernacle of David

Among the essential elements of Restoration is what is called, "The Tabernacle of David." This means that, before the Church can be perfected and establish dominion, it must restore praise and worship as a means to enter into the presence of God. Only then will His blessings be poured out upon His people and they will be given the power to subdue spiritual principalities.

The praise and worship that has come forth through those who propagate these teachings are truly beautiful to the human ear. Instrumentation for full orchestration, and professional-quality vocalization and dancing are often incorporated. Those not so professionally inclined nevertheless are encouraged to enter into fervent praise and joyful, loud singing, sometimes in tongues.

There is little that can be said against this element of Restorationism. All true believers in Jesus owe Him loud Hosannahs, and we love to praise Him for His great love and mercy. But for the dominionists there is an added incentive which clouds the purity of motive that should accompany all true worship and praise. That added incentive is to move God to destroy their enemies and to establish them as supreme in the earth. Much of the music does not exalt God, but the Church.

Consequently, we find in the dominionists' ointment of praise a fly of carnality. What is perceived as spiritual is in reality soulish, contributing to a euphoric state of altered consciousness from repetitious choruses that follow one upon the other. The mesmerizing effect of the music creates a frame of mind open to suggestion by the subsequent preaching of dominionist teachers who build on the fervor of the moment with messages of future power and glory.

The dancing is usually choreographed and it is common to find women and girls especially participating. The usual formula is to dance in a wide circle, and the costuming includes a garland of flowers around the dancers' heads.

Where this form of dancing originated in the Church is not to be found. But it is very similar to that engaged in by the ancient Druids who worshiped nature, and their modern counterparts involved in Wicca, or witchcraft religion. The circle is a magic form, the garlands of flowers magic talismans.

If this seems an unfair assessment, the reader should keep in mind as he reads, the many similarities of pagan practice that have been incorporated into the churches throughout the centuries.

POSITIVE CONFESSION

If there is one teaching of dominion theology that has come to characterize the Positive Confession movement of late, it is the deification of man. While most of the aforementioned movements employ this theme, Positive Confession brings it to the forefront with teachings that we are little gods and are equal to Jesus.

This is a paradox of sorts, because there are many in Positive Confession who are not consciously linked to dominion theology, but are looking instead for the imminent return of Jesus, whether pre-, mid-, or post-tribulational. They do not see man's efforts as a solution to the world's ills. They would reject the idea that they are or can be gods, even though in their acting out the Positive Confession scenario they are acting out the role of God. This by their insistence that, just like God, they can speak into existence things that are not as if they are, in accordance with a gross misinterpretation of Romans 4:17.

But it isn't the conscious adherence to dominion theology that makes Positive Confession compatible with it (though the numbers who do agree with dominion theology are growing rapidly). It's the strong dominion mindset and the increasingly prevalent teachings on the believer's alleged "god-likeness" that will eventually draw the bulk of Positive Confession people into the dominionist camp.

Reconstructionist Gary North, in his book, *Unholy Spirits*, demonstrates how the Reconstructionists have influenced the charismatics and, most especially, the Positive Confession movement, without their being aware of that influence:

> Some of the charismatic groups believe in tightly knit church covenants. The reconstructionists have been the major theologians of the biblical covenant. Other charismatics have preached personal financial victory and health through prayer and by obeying God's "principles." The reconstructionists have been the major defenders of the continuing legitimacy of God's law in New Testament times. Some of these "positive confession" charismatics (also called "word of faith") have begun to preach that the optimism which God offers to individuals also applies to God's other covenanted associations: families, churches, and civil governments. This represents a major break with the traditional pessimistic eschatology of fundamentalism, called dispensationalism. These charismatic leaders have not self-consciously made the break from premillennialism to postmillennial optimism, but the term "dominion" implies it. Again, the reconstructionists are the only Protestant theologians to have forthrightly preached postmillennialism after 1965. (R. J. Rushdoony was the pioneer here.) Thus, the ideas of the reconstructionists have penetrated into Protestant circles that for the most part are unaware of the original source of the theological ideas that are beginning to transform them.[7]

The concept of dominion fits the Positive Confession mold perfectly. If all that's necessary for the Church to take dominion is to speak and act "in faith," then the only problem is to get enough Christians to do so.

Positive Confession's belief in faith as a "force" into which anyone can tap is a tenet of witchcraft. It places God at the disposal of anyone who can learn the formulas (or "principles") of "faith," and tries to force Him to work on their behalf regardless of His will.

Positive Confession is not prayer; it's not communication with the Father. Rather, it is mental and verbal affirmation of what the person "confessing" wants accomplished. There is little or no practical consideration of what God's will might be. And there is little or no practical difference from the beliefs of religious science. Although Positive Confession has no definitive eschatology, its teachings establish a dominionist mindset.

SHEPHERDING-DISCIPLESHIP

The most influential movement to affect the Church in this century is that of Shepherding-Discipleship. For this reason we must consider some extremely important details regarding its history.

In the mid- to late sixties, two young Catholics who were on the secretariat of the Cursillo movement (a Roman Catholic advocacy group) became deeply involved in the Charismatic Renewal. In 1967 these two young men, Steve Clark and Ralph Martin, decided to hold meetings in their apartment. From the initial meeting of fewer than a dozen persons grew the Word of God charismatic fellowship. The Word of God group grew to 100 people within four months and, within seven years, had attained a membership of some 1,000.

Today, through a subsidiary organization known as the Sword of the Spirit, they control an international network of some 20,000 members who, in turn, affect the spiritual and social lives of millions of people.[8]

For the first three years, the Word of God structure was loose, focusing primarily on interpersonal relationships and seeking a deeper walk with the Lord. In September, 1970, however, Clark and Martin began to introduce more stringent structures, creating coordinators and district subgroups called "subcommunities." They also began formal initiation into membership, requiring each member to make public commitments to the group through covenants.[9] Russ Bellant, writing for the *National Catholic Reporter*, quotes a former member of the Word of God:

> "From that point onward," says former member Tom Yoder, "coordinators had increasing control. By mid-1972, they had total control."[10]

> "In the eight and a half years I was in the Word of God," says Yoder, "I witnessed, or heard stories from those involved, of situations that most people would consider bizarre. Some examples are: arranged marriages, expulsion due to unapproved marriages, people compelled to live in houses not of their choosing, a man forcing discipline on a woman by tying her up, and members submitting advance schedules to their 'head' on a weekly or monthly basis for approval. What they call 'headship' or 'pastoral leadership' goes far beyond what you'd find even in a cloistered monastery or in military life."[11]

Under Clark's and Martin's leadership, the Word of God set out to save the world:

> It has also created a far-flung network whose aim is to save the world. To do this, its members feel, it must first do battle

with the world's enemies and eventually prevail over them. To this end, it has allied itself with conservative elements in the U.S. church and in the Roman curia, with right-wing activists that include Nicaraguan contras, their U.S. supporters, the CIA and conservative business people with a wide range of radical agendas.[12]

It is reported that, at least as late as 1986, Pope John Paul II looked with favor on the Sword of the Spirit in spite of difficulties:

> The pope's views on Sword of the Spirit have not been fully clarified. But a conference of Word of God members and associ-ated groups held at the University of Steubenville last spring included several prelates close to the pope (*NCR*, April 8). Cardinal Edouard Gagnon, president of the Pontifical Council for the Family (PCF) said of the movement, "The pope accepts them. He is ready to accept them even if at times they exaggerate on one point or another. . . . The pope has a very solid trust in them."[13]

New Covenant Magazine

In 1971 Martin and Clark began to publish a pastoral letter called *New Covenant*. Within six years, the letter grew into a full-fledged magazine with circulation of 65,000. This growth was due in large part to Charismatic Renewal Services in South Bend, Indiana, which acted as a major supplier of books, music and cassette tapes for Servant Publications, the publishing arm of Sword of the Spirit.[14]

The Council

In the early 1970's Clark and Martin began to make contacts with the leaders of Christian Growth Ministries in Fort Lauderdale, Florida, led by the men who would become known as the "Fort Lauderdale Five": Bob Mumford, Derek Prince, Don Basham, Ern Baxter (who had been an associate of William Branham), and Charles Simpson. By 1974, these five, plus Clark and Martin, along with John Poole, formed a secret group called "the Council." The purpose of the Council was to coordinate efforts between the Word of God and Christian Growth Ministries in a common cause to convert the world through ecumenical cooperation in a tightly controlled spiritual environment.

Eventually, others became involved in the Council, including Tom Monroe, Dick Key, Ray Ostendorf, Larry Christenson, Kevin

Ranaghan, Paul DeCelles, Jim Cavnar, Don Pfotenhauer, and Dick Coleman. The purpose of the Council was stated as such:

> The Lord is giving us a work that many in the church do not understand: bringing believers together in a committed disciplined submitted relationship to be a network of bodies that can be a servant to God in the world. That is our primary call. Out of that work, we will be able to speak to the charismatic renewal, to the church and to the world, but our primary concern is with the bodies.[15]

The method of operation for the Council was to offer support and advice to major charismatic leaders. For example, Derek Prince was authorized to produce a curriculum for Morris Cerullo and to work on the board of one of Cerullo's institutes.[16]

During a pilgrimage to the Holy Land in 1977, the Council began to enter into relationship with León Joseph Cardinal Suenens. At their June 1 meeting at St. Catherine's Monastery in Mt. Sinai, Israel, Clark and Martin informed the Council that Cardinal Suenens wanted to enter into a covenantal relationship with them. The Council decided that they should relate to the Cardinal in some "significant manner," and that they should work with him and his people as "one module."[17]

The Council drafted a statement to be read to the Cardinal at their June 2 meeting:

> Preamble:
> In light of Cardinal Suenen's gracious invitation to the Council to accompany him on the pilgrimage and his hospitality in Belgium in the historic room of the Maline Conversations, and as one practical step to move us ahead from the spiritual victory we achieved together on the day of Pentecost; we offer the following statement:

> 1. We, as a Council, are committing ourselves to work together with the Cardinal for the restoration and unity of Christian people and world evangelization in projects to be mutually agreed upon.

> 2. In each project, headship, authority and method of functions will be mutually determined by the Cardinal and the Council in the light of the requirements of each situation.

3. Our normal procedure would be that the Council would relate to the Cardinal through its acknowledged head or through a representative delegated by its head.[18]

Out of this collaboration with Cardinal Suenens came a startling proposal for the Council's Leadership Training Institute:

Cardinal Suenens is interested in a training institute where men could be ordained into the R.C. priesthood and diakonate.[19]

Due to the secret nature of the Council and the tightly controlled authoritarian structure of the communities over which it presided, it is difficult to know whether or not Cardinal Suenen's proposal was implemented and, if it was, who may today be Roman Catholic priests working as a fifth column within the Protestant charismatic movement.

Considering that the purpose of the Council was to establish a network of committed, submitted bodies under an authoritarian structure, its collaboration with the Roman Catholic Church is significant. It was largely the Council's work that put together the historic Kansas City Conference in 1977 and, subsequently, the Washington for Jesus Conference in 1980, with the desire to demonstrate unity of the Spirit in an ecumenical environment, without regard to doctrine. At Washington for Jesus, for example, the people were told by Roman Catholic priests that the departed saints were among them, blessing them for their participation.

It has become obvious that Shepherding-Discipleship is not merely an aberration that affects individual personal lives, but is a broad-based ecumenical outreach designed to conform the entire Church to an authoritarian structure with the purpose of achieving dominion over the temporal world system. It laid the groundwork for current ecumenical outreaches, such as North American Renewal Services Committee (*AD2000*), sponsor of Indianapolis 1990. The purpose is to funnel converts into any church, with little regard to doctrine, including covenant-oriented and Roman Catholic churches. At the same time, it has neutralized attempts to minister the Gospel to Catholics by giving them the impression that the Roman Catholic Church's errors are inconsequential.

In view of the disregard for sound doctrine, upon which disregard these ecumenical evangelistic outreaches are based, it seems that the real purpose is not to bring people to Christ (although by His grace that does happen), but to bring them to unification under a religious hierarchy. And who will ultimately head this hierarchy? Certainly the papacy will never relinquish its claim to absolute authority; to do so would mean the dismantling of a religio-political institution whose purpose since its inception has been to establish its authority over the kingdoms of the world.

With one billion adherents worldwide, as well as universal popularity among the leaders of the world's religions—both Christian and non-Christian—the pope holds the trump cards.

Authoritarianism Needed

The Shepherding-Discipleship movement exemplifies the authoritarianism needed to implement and sustain any attempt at establishing a theocratic or theonomic state. In spite of extreme abuses against personal freedom in Christ, the thought control that characterized the Shepherding-Discipleship movement continues among dominionist groups. And its leaders have gained new respectability both inside and outside the charismatic camp.

The extremes of Shepherding-Discipleship were addressed by Bob Mumford in public apologies in print and on television for the abuses in which his movement engaged. Yet in his apologies he has gone only so far as to say that the abuses were wrong and that the movement was wrong in not taking sufficient action to stop them. He continues to affirm, however, that the principle of Shepherding-Discipleship is valid. But with this we must disagree. The very concept of Shepherding-Discipleship is ungodly. All forms—particularly that which Mumford still maintains is valid—stifle the individual believer's personal relationship to the Father and subordinate it to the corporate structure of the religious society. This is the priestcraft that maintained for centuries the Roman Church's control over kings and other government magistrates.

It's no news to those who suffered under the Shepherding-Discipleship abuses that those abuses occured or that they were wrong; Mumford pretty much admitted to something everyone had been aware of for some time.

And despite Mumford's apologies, the same abuses continue in many churches today, particulary those in the dominionist circles. This is because such a mentality is critical to dominion theology. For how can the leaders of the movement gain dominion unless Christians are made to conform to the dictates of the apostles and prophets?

And how can Christians be made to conform except through fear and guilt? No one wants to miss out on what appears to be a move of God. Ignorance on the part of those who are unsure of their relationship to God breeds indecision which, in turn, results in acquiescence to authority at the expense of their personal relationship to God.

Today the principles of the Shepherding-Discpleship move-ment are implemented in dominion theology through the use of covenants. This will be explored in a future chapter.

CHARISMATIC RENEWAL

The Charismatic Renewal places a heavy emphasis on unity based on the outward evidence of speaking in tongues. This af-finity toward unity is natural among charismatics because of their common tendency toward mysticism. Charismatic Protestants are very ecumenical in their outlook, and are overtly working toward unity with the papacy.

The charismatic ideal seems to have developed into this: in the interest of unity we must overlook differences in the doctrines of those who confess Jesus and appear to exhibit the gifts of the Spirit—particularly speaking in tongues.

It is on these points that Roman Catholic priests have been given platforms to teach on Christian television, and that Mormons have been welcomed into fellowship among some charismatics. (What could find more compatibility between Mormons and dominionists than the idea that men are gods?)

If there is any rhyme or reason to this widespread mysticism it is that many charismatics, having come out of denomination-alism, have lacked sufficient grounding in God's Word to be able to separate the true work of the Holy Spirit from that of Satan. Having had little or no experience with supernatural power in their denominations, they sorely lack discernment in that area.

Many of today's most prominent leaders in charismatism are Pentecostals who believe that the Holy Spirit is at work in the movement. On that basis, they have carelessly embraced false teachers and opened the door to great deception. Such is the case with the late David DuPlessis whose overtures toward the papacy have resulted in many other Protestants, both Pentecostal and non-Pentecostal, sliding wholesale into the papal web of dominion. The disastrous results of this move toward the Vatican state will only be discerned when it's too late.

This merely demonstrates that, whether traditional or Pente-costal, when one attaches more importance to experience than to the rightly-divided Word of Truth, the chance for error is greatly increased. Due to its interdenominational thrust, charismatism presents especially fertile ground for the propagation of unity with the papacy. The saying, "All roads lead to Rome," isn't limited to the heyday of the Caesars or to the papacy's former domination of Western culture. It applies today to the charismatic movement that is affording Roman Catholicism much credibility among Protes-tants and other non-Catholics. The Vatican is capitalizing on that credibility to make overtures for unity in traditionally Protestant countries while continuing to persecute evangelical Christians in countries where Roman Catholicism is dominant.

The naivete of Protestants who have forgotten the reason for the Reformation is being exploited by Catholic clergy who, though professing love and unity toward non-Catholic Christians, refuse them the elements of communion on the basis that non-Catholics do not recognize the pope as their spiritual leader. In order to achieve true unity, this will have to be corrected; and it's not as far off as many would like to believe.

The danger to the purity of the Faith is genuine. The Charismatic Renewal has opened doors it may find difficult to close when Satan's demonstrations of signs and wonders increase to the point where physical as well as spiritual life or death hang on the balance of one's discernment.

FEAR AND GUILT

Were we to analyze each movement germane to dominion theology we would find strong elements of fear and guilt at the core of their structures. To illustrate, let's take the movements with which we've already dealt (we've already noted the problems with Shepherding-Discipleship) and briefly see how fear and guilt play a part in their propagation.

Identity: Fear and guilt are essential ingredients in any racist, authoritarian structure—especially where paramilitarism is a major factor in its operation.

Manifest Sons of God & Kingdom Message: Extreme fear and guilt is instilled in those who do not move forward to perfection. Fear of death is instilled in many, because death means failure to reach spiritual maturity.

Restoration: A strong condemnation for using judgment breeds guilt in those who question the teachings of their leaders. This results in fear of God's displeasure. This applies even to the righteous judgment of sin and doctrinal error.

Positive Confession: Fear is induced by belief that if one doesn't act and speak in a prescribed manner, God will not answer. Guilt arises from belief that one's faith is deficient should his prayers not be answered to his satisfaction.

Charismatic Renewal: Guilt is instilled in those who balk at attempts to meld them into unity with others whose doctrines are in serious conflict with Scripture. This results in fear of reprisals for speaking out against error. Mysticism lends additional validity to alleged signs and wonders and causes guilt, fear, and at least doubt among those who cannot reconcile them with Scripture.

CONCLUSION

These are sketchy but accurate assessments of how religion based on fear and guilt has encroached upon the modern Church. The Christian's personal relationship with the Father is a sacred trust to be nurtured and strengthened by the teaching and counsel of the elders in the Church. While the corporate expression of faith is vital to the life of the Church, that life is only as strong as the strength of the individual links in the corporate chain.

The subordination of the individual to the corporate body at the expense of personal freedom in Christ weakens the Church in its ability to stand against deception and, ultimately, against the overt evil influences of the world. Dominion theology, in all its forms, can only be likened to a cult within the Church—a subculture that threatens to tear asunder the delicate fabric of true unity based not on external piety, but upon the indwelling presence of the Holy Spirit.

3
Dominion Teachings

The more important teachings of dominion theology reveal basic problems that lie primarily in the authoritarian structure necessary to implement and maintain the dominionist agenda. Dominionist teachers of every persuasion are exhibiting cultish traits that rob individual believers of a true understanding of their personal relationship with the Father and their freedom in Christ.

There are also dangers in the elitist mentality that naturally progresses from the idea that somehow, due to God's grace or one's own personal righteousness, the lives of the elite are more valuable than the lives of the masses. This is evidenced by teachings that call for the death penalty against dissenters who would challenge the theonomic or theocratic structure of God's government administered by the overcomers.

An additional problem is that followers of dominion theology are easy prey for political extremists. There are those who play upon the concerns of all Christians who naturally desire to see eradicated such evils as abortion, pornography, homosexuality, child abuse, drug dealing, and crime in general. The fact that many in the "Christian right" are already united with Sun Myung Moon and the Mormon Church is sufficient reason to suspect that, in the long run, no theocentric form of government will reflect the true biblical pattern for society.

Morality and righteousness are wonderful traits when manifested as a result of Spirit-filled living. When manifested as a result of religious fervor, these traits become precursors of a totalitarian state. We would do well to take a lesson from history and remember that Adolph Hitler made his plea for acceptance of Nazism based upon a platform of anti-communism, anti-homosexuality, patriotism, and morality. Many German Christians rejoiced when he assumed power.

In light of these dangers we must identify the sources of dominion theology so that the Body of Christ may be cautious of involvement. Naturally, if someone desires to believe in dominion theology that is their business. When they teach it publicly, however, it becomes everybody's business. They should be willing to have their teachings challenged without the adverse reaction that has characterized their responses to legitimate criticism.

Naming Names

In order to do justice to this complex subject, it's necessary that we name those involved, and particularly those in the vanguard of dominion teachings. Some find this distasteful and will perceive it as a personal attack against men and women of God with whom I disagree. On the contrary, it is my position that we must be careful not to condemn those who are caught up in error, but pray for them, recognizing that God's grace is extended to all.

No one should mind criticism of their teachings as long as they are treated honestly and in context. Those who scream foul when they're challenged for what they teach publicly should be suspect.

Some dominionists may be deceivers engaged in a power struggle for personal gain. Some may also have designs on leading the Church into areas of compromise with political extremists. Some may even be agents of the Vatican. But I believe some are brethren in Christ who sincerely perceive that the dominion message is a viable means by which to engage in evangelization.

It would be a mistake to consider all who believe or even teach error our enemies. Granted, their beliefs are dangerous in many of their implications, but some followers are temporarily deceived, and will one day recognize the errors they've been led to believe. None of us knew better before the Holy Spirit did His work in us.

It will be asked if I went to these people before challenging their teachings openly. Every attempt I did make either went unanswered or was met with untrue denials of having stated what they did. Only Jay Grimstead of COR gave me any time. This is typical and can be attested by others who have tried. And even if I could reach every person whose teachings I question, it would take years and far more financial resources than I have. In the meantime, it is vital that this information be exposed to the Church.

However, if in our zeal to expose those in error we obtain a certain amount of glee in discovering their feet of clay, we'd best take inventory of our own motives and question whether they are based upon love or a contentious spirit that enjoys exposing the errors of others. We may rightly quote Jude 3 as justification for earnestly contending for the Faith, but if we forget I Corinthians 13 we are no more free from error than those whose errors we expose.

THE DOMINION MANDATE

Dominion theology is predicated upon three basic beliefs: 1) Satan usurped man's dominion over the earth through the temptation of Adam and Eve; 2) The Church is God's instrument to take dominion back from Satan; 3) Jesus cannot or will not return until the Church has taken dominion by gaining control of the earth's governmental and social institutions. The following are only a few among the many proponents of these beliefs:

Earl Paulk

Paulk is the senior pastor of Chapel Hill Harvester Church in Atlanta, Georgia. In his church's publication he is referred to as a "prophet" of today's Kingdom Message:

> If there is a prophet today who speaks the truth God wants His Church to hear, it is Earl Paulk. He is the leading voice today in preaching the message of the Kingdom of God ... a man driven compulsively to show this generation that God is waiting for us to do something that will bring Christ back to earth.[1]

Paulk himself has stated:

> Christ in us must take dominion over the earth. . . . The next move of God cannot occur until Christ in us takes dominion.[2]

> The next move of God will unite His Son in marriage. The marriage supper of the Lamb, the completion of establishing the Kingdom, the eternal rule of God, will finally take place.[3]

We see that Paulk believes the marriage supper of the Lamb cannot take place until after the Church ("Christ in us") has taken dominion. But does Paulk mean that Jesus will already have returned and been with us in order for us to have taken dominion? No, he doesn't. Otherwise he would have said that the next move of God is for Jesus to come back and *then* for the Church to take dominion under His kingship. And he would not have used the term "Christ in us." In its proper biblical context that is a valid term. But in this case its use implies that Jesus will take dominion through the Church while He remains in heaven.

The office of Christ cannot be separated from the person of Jesus. He is the *only* Christ of God. It is Jesus, when He returns, who must take dominion and establish the visible Kingdom of God on earth, not "Christ in us." But does Paulk understand this, or are his statements nothing more than poor choices of words? Let's see what he himself reveals about this:

> Christ was one person, limited to ministry in only one place at a time. In order to minister as an omnipresent Spirit, Jesus relinquished His fleshly dimension with its limitations of time and place. He entered a higher realm of restoration and love by becoming an indwelling Spirit.[69]

Either Paulk's Christology has taken an aberrant turn, or he's had a mental lapse. Now, I've often heard people, in one breath, address their prayers to the Father, and, without breaking continuity, address Jesus as if he were the Father—a "Jesus only" mental glitch. I can understand that mistake. However, when someone *publishes* a statement that says Jesus became the Holy Spirit, I would think that takes more mental affirmation.

It isn't that Jesus *was* one person; He *is* one person: Jesus of Nazareth, God in the flesh, born of a virgin, *raised in the flesh*! When the Scripture says, "Christ in you, the hope of glory" (Colossians 1:27), it in essence affirms that we are united with Him by the Spirit of God. He is "in us," and we are "in Him." It does not mean He relinquished His flesh to become "an indwelling Spirit." He is "flesh and bones" (Luke 24:39). In His resurrected body, He is in a specific location, heaven, at the right hand of the Father.

The Holy Spirit is omnipresent. Although the Holy Spirit is called the Spirit of God, the Spirit of Christ, and the Spirit of Jesus, a distinction must be made. It is the Holy Spirit, not the bodily-resurrected Jesus, who is the indwelling Spirit of true believers.

This is more important than it may at first appear. For without a proper Christology one cannot have a proper eschatology. In this case, Paulk sees Jesus as "an indwelling Spirit." On this basis he claims that the Church is the "ongoing incarnation of God." This parallels the Manifest Sons of God doctrine that the Church is now Christ, and all Scriptures pertaining to Christ's ruling on earth are really referring to the Church.

We'll deal with this in more detail in another chapter. For now, we'll examine further Paulk's views on dominion:

> When the apostles asked Jesus if He would now restore the political kingdom, He said, "It's not for you to know the times or the seasons. But I will tell you what will take place in your life, and when you have received what I'll tell you about, you will be able to bring in the Kingdom of God."
>
> How will the Kingdom of God be ushered in? In Acts 1:8, Jesus said, "But ye shall receive power, after that the Holy Ghost is come upon you; and ye shall be witnesses unto me both in Jerusalem, and in all Judea, and in Samaria, and unto the uttermost part of the earth."[5]

Notice how Paulk puts words in Jesus' mouth by having Him say, "you will be able to bring in the Kingdom of God." Nowhere in Scripture is such a statement found. Evidently the first-century Church did not have enough faith or maturity to accomplish this feat, so it's up to today's Christians to do the job.

> What are we waiting for? Why is Jesus waiting in heaven at the right hand of the Father? [I thought Paulk said Jesus shed his flesh to become an "indwelling Spirit." Is Jesus fragmented or something?] Who is He waiting for? He is waiting for you and me to become mature, so that He can come again. Did you know that God has done everything He can do? If anything else is going to be done, we're going to do it.[6]

> In Matthew 24:14, Jesus clearly says that He cannot return for His Bride until she has demonstrated the Gospel of the Kingdom to all the nations of the earth. Until the church can demonstrate the alternative Kingdom, Jesus cannot come again. God no longer has the authority to send Christ back to earth, because He will not circumvent His eternal plan. While no man knows the day or the hour, I can say with the authority of God that **Christ cannot and will not come back until we have demonstrated the Gospel of the Kingdom to the nations of the earth.** That task demands a mature church, which will have become an alternative to the kingdoms of the world. **That is what the church is all about and Jesus Christ's return is up to us.**[7] (Paulk's emphasis)

In keeping with the dominionists' desire to take God's place, Paulk believes God no longer has the authority to send Jesus back to earth; His return is up to us. So God has taken control out of His own hands and placed it in Paulk's and his followers' hands.

Now it's true that "He will not circumvent His eternal plan." But He has revealed in His Word the manner in which He will accomplish His eternal plan. Contrary to Paulk's surmisings, God's eternal plan is not that the Church will take dominion on its own, but merely that the earth will be redeemed. Many of the details of that redemption have not been revealed, but in order for the dominion concept to apply, one must spiritualize what he believes the Word says rather than take it literally. What it does say clearly is that God's plan for the world's redemption includes Jesus' bodily return to establish the visible Kingdom of God over the nations before the creation of the new heavens and new earth (Revelation 20:2-21:5).

Paulk misreads God's eternal plan by spiritualizing Matthew 24:14, which simply states, "And this gospel of the kingdom shall be preached in all the world for a witness unto all nations; and then shall the end come."

It's one thing to preach the Gospel of the Kingdom; it's quite another to institute—or "demonstrate"—the Kingdom according to Paulk's interpretation. In the first place, this is not Paulk's original thinking. It is pure Manifest Sons of God teaching which was in effect before Paulk was dismissed by the Church of God, Cleveland, Tennessee, and fell into the Manifest Sons of God mold. Before he was dismissed by the Church of God, his teachings were in direct opposition to what he is teaching today.

Another point with which we must take issue is Paulk's separation of the Gospel of the Kingdom from the Gospel of Jesus Christ. There is only one Gospel: the Gospel of salvation through faith in Jesus Christ. Within that Gospel is the gospel (good news) that Jesus is coming again to establish His visible earthly reign. That is the "Gospel of the Kingdom" we are commanded to preach, not this counterfeit dominion theology which exalts man above what God intended.

Yet in spite of his erroneous applications of Scripture, Paulk equates his own words with Holy Writ: "I can say with the authority of God . . ." Such a statement reveals an "apostle complex" characteristic of dominionist teachers. Within Evangelical Christianity have arisen those who see their "magisterium" or teaching authority to be equal to God's Word.

Pat Robertson

As a well-known public figure and founder of the Christian Broadcasting Network, Pat Robertson is more careful than most in revealing his belief in dominion theology. He claims to believe in a literal rapture, but not until there has been a great revival that will result in a godly society run by the Church. In his keynote address to the Dallas '84 convention for Bob Weiners' Maranatha Campus Ministries, Robertson made reference to the late John Lennon's song, *Imagine*, in which Lennon imagined a world of peace wherein no religion existed to engender strife. Paraphrasing Lennon, Robertson said:

Imagine a world when no more little babies are slaughtered in the womb.

Imagine a world where there are no more homes torn apart because of alcoholism.

Imagine a world where there are no more young men and young women spaced out and glassy-eyed on account of drugs.

Imagine a world when there are no more crime lords selling prostitutes, selling pornography, selling gambling devices, selling drugs, and stealing from legitimate business.

Imagine a world where nobody hates anybody any longer, where there is no more fighting and no more killing.

Imagine a world where you can walk down the streets of the city—or any city—safely at any hour of the day or night without fear of your life.

Imagine a world where men and women [are] married in holiness and godliness, and women were not being used as cheap, exploitive [sic], devices to satisfy the lust of men. And imagine a world where there was no more perversion, and homosexuality, and lesbianism, but men and women functioned as God made them, where they brought up their children together in love, where there was no more divorce, and where little children knew who their mothers and fathers were.

Imagine a world where the Word of God was honored and people said, "this is the answer to life's problems." Hallelujah!

And imagine a world where those who brought that book, and those who had the message of Jesus, were the honored representatives of society where men and women said, "Welcome into our community; you have come with the Word of God."

Now, you say, "That sounds like the Millennium."

Well maybe some of it does, but some of it we're going to see.[8]

What Robertson described is a utopian society based on peace and love. And in making these statements he was well aware of the dominionist stance taken by Weiner and Maranatha Campus Ministries. But regardless of what Robertson and Weiner say, no such society can exist as long as men live in corruptible flesh. Unregenerate men, as a whole, will not welcome the Word of God because, properly communicated, the Word of God will convict of sin and the need for repentance.

> But the natural man receiveth not the things of the Spirit of God: for they are foolishness unto him: neither can he know them, because they are spiritually discerned (I Corinthians 2:14).

By saying that "some of it we're going to see," Robertson infers that some, if not all, of these scenarios are possible in present society. Yet there is not a single one that is possible given mankind's sin nature—unless ninety-eight percent of the human population were wiped out, leaving only conscientious Christians and some unbelievers who are naturally moralistic. Apart from a police state of greater magnitude than that of Hitler's Germany, these evils will persist in increasing intensity until Jesus returns.

Even during the Millennium, with Jesus reigning in person, there will be those who will rebel against His government. That's why He, along with His resurrected saints, must rule the nations with a rod of iron (Revelation 2:27; 12:5; 19:15).

There cannot be a perfect society until only the saints of God, in their resurrected bodies, occupy the earth. That will take place after the Millennium and during eternity in the new heaven and new earth (Revelation 21).

If Scripture does not promise such a society before then, what hope is there that, under the fallible rule of supposed "overcomers," even a substantial portion of sinful humanity will obey God's laws for any reason, whether beneficial to them or not.

Robertson's error is the same as that of all dominionists: he applies to the Church certain Old Testament Scriptures that relate to the Millennium and to eternity, and that promise the restoration of a remnant of natural Israel to faith in their Messiah. Another error is his belief that there is a raising of human consciousness toward righteousness in Christ. That belief, based upon a Gallup Poll commissioned by CBN, reveals a lamentable naivete:

> George Gallup discovered that something happened in America about four or five years ago. Because we said, "We want you to go back and survey people and find out the difference of their attitudes today versus 1979 about religious matters."
>
> George Gallup went to the campuses of America. He surveyed with extremely accurate testing methods the attitudes of college students on the campuses of America. Fifty percent of those on the college campuses said, "We are more religious today than we were five years ago."
>
> Of the general population, sixty percent of the people in America said, "We are more willing to accept religious solutions to life than we were five years ago; we are more religiously inclined than we were five years ago; we are looking for answers from God more than we were five years ago; we are turning away from science, from humanism, from materialism, and we're saying, 'God, you've got to have an answer.'"
>
> Now that's what America told Gallup, and he in turn told us. Now what does that mean? Well what it means is we are on the verge of one of the greatest spiritual explosions in the United States that this world has ever known. That's what it means.
>
> It means that millions and millions of people are open to Jesus Christ.[9]

All Gallup's poll really means is that people in the United States are becoming more religious. What does religiosity have to do with faith in Jesus? In fact, the religious entities enjoying the largest surge of interest are Islam and various elements of the New

Age Movement. These include the entire spectrum of occultism from witchcraft to the human potential programs of EST, TM, Eckankar, the Pacific Institute, Scientology (Dianetics), and their like, to the eastern religions of Buddhism, Hinduism, and even most schools of modern psychology.

A later Gallup Poll found that, while there definitely is an increase in the number of people in the United States who profess to be "born again," their answers to questions about their lifestyles revealed that their moral values are identical to the rest of society, no better.[10]

This is borne out even by Pat Robertson's attitude about how his CBN Bible, *The Book*, was advertised when it first came out in 1984:

> And at the end of September we're going to start perhaps the biggest advertising blitz for this particular product that's ever been put behind any book in history. And we've even got guys like Bubba Smith to stand there and say, "I read *The Book!*" ... And Donna Summers, and a couple of stars from *Dallas*, and one of them from *Dynasty*, and all these are going to say, "We read *The Book!*"
>
> And reading the Bible, in America, may get to be one of the most "in," important things people do![11]

It seems not a little incongruous that people who represent some of the most ungodly media productions were used by Robertson to sell Bibles in the interest of converting society from ungodliness.

Robertson also believes that, in this present age, the wealth of the world will be turned over to God's people, along with the responsibility of ruling society:

> Somebody has got to sew some tents together, and sew some nets together, and get the literature together, and all the things that are going to be needed to handle 400 million to a billion souls that are going to be saved in the next few years! I mean, it's a staggering task and God's going to give it to us! Someone has got to train the future leaders of this world, because God is going to put us in positions of responsibility.
>
> Let me ask you this question: Assume that the Lord took away from the governments of this city, this state, other states, the nation, all the ungodly and the sinners. Assume they were just taken away. What would happen then if He said to His people, "Go in; it's yours"?
>
> I don't know how to run a sewage system—do you? How do you run these things? What do you do with a tax policy? What's the foreign policy of the United States, or of a state? How

do you handle the various taxes and imports and duties? How
do you run the various social welfare and social service opera-
tions? What about the welfare of great numbers of people? What
about the major educational programs?

And you could go on, and on, and on, and on. God's
people have got to be ready for what He's going to do. It's one
thing to sit here and say, "Hallelujah! There's going to be a
revival!" But what are you going to do when it comes? . . .

There has to be preparation; there has got to be training.
There has to be a teacher corps ready to train young converts in
the Lord. If you want to concentrate on something while you're
here, concentrate on the plan you're going to have for the next
five years. What's going to happen when all these things that
we talk about take place? We will see them happen![12]

There are going to be taxes in the utopian society? And social
welfare? Obviously Pat wasn't talking about the Millennium. In
fact, he has revealed something about his own approach to tax
policy by stating that the state should tax the people to pay for
religious training.[13] How this escaped the secular media during his
candidacy for President of the United States is a mystery.

Also, the question arises as to how God is going to remove the
"ungodly" and the "sinners" to the point where we will have a
godly society before Jesus returns.

Actually, Robertson's description of the problems in running
secular society point out how woefully inadequate the Church is
to cope with those problems. In two thousand years it hasn't
learned to handle its own problems well enough that it should
desire to run society.

It should be of concern that anyone would believe that a godly
society could be established among unregenerate mankind to the
degree that there would not even be a need for prisons. Will human
nature change? Not likely. The outward manifestations of evil such
as crime and immorality are merely the fruit of man's inner nature
of sin. They are reflections of the inward thoughts and intents of
the heart (Jeremiah 17:9). Unless man's heart is changed, his actions
cannot be controlled without great expense and suffering.

Robertson believes that a coming revival will change the
hearts of mankind sufficiently to allow godliness to prevail upon
the earth. Scripture, however, tells us that toward the end of this
age the love of many will grow cold because sin will abound
(Matthew 24:12).

While we know that "the wealth of the sinner is laid up for the
just" (Proverbs 13:22), it is not a given that we will take over the
world before Jesus returns. Though we may point to isolated
testimonies of inheritance from sinners, we will not inherit the

earth in its totality until after we stand before Jesus to give an account of the deeds done in our flesh (Romans 2:6; II Corinthians 5:10). Yet Robertson believes that Jesus will not return until after the Church has taken control of society and judgment has come upon the ungodly. In the meantime, we are to prepare ourselves to take dominion:

> Now what do you do? What do I do? What do all of us do? We get ready to take dominion! We get ready to take dominion! It is all going to be ours—I'm talking about all of it. Everything that you would say is a good part of the secular world. Every means of communication, the news, the television, the radio, the cinema, the arts, the government, the finance—it's going to be ours! God's going to give it to His people. We should prepare to reign and rule with Jesus Christ.[14]

At this point Robertson called for preparation to begin with prayer, after which he led the Maranatha Campus Ministries convention in a prayer for revival as a prelude to taking dominion.

Obviously Pat wasn't talking about the new heaven and the new earth when he said everything that is "a good part of the secular world" would be ours. He was speaking of taking dominion before Jesus returns. This is borne out by his reference to the "good" part of the secular world. There will be no secular world in the new earth. Nor, for all practical purposes, will there be a secular world during the Millennium, at least in terms of government, since the government will be administered under the direct, visible kingship of Jesus.

The inconsistencies in Robertson's eschatology that teaches both dominion and a rapture are recognized even by Gary North, one of the leading advocates of dominion eschatology. Referring to the effect of David Chilton's *Paradise Restored* upon television ministers, North says of Pat Robertson:

> Pat Robertson was so concerned that his evangelist peers might think that he had switched to Chilton's version of postmillennialism that he wrote a personal letter to many of them (including one to me) in the summer of 1986 that stated that he had not adopted Chilton's theology. He mentioned *Paradise Restored* specifically. Then he outlined his own views, in which, as a premillennialist, he somehow completely neglected to mention the Great Tribulation. That a doctrine so crucial to premillennnial dispensationalism as the Great Tribulation could disappear from his theology indicates the effect that Chilton (or someone) has had on his thinking. . . .

The change in Pat Robertson's thinking (and the thinking of many premillennialists) had begun several years before *Paradise Restored* appeared. Rev. Jimmy Swaggart begins a highly critical article against "kingdom now" theology, including Pat Robertson's version, with a lengthy excerpt from a speech given by Rev. Robertson on Robert Tilton's Satellite Network Seminar on December 9-12, 1984. This was several months before I handed Rev. Robertson a copy of *Paradise Restored*, and about a month before the first edition of the book was published. He had already made the switch away from traditional dispensationalism.[15]

Pat Robertson has presented a message so completely postmillennial in its tone that it is difficult to understand why he continues to insist that he is still a premillennialist. I have never seen a public pronouncement of any postmillennialist that is more detailed in its description of a coming era of external blessings. I know of none who thinks it is coming in the next few years, but Pat Robertson did, in late 1984.[16]

No doubt those who believe Pat Robertson's scenario are sincere in their desire to see righteousness prevail on earth. But danger lies in expecting more than God's Word promises. At the proper time the earth will be ours as joint heirs with Jesus Christ. Until then we should not try to take for ourselves what He has not ordained. God allows evil to exist in the world, and it will continue to exist, if for no other reason than to test the hearts of men so that none will be without excuse when they stand before their Judge. God is the final arbiter of when evil will be done away with once and for all. Our responsibility is to rescue souls from the consequences of sin; it is not incumbent upon us to rescue the world system from the consequences of God's judgment.

PURGING THE EARTH

A sure sign of religious authoritarianism is a zealousness to rid the world of opposition to one's peculiar tenets. In the minds of many dominionists the authority of the apostles and prophets must not be questioned. Their rulership in the Kingdom of God (as they understand it) must be free from dissent. Therefore it will be necessary that those who challenge their teachings and their authority be removed.

There are differences of opinion among dominionists as to how dissenters will be removed, but there are essentially five ways in which that may occur: 1) God will supernaturally strike dead those who oppose His apostles and prophets; 2) God will send, or allow satanic forces to send, plagues upon dissenters; 3) the Church (or certain "overcomers") will pronounce God's judgment upon dissenters, thus moving God to destroy them; 4) the Church will, out of "necessity," use physical force by which it will judge, sentence, and execute judgment (including death) upon dissenters; 5) all or any combination of the above may take place.

According to some dominionists, in order to effect this purging of the earth the overcomers must attain immortalization, thus becoming immune to any physical resistance to their program. Becoming immortal, and thus impervious to injury or death, will be the result of having attained spiritual perfection through obedience to the apostles and prophets.

We will deal with the teachings on immortalization in a later chapter. The subject at hand is the purging by the overcomers of not only the earth, but of the Church as well.

Franklin Hall:

In his book, *Subdue the Earth, Rule the Nations*, Hall quotes Revelation 12:5, and equates the man child of the sun-clothed woman with the overcomers:

> The man-child company will have dominion of this planet first. Those who possess a house may decide who shall occupy it. In the same manner, as a group from the church take up their authority and rulership of the planet that God gave them, they will likewise be able to choose whom they will, to occupy it.[17]

> The man-child group of the sons of God will be required "to rule all the nations with a rod of iron" (Revelation 12:5). To those not accepting this invitation into Holy Ghost Light of fire, there is but one alternative: the opposite to light is DARKNESS. The Light of Life will be to them a blinding and consuming fire of destruction![18] (Hall's emphasis)

This fanciful interpretation of Revelation 12:5 is not consistent with Scripture. While the symbolism of the man child is open to interpretation (whether he is Jesus, Israel, the Church, certain overcomers, etc.), the fact remains that the man child is caught up to heaven while the woman who gave him birth is driven into the wilderness. If the man child is in heaven while the earth is being purged, then he cannot rule with a rod of iron until after he returns to the earth. He cannot exercise dominion prior to his return which, if he is the Church (or overcomers within the Church as Hall claims), will be with Jesus at *His* return (Jude 14-15).

Hall states that the man-child company can choose who will occupy the earth. Excluding the possibility of exile to other planets, this can only mean that those who do not find favor with the man-child company will be executed.

Royal Cronquist:

Royal Cronquist is an apostle of the Manifest Sons of God movement. Cronquist continues to teach the Manifest Sons of God doctrines, and is influential behind the scenes of some of today's Charismatic Dominion teachers.

> The greatest decision that the church is going to have to make in these days ahead (and especially the ministries in the body of Christ) is to have to face that there are apostles of God, and that they must submit to that authority and to that office; they must submit to that foundation as though it was Jesus Christ, and whoever will not submit to that authority shall be destroyed from among the people.[19]

> Jesus cannot, will not return, until there literally exists this kind of church, body of Christ. This Church (remnant) is to be . . . executing deliverance and judgment, in all authority and power, to all the people of the earth, first to and in the Church, then to all the nations of the earth.[20]

> The kingdom of God is now ready to appear, now ready to be literally established in all its fullness within the earth. The first-fruits people will be counted worthy to escape the things that are to come to pass upon the earth. They will have absolute immunity to destruction and death in any form. Even vengeance and wrath which is about to come, will not touch them, but they themselves will be the execution of this vengeance and wrath.[21]

If an attempt to execute vengeance is to take place, those doing the executing had better be under absolute control by the Holy Spirit. The problem with Cronquist's scenario is that the premise upon which it is built (immortalization before Jesus returns) is unscriptural.

Earl Paulk:

In his book, *Thrust in the Sickle and Reap*, Paulk quotes Matthew 13:40-43 (NKJV):

> *Therefore as the tares are gathered and burned in the fire, so it will be at the end of this age. The Son of Man will send out His angels, and they will gather out of His kingdom all things that offend, and those who practice lawlessness, and will cast them into the furnace of fire. There will be wailing and gnashing of teeth. Then the righteous*

will shine forth as the sun in the kingdom of their Father. He who has ears to hear, let him hear!

Applying his personal interpretation that the angels who will accomplish this task are ministers of the Church rather than the angels of heaven, Paulk calls upon God's people to rise up and judge the kingdoms of the world:

> The book of Revelation makes it clear that John wrote his letters to the angels of the Church. Who are the angels that God will use? They are ministers called by God to boldly proclaim the Word of God. They will sound the trumpet. One should never separate prophecy of the New Testament from prophetic Old Testament scriptures. The trumpet sounded in the Old Testament as a warning. Today the trumpet sounds from the angels of the Church, God's ministers who cry out, "It is harvest time!" Witnesses to God's power will shine as never before. God will gather righteous people together to raise up a witness of Jesus Christ and judge the kingdoms of this world.[22]

Paulk goes on immediately to say that the first sign of the time of harvest is an answer to Jesus' prayer in John 17, "that they all may be one just as We are one."

Unity aside, the chilling aspect of Paulk's reasoning in these passages of his book is the realization that he is looking forward to the day when the "angels" (i.e., he and other "ministers of the Church") will gather out of God's kingdom "all things that offend, and those who practice lawlessness, and will cast them into the furnace of fire." I hope I'm misreading his intentions.

IMMORTALIZATION

It is an essential ingredient of dominion theology (particularly among the Charismatic Dominionists) that the "overcomers" attain immortality. If the dominionists are to be God's instruments of destruction upon not only unbelievers, but believers who do not submit to the authority of the apostles and prophets, they will need immunity from reprisals. This, it is believed, will result from their living a perfect, sinless life, and will make them impervious to injury and death.

It is because of this doctrine that death among Charismatic Dominionists is a tragedy—especially the death of a prominent leader. If God does not count such people worthy to escape death, then those close to him must make excuses such as equating his death with vicarious suffering for the Body of Christ, or admit that the one they were following to perfection wasn't perfect himself.

Of the fringe movements in dominion theology, Positive Confession is most susceptible to the immortalization theory. The believe-it-and-receive-it mentality of Positive Confession must logically result in the belief that if one can muster enough "faith" to live in "divine health," he can also muster enough faith to believe for immortality.

We've already seen that the roots of the immortalization doctrine go back at least to Franklin Hall. Those who have carried his torch through the Latter Rain Movement and the Manifest Sons of God are still actively propagating this teaching today.

Of course, it is believed that this final state of physical perfection will come about only through the attainment of spiritual perfection. The reason is that death is the final enemy to be conquered (I Corinthians 15:26).

David Ebaugh

David Ebaugh is a leading apostle of Identity. In a communication to his followers, Ebaugh reprinted a proclamation by a "Rev." Dean Goss entitled "Melchisedec Order Decree," and offered it free on request to those who would write to his organization, Word by Word Association. This decree, affirming belief that the end-time overcomers will be a part of the "Melchisedec Order" of priests, states in part:

> In the name of the Lord Jesus Christ, through his blood, fire, water, and Spirit, I receive glory, honor, and immortality by imparting his now-blood, liquid streams of living light into my blood. My whole spirit by faith, soul by works, body by hope is now being preserved blameless until the coming of the Lord. When I decree a thing, it is established unto me; and your light shines upon my ways. I decree that the full manifestation of the Kingdom of God from within me now come forth. I decree that every atom within my earthly, physical body bring forth health, light, life, and immortality. My light is now coming forth as the morning, and my health is springing forth speedily, and my righteousness goes before me. Your glory is my rear guard. For I am made in the image of Elohim, after Elohim's likeness. I have dominion over the fish of the sea, and over the fowl of the air, and over the cattle, and over all the earth, and over every creeping thing that creepeth upon the earth. I am helping to bring about the revelation and restoration of all things which you have spoken by the mouth of all your holy prophets since the world began.[23]

The doctrine of immortalization is only one of several that tie Identity to the Manifest Sons of God.

Sam Fife:

In his book, *One Corporate Man*, this leading apostle of the Manifest Sons of God stated:

> Therefore let all men know, that in this dispensation of the fulness of times, God is going to fulfill His purpose to bring together into one, all things that are in Christ, both in the earth and in heaven, and make of all the twos, one new many-membered man, who lives after the order of Melchisedec. When He has finished preparing this many-membered man, He is going to purge the earth of every other man by His Judgment Day, and there will come in a new age, and a new earth, with a new man living in a new order, where every member is so dead to self that he lives unto the rest of the Body, and that order shall perpetuate eternal life.[24]

Paul Cain:

Paul Cain is a William Branham disciple well known in today's charismatic circles, and associated with John Wimber and the Vineyard movement.

> If you have intimacy with God, they can't kill you. they just can't. There's something about you; you're connected to that vine; you're just so close to Him. Oh, my friends, they can't kill you.[25]

> If you're really in the vine and you're the branch, then the life sap from the Son of the living God keeps you from cancer, keeps you from dying, keeps you from death . . . Not only will they not have diseases, they will also not die. They will have the kind of imperishable bodies that are talked about in the 15th chapter of Corinthians . . . this army is invincible. If you have intimacy with God, they can't kill you.[26]

Earl Paulk:

> The fifth function of the church is to conquer the last enemy, which is death, and to bring redemption to the Body of Christ. When the Apostle Paul says that redemption has not yet taken place, he speaks, I believe, of the redemption of the individual body; yet in my spirit I perceive that he speaks also of the redemption of the Body of Christ.
>
> Jesus Christ Himself overcame death individually, and **when the church becomes so conformed to His image that those who die do not pass through the grave, but become instead gloriously changed in the twinkling of an eye, it will**

be that church which will bring the Kingdom of God to pass on the earth. [Paulk then quotes Romans 8:18, 22-23, and Ephesians 13-14, and goes on to say:]

We have received the earnest of the **expectation** through the baptism of the Holy Spirit, but we must move on to the **possession**, which is overcoming the last enemy, death. Sometimes the interpretation has been made that Jesus Christ conquered death, but if that were so, why would Paul's epistle to the Corinthians, written at least ninety years later, say that the last enemy that **shall** be destroyed is death (I Corinthians 15:26)? **Jesus Christ conquered death individually, but it is left to the church to conquer death on a corporate basis.**

Is it possible that there will be a people who so possess the authority of Almighty God, as Elijah did, that they, as a group, will say to death, hell, and the spirit of Satan, "We will **not** die. We will stay here and be changed, and we will call Jesus Christ to return to this earth as King of Kings and Lord of Lords"? Yes, that is what I believe the church must do! But it will not be easy, because **God is looking for the manifestation of a mature church who can speak with the authority Jesus had when He stilled the winds and called Lazarus forth from the grave.**

An exciting prospect? Oh, yes! We are God's people, called to do the will of God in the world today and to see the King of Glory return to establish His Kingdom on earth! Jesus Christ had the authority to say "No" to death on earth, and He is waiting for us to come to that same authority He had so we can say, "The last enemy—death—has been conquered!" . . .

Jesus Christ, as the firstfruit of the Kingdom, began the work of conquering death on an individual basis, but we, as His church will be the ones to complete the task. Jesus said (Matthew 28:18), "All power is given unto me in heaven and in earth," and the church today has that same power. Death will not be conquered by Jesus returning to the earth. It will be conquered when the church stands up boldly and says, "We have dominion over the earth!" How else will God be able to show Satan a people for whom death holds no fear, over whom death no longer has any power? When God can do that, Satan's hold on us will be broken forever![27] (Paulk's emphasis)

Both Scripture and history demonstrate that true believers needn't be immortal to be free from the fear of death. It is *perfect love*, not perfect living, that casts out fear (I John 4:18). It is by the faith that assures us of eternal life, that God's saints suffer death rather than serve sin (Hebrews 11:36-40).

I suspect that those who so earnestly desire immortalization that they will twist Scripture to fit that desire are the ones who are not made perfect in love and, therefore, fear death. So great is that fear that they have deluded themselves into believing they can overcome death through their own works of righteousness.

This is why so many demonstrate such an outward fervor toward God. It isn't so much that they fear Him as it is that they fear death and its consequences if they haven't proven themselves worthy of eternal life. It becomes increasingly obvious that at the root of dominion theology is a works-oriented salvation rather than a faith-oriented salvation.

Contrary to what these people teach, when immortality does come it will be *after* the dead in Christ rise at the Lord's return to take His people out of the earth. Then, from the heavens, He will pour out his wrath upon the nations. (I Thessalonians 4:13-17).

This immortality, the hope of our salvation, will occur suddenly and will take effect throughout the Body of Christ, not just among a select few at individual moments when they attain spiritual perfection. It won't occur because we happen to come to the realization that we can speak it into existence because of our attainment to holiness through outward works of righteousness.

The very Scriptures Paulk cites *contradict* his belief that the Church will destroy death. For verse 26 of I Corinthians 15 says, "For he [Jesus] must reign, till he hath put all enemies under his feet. The last enemy that shall be destroyed is death."

Jesus, when He returns (not the Church prior to His return), is the one who will put all enemies under *His* feet. He must reign on earth until that is accomplished. The context of these verses shows clearly that death will not be destroyed until *after* the Millennium, when Christ "shall have delivered up the kingdom to God, even the Father" (I Corinthians 15:24).

The dominionists take Scriptures relating to entirely different time periods and apply them to the present age. Much of what is said is true if placed in proper context relative to the millennial reign of Jesus for which it is meant. Yet the dominionists can quote Scripture, seemingly with authority, to "prove" their hypotheses.

What the immortalization theory fails to explain is how, if death is the *final* enemy to be conquered, there will still be other enemies left to be conquered by those who have conquered death.

Of all the bizarre elements that make up dominion theology, the one that caters most to spiritual pride is immortalization. And when one comes to the place where he believes he has no sin, he will move into an amoral mindset that justifies any action in the name of God. Earl Paulk gives a clue to such reasoning by suggesting that whether or not one sins depends upon his motive:

The accusers said to Jesus, "We have Moses as our father, and Moses said, 'Thou shalt not commit adultery.'" Jesus replied, "I believe that too, but let me carry you to a heavenly dimension. If you don't lust in your heart you cannot commit adultery." They said, "The law says, 'Thou shalt not kill,'" And Jesus replied, "I believe that too, but let me speak to your heart. If you don't hate first, there is no possibility of murder." How wise Jesus was![28]

And how wise those who put words in Jesus' mouth are. Paulk presents a perfect example of twisting Scripture to fit his premise. While motive does play a role in sin, there are objective standards instituted by God and revealed in His Word which cannot be abrogated simply on the basis of one's personal convictions.

How many people "fall in love" with another man's wife, not out of lust, but a genuine caring? Would it not be adultery if, in an expression of their love they engage in sex? Not all sexual activity is in response to lustful thoughts. Otherwise the marriage bed itself would be defiled. Perhaps Paulk would condone wife-swapping as an expression of love provided "lust" is not involved.

Hit men for the mobs don't necessarily hate their victims—for the most part they're indifferent to them. Using Paulk's rationale, they are innocent no matter how many people they kill. If, as so carelessly stated by Paulk, "you don't hate first, there is no possibility of murder," then out of a motive of purifying society, and with a "heavy heart," dominion "overcomers" may put dissenters to death at will. Many Inquisitors mourned for their victims, believing that they had rejected God.

Sin is sin, regardless of the motive. Where motive matters is in works of righteousness, not in sin; even our righteous acts are sin when performed apart from pure motives.

There is a strange paradox revealed among those who, on the one hand make pleas for love and unity, and on the other hand, passionately look forward to the day they can "speak the word" or pull the trigger that will destroy "sinners" (and unyielding Christians) that they perceive as God's (i.e., their) enemies.

Yet if the utopian society of the dominionists is to be realized before Jesus returns, a holocaust worse than any history has ever witnessed must take place. The "holy wars" of the early Holy Roman Empire may yet be revived.

THE CLOUD OF WITNESSES

Among Manifest Sons of God and Kingdom Message people there has developed a teaching alleging that there is an "interaction of the worlds." That is, that the directions for establishing the Kingdom of God on earth will come through the departed spirits of the saints who have gone before. These supposedly comprise the "great cloud of witnesses" of Hebrews 11:4-12:1.

Earl Paulk claims to have already had some communication with the departed. In a sermon entitled "The Next Move of God," aired over the PTL Network in August, 1985, Paulk described his contact with his deceased sister, Joan Harris:

> I was communicating with the Lord and the spirit of Joan came to me. I was so hungry and so much in need of that, for I miss her—I miss her greatly. I find myself still hearing her voice in the hallways. She's fresh in my spirit.
>
> And I was somewhat dismayed when I got up this morning and saw the rain falling, for I know the people in Atlanta. They not only will not come through the snow and the sleet and the storms, but many of them will not come through the drizzle.
>
> And so I said, "Lord, you know, I know you have something for the people today."
>
> And the spirit of the Lord just stopped me and said, "The people that I want to hear you will be there today, and the people who need to know my message will receive it one way or the other."
>
> And then came the spirit of Joan. And so beautifully she said to me, "You know, I'm gathering on the Hillside of Glory this morning people to hear the message from Chapel Hill." And she said to me, "You know, our hope in Glory is Christ in you on planet earth."
>
> Now how many of you understand that?
>
> You see, everything in Glory, Hebrews 12, are compassed about with a great cloud of witnesses.

Later on in his message, Paulk was pleading with his congregation to live righteously, when he again made reference to his "communication with Joan":

> You gotta realize He said the law is dead! And now you come to something new: I say to you, that if you look upon a woman to lust; I say, if you covet in your heart; I say, if you let it be in your spirit.
>
> That's why I plead over the spirits of you that sing in this place. That's why I lie before God and say, "God, don't let them get tainted with the things of this world. Don't let them get their minds off of their calling!"
>
> In my communication with Joan this morning—and I know so much how God used it—she reminded me of some of you that she ministered to. Have you so quickly forgotten? Have you so quickly walked away and forgotten? No wonder He said, "if someone come forth out of the grave you wouldn't hear it because you won't listen to your prophets!"

Some may legitimately ask whether Paulk's strong statements were merely a passing reference to *thinking* Joan would say these things. I would not quarrel with Paulk's statement that he still hears "her voice in the hallways." That could certainly be a metaphor. But one must admit that quoting her "spirit" as saying that she was gathering the saints on the Hillside of Glory" is inflammatory and requires explanation.

When I questioned him personally by phone while he was guesting on a local radio program in the Los Angeles area, Paulk denied that he ever made such a statement, or that communication with the dead was to be desired. Although he denied making the statement, he also stated that the statement (which he denied making) was a message meant only for his congregation, and was not meant to be taken outside. Yet there are other statements that bear on what Paulk believes about communication with the dead, one of which was revealed in another of his sermons aired over the PTL Network. In a portion entitled, "A New Dimension of Looking at the Spirit World," Paulk stated:

> It says in Revelation that there are saints, that their spirits are crying out, "How long, O Lord, how long, O Lord?" Now get this: I believe departed saints like my little sister Joan that stands before the face of God is saying, "Father, is this the hour? Is this the time? Father, I have brothers and sisters who are warring the battle. I want you to see them!"
>
> You say, "Well, God knows it." Sure He knows it! But God's always subjected Himself to His creation! Always! And God cannot, and will not act until the time is right! And for the time to be right there's got to be a persuasion in heavenly places.
>
> Our boys and girls must learn not to go to the old seance idea and not to become a mystic. But they've got to learn there is an interaction of the worlds—just men of God—saints of God—their spirits!
>
> This coming generation has got to learn there is an interaction of the worlds, because the Bible said we've got to learn how to bind the strong man, if you will.
>
> Honey, we can't release God's power until we learn to bind the strong man!
>
> And this business of binding and loosing on earth as it is in heaven, and having the authority God has given us is something our boys and girls must learn first-handed.[29]

Paulk has made some curious statements. First he states that "God always subjected Himself to His creation. Always." This is error. God never has subjected Himself, nor will He ever subject Himself, to His creation. Certainly He will on occasion respond to what man does; He answers prayer, for instance. But every response is in accordance with His sovereign will, and is not predicated upon any inviolable law. To say He "always" subjected Himself, and "He cannot and will not act" until there is a persuasion in heavenly places, puts man in control of God.

The implication that the spirits of just men of God interact with those on earth leaves us to draw but one conclusion: Paulk does believe that communication with the dead is not only possible, it is not only desirable, it is imperative for Christians who desire to engage in spiritual warfare.

The great cloud of witnesses to which Paulk refers will be instrumental in bringing about the new revelations needed to establish the Kingdom of God on earth. This is why Paulk insists that the younger generation must learn that there is an interaction of the worlds between those on earth and departed saints.

Of course, Paulk does decry "the old seance idea." But that is a diversion from the fact that *any* attempt at communication with the dead is forbidden by God's Word. His statement implies that we must be open channels through which "just men of God—saints of God—their spirits" may give their revelations. This may not be "the old seance idea," but it is akin to spirit channeling or mediumship.

In spite of Paulk's denial, there is further evidence that his does believe that communication with the dead is acceptable:

> My son-in-law, Steve, told the story of going out to Stone Mountain to run the morning after Joan died. He prayed, "Lord, I would like to communicate with Joan." I understand the dangers of seances and all the prostitutions and counterfeits of supernatural communication. But for every counterfeit, a reality exists. Moses and Elijah stood with Jesus as He was transfigured. Stephen, as he was being stoned, saw Jesus in the heavenlies. The rich man begged to send someone from the dead back to earth to warn his brothers. Interaction between the worlds of the natural and spiritual happens according to scripture.
>
> Steve simply wanted some communication with Joan's spirit. He thought that talking to himself would bring back memories of some things that Joan had said to him. But Steve said that the Spirit of the Lord quickened his spirit saying, "No, I will grant a spiritual communication." Steve said he could hear the voice of Joan's spirit saying to him, "Steve, it is great over here! Everything we regarded as mystery—things we have been preaching and teaching and trying to understand—I understood instantly. I completely understand redemption—all those things I wondered about, I understand! Now, I see," Paul said,

"We shall know fully even as we are known." Joan said, "I see it now, Steve. The place, the dimension in which I exist now is beyond anything I can describe." The Apostle Paul said, "I cannot describe it."[30]

> We're told that we are surrounded by a cloud of witnesses (Hebrews 12:1). Why does the Word tell us about "the cloud"? I've been with hundreds of people when they died. Almost every dying saint I've ever prayed with has talked about seeing somebody they had known who had died previously. They have talked about seeing tremendous light.
> Why did Jesus go to the mount of transfiguration? Whom did He see there? He talked with Moses and Elijah who had been dead many years. I believe that God desires interaction between planet earth and the heavenlies unlike we've ever known.
> I believe that Joan is before the throne of God as one of those witnesses that the book of Hebrews talks about. She stands before God as an overcomer and intercessor urging us on. She encourages Christians on earth to be overcomers also.[31]

To use the Lord's conversation with Moses and Elijah as justification for seeking communication with the dead goes beyond the liberty afforded us. In the first place, Elijah did not die, but was taken to heaven bodily. As for Moses appearing with him, we do not know the nature of this interaction, but it is obvious that Moses had a particular dispensation to appear with Elijah. But this was at the instigation of God, not man; and it involved Jesus, not sinful humanity.

When Saul went to the witch of Endor to have her call up Samuel's spirit, it was clearly sin even though it was Samuel and not a familiar spirit that appeared. Saul broke the law forbidding communication with the dead, no matter the method.

Interaction between the natural and spirit realms does occur. But in the context of Paulk's messages, he is referring to communication between Christians and departed saints for the purpose of receiving revelations of truth. God's Word is clear that it is the Holy Spirit to whom we should look in order to understand God's direction and to discern truth in every matter:

> *Howbeit when he, the Spirit of truth, is come, he will guide you into all truth: for he shall not speak of himself; but whatsoever he shall hear, that shall he speak: and he will shew you things to come.* (John 16:13)

Nowhere does God's Word tell us that we must look to departed saints for new revelations. Yet while Paulk says we must learn not to become mystics, his teaching is mysticism of the highest order, akin to seeking apparitions of the Virgin Mary and patron saints common to the Roman Catholic Church.

Paulk is obviously very fond of his sister. And no doubt she was the beautiful, loving woman he portrays. But let us consider the ramifications of desiring communication with the dead.

How we all miss our loved ones. And how much we would love to speak to them after they've gone on. But actively seeking or even desiring such communication by any means leaves one open for contact by familiar spirits—demons impersonating the deceased. This is expressly forbidden in God's Word (Leviticus 19:31, 20:6- 27, Deuteronomy 18:11; I Samuel 28:3; etc.).

According to Paulk, the "cloud of witnesses" does not include only the departed saints; it also includes angels:

> Secondly, we enlarge our vision to a spiritual dimension. Individual efforts alone will never work. We enlarge our vision to spiritual proportions which include the angels. The Bible says, "... the angels rejoice when one is converted." "We wrestle not against flesh and blood but against powers and principalities." There's "a host" warring against us, but there's "a cloud" of witnesses cheering us on. We must broaden our perspective by saying, "God, we stand before You, the holy angels, and the powers and principalities."[32]

Including angels in the cloud of witnesses with whom Paulk believes we should communicate, implies that communication with angels is to be sought as well as communication with the dead. There are many voices today claiming that the way in which we will receive God's strategy for dominion is through angelic visitations as well as visitations from departed saints.

We are witnessing today claims by many leaders in the churches of having communication with angels. And it is an important element of word-faith or Positive Confession teaching that we can command the angels to do our bidding.

Roland Buck's book, *Angels on Assignment*, took the Christian book market by storm several years ago with claims that angels are manifesting themselves in great numbers to prepare the Church for victory over the world system. The discrepancies in that book bear out the demonic sources of Buck's angelic visitations.

Frank Peretti's best-selling books, *This Present Darkness* and *Piercing the Darkness* have erroneously expanded the thinking of hundreds of thousands, if not millions, of Christians to think that their prayers control the angels. His fanciful depiction of spiritual warfare is not scriptural, yet many have taken his fantasies as textbooks on spiritual warfare. (See the Media Spotlight book reviews, "Angels on Assignment or Demons of Deception?" and "This Present Darkness: Spiritual Warfare—Fact or Fantasy?")

The Latter Rain period saw William Branham operating under the influence of a "Voice" that turned out to be an angel. Today, one of Branham's disciples, Paul Cain, has reappeared on the international scene with claims that he, too, hears a "Voice" which is that of an angel. So, too, does Bob Jones, another Latter Rain product associated with Cain through the Kansas City Fellowship in Kansas City, Missouri. All these "Voices" and/or "angels" give revelations contrary to Scripture or that do not come to pass. We examine Cain's and Jones' claims in the next chapter.

What lies ahead for the Church if it accepts the teaching that its boys and girls must learn to seek communication with departed saints, and it begins to intrude into the spirit realm of angelic beings in order to receive power?

FIVE-FOLD MINISTRIES

Those whose teachings center on or are substantially concerned with the five-fold ministries (Ephesians 2:20; 4:11) are convinced that there can be no unity in the Body of Christ, and no perfecting of believers until all Christians (or at least a vast majority) submit without questioning to the authority of the latter-day "apostles" and "prophets." By perfection is meant overcoming sin and living such righteous lifes as to not have to suffer death.

Earl Paulk:

> That's what we're doing as the five-fold ministry—the apostles, prophets, evangelists, pastors, and teachers—is equipping the saints, maturing the Body of Christ. But see, even that frightens us because we say we've got pastors, we've got evangelists—we talk about apostles and prophets, we get afraid. And yet they've got to come back with authority and power.
>
> Ephesians 2:20 says the Church is built not on Jesus (a lot of folk don't know that), but it's built on the apostles and prophets, and Jesus Christ being the chief cornerstone. He's the cornerstone, but the apostles and the ministry of the prophets is the foundation.
>
> What God is doing today is raising up prophets. I don't have any doubt in my mind that Oral Roberts is a prophet to the Church to bring us back to the healings.
>
> Many of them—Branham and many others—I believe that the Hagins and the Copelands, we have varying doctrines here, but I believe they brought us back to understanding the power in God's Word. They were apostles toward that. I believe there are other apostles and prophets God is raising up.[33]

Calling Kenneth Hagin and Kenneth Copeland apostles seems ludicrous in view of these men's teachings that we are not saved by Jesus' death on the cross, but by His suffering under Satan in hell! This is nothing less than a denial of Christ's blood!

We see also that Paulk believes William Branham was a prophet of God in spite of his aberrant doctrines. In addition, one would think that Oral Roberts' false prophecies relating to the destiny of his medical school must cause some concern that the term "prophet" is so loosely bandied about. Add to this Roberts' calling Jim Bakker a prophet, and we can see how desperately in trouble are those who follow these men.

If we apply any formula for consistency to Paulk's words, we would have to assume that Jesus has taken a minor role in the governing of His Church. The following statement, taken with the understanding that Paulk considers not Jesus, but the apostles and prophets, to be the foundation of the Church, removes Jesus from the position of the Rock upon which the Church is built (Matthew 16:18), and assigns that title to the people who comprise the five-fold ministries:

> The fourth issue at stake is the true unity within the Body of Christ. To build upon anything less than the true Rock, the only lasting foundation, would be only to see the entire building fall. Paul made it clear that the Cornerstone had been "rejected by the builders." The only solution was to bring forth new builders—whom Paul defined as apostles, prophets, evangelists, pastors and teachers—to build up a people fitly joined together whose head is Jesus Christ Himself. We are further given the warnings as to how we build on the foundation. To talk of unity without truth is to build with wood, hay and stubble (I Corinthians 3).[34] (Paulk's emphasis)

Some logical, deductive reasoning would assume that Paulk is calling the five-fold ministries the Rock of our salvation: Jesus is not the foundation, He is the Cornerstone; the five-fold ministries comprise the foundation; the Rock is the only lasting foundation; ergo, the Rock is the five-fold ministries. In Roman Catholicism, a direction in which Paulk is heading with his latest teachings, the chief apostle, Peter, is believed to be the Rock (Matthew 16:18) upon which the Church is built.

During a *Praise The Lord* program on TBN in July 1987, Paulk was challenged by Hal Lindsey regarding some serious errors in his teachings. Paulk denied believing what he had written in his own books. Yet he so much as admitted to them by suggesting that Hal wasn't able to perceive the true meanings of his writings because people who do not have the Spirit of God cannot understand what can only be spiritually discerned.

By making such an incredible statement Paulk not only insulted Lindsey (while making pleas for unity), he placed his own writings on a par with Scripture, and limited understanding of his esoteric "truths" only to those who see things his way.

Such statements hinder greatly attempts to bring unity to the Body of Christ under the truth of God's Word.

Paulk goes one step further in his teaching on the role of the alleged latter-day apostles and prophets, equating them with God in the flesh:

> How else will God speak today other than by written revelation in His Word and prophetic voices? Anointed teachers interpret revelations so God's people can understand. But prophetic voices of God must take the lead in speaking as God in the flesh. In I Peter 2:2, Peter refers to this as "... the pure milk of the word," which brings life, direction and healing.
>
> For that reason, God has placed in the Body of Christ not only apostles who establish churches under His anointed direction, but also prophets. What can a prophet do unless he prophesies? Why would God anoint a prophetic voice if prophecy does no more than teach that which has already been revealed? Prophecy is not teaching revealed truth. Prophecy opens us up to revelation, insight and direction. It moves God's people to spiritual levels of maturity they have never known before. The Church can never become the glorified Church God intends it to be until its ears are opened to hear God's prophetic words.[35]

It's bad enough that Paulk considers himself (as a prophet) to speak as God in the flesh—a Protestant pope of sorts. But just as bad is his teaching that the Scriptures are insufficient to bring believers to maturity; there are new revelations by which this will be accomplished that can only come through himself and other latter-day prophets. This is a basic tenet of Manifest Sons of God theology, a major spokesman of whom we will examine next.

Royal Cronquist

Cronquist's interpretation of Ephesians 2:20 is classical Manifest Sons of God:

> Who is the foundation? The apostles and prophets. Is Jesus Christ the foundation? No. He is the foundation of all things, but literally, to the church, He is the cornerstone, and upon Him come the foundation of the apostles and prophets to put the foundation of all doctrine, of all revelation, of all experience, of

all truth, of all anointing, of all authority, of all power, not only upon, but under all the people of God.[36]

Cronquist does say that upon Jesus "come the foundation of the apostles and prophets." Certainly we can find no fault with that order except to remind him that the cornerstone itself is merely a part of a foundation, albeit the part that holds the whole together. The foundation does not rest upon the cornerstone.

However, as is the case with dominion teachers, Cronquist assigns to the latter-day apostles and prophets powers beyond those assigned by God's Word. He believes that the apostles and prophets are not only the foundation of our very lives, he also believes that they create God's will for our lives:

> The whole purpose of the foundational ministry, and especially the foundational ministry, is to equip you in a very private, particular way to inform, to undergird, to strengthen, to encourage, to qualify, to create the will of God for your life. Can you imagine how the body of Christ is still in the baby infancy stage, because they have really denied the foundation that is to their lives, and if they deny the foundation of their life, there is no way that the foundation can be built within them.[37]

Cronquist errs in suggesting that the five-fold ministry is "the foundation of their life." Those in whom God has placed responsibility to build up the saints and bring them to maturity are to be honored and obeyed, insofar as they teach and practice truth. But Jesus is the only foundation of our spiritual life; it is to Him that we owe our very being and substance (Acts 17:28).

And how can the apostles and prophets "create the will of God" for our lives? Only through total submission of our minds and wills to theirs will we be made to believe that they are ordained by God to direct our every move.

While submission to authority in the Body of Christ is of great importance, it is within the local body that that submission must take place, and only to the degree that the authority operates in conformity to God's Word. It is only in the local body that anyone ministering the prophetic gifts or administering authority can know enough about the believer to guide him. But the dominionists want us to believe that there are apostles and prophets at large who are coming on the scene with new revelations to which every believer must adhere without question. There is no accountability of these apostles and prophets to the elders of the local churches, but only to one another. This very subjective authority must be taken on faith by the individual at the risk of his being deceived:

And so we are going to have to be willing to let our mind be changed by the Holy Spirit in the way that we think and the way we understand. He did promise that "albeit when He, the Spirit of Truth is come, He will guide you into all truth." In 2,000 years no one has ever been guided into all truth. Why? The only thing I can think of—and I don't know everything yet because I haven't yet become glorified, but I believe that God is now beginning to remove the seals from the secrets that have been hid from the foundation of the world. I believe that He is now going to begin to reveal unto the holy apostles and prophets the foundation of the kingdom that will unfold the truths of God to His people so that they can literally become the very divine substance of Jesus Christ in their spirit, soul, heart, mind, and body.[38]

This statement is fraught with error, not the least of which is the idea that men can "become the very divine substance of Jesus Christ in their spirit, soul, heart, mind, and body." This is nothing less than the deification of man.

In addition, if what Cronquist (and Paulk) says is true, then the Holy Spirit did not guide the writers of the Scriptures into all truth. The problem with Cronquist's reasoning is that he interprets *all truth* to mean *all knowledge*. There is a difference.

God has chosen not to reveal all knowledge to man—even to His adopted sons—as long as we are in sinful flesh. But He has revealed all truth in terms of what is necessary to effect the maturing of the saints. Those truths are contained in the written Scriptures (II Timothy 3:16--17). Any new "truths" added to the Scriptures and deemed necessary for belief by the Body of Christ are of Satan, not of God. Collectively, the Scriptures comprise "all the truth" promised by Jesus.

The dominionists, in effect, tell us that God planned for the Church to walk in darkness, unable to grasp the truths necessary to mature believers to the stature (and even the nature) of Christ, until latter-day apostles and prophets arrived on the scene. But what do the Scriptures say?

> For whom he did foreknow, he also did predestinate to be conformed to the image of his Son, that he might be the firstborn among many brethren.
>
> Moreover whom he did predestinate, them he also called, and whom he called, them he also justified: and whom he justified, them he also glorified.
>
> What shall we then say to these things? If God be for us, who can be against us?
>
> He that spared not his own Son, but delivered him up for us all, how shall he not with him also freely give us all things?

> *Who shall lay any thing to the charge of God's elect? It is God that justifieth.* (Romans 8:29-33)

> *But evil men and seducers shall wax worse and worse, deceiving, and being deceived.*
> *But continue thou in the things which thou has learned and hast been assured of, knowing of whom thou has learned them;*
> *And that from a child thou hast known the holy scriptures, which are able to make thee wise unto salvation through faith which is in Christ Jesus.*
> *All scripture is given by inspiration of God, and is profitable for doctrine, for reproof, for correction, for instruction in righteousness:*
> *That the man of God may be perfect, throughly furnished unto all good works.* (II Timothy 3:13-17)

It is not today's "apostles" and "prophets" who are going to perfect the saints (bring us to maturity). It is the Word of God, working on our hearts through the power of the Holy Spirit, who will bring us to maturity as we learn to submit to God and to one another in love. All anyone can do, whether he calls himself an apostle, prophet, evangelist, pastor or teacher, is instruct us in the Word of God rightly divided, and encourage us to follow its directives with pure motives. There are no new revelations by which we must be saved or grow to maturity.

Now, however, we are being asked to believe that men who cannot rightly divide the Word of Truth where its meaning is obvious even to babes in Christ, are going to give us "new truths" by which they will direct our paths toward perfection. What Cronquist means by saying we will become "the very divine substance of Jesus Christ" is not clear. But this statement fits the theory of the deification of "overcomers" held by many dominionists. How will we achieve this? Cronquist says:

> You therefore shall be complete, even as your heavenly Father is complete. How do you suppose that is going to be done? It's going to be done by holy apostles, prophets, evangelists, pastors, and teachers who become the experience themselves, who equip you with the experience that they have, who give you the rules, the laws, the ways, and the how-tos to literally cooperate with God's Holy Spirit so that it again can be performed.[39]

The rules and laws by which we exercise our faith are already established in God's Word (Revelation 22:18-19). Those who would burden the Church with new, man-made rules and laws according to their own experiences are legalists of whom Paul warned us:

> *Beware lest any man spoil you through philosophy and vain deceit, after the tradition of men, after the rudiments of the world, and not after Christ.*
> *For in him dwelleth all the fullness of the Godhead bodily.*
> *And ye are complete in him, which is the head of all principality and power.* (Colossians 2:8-10)

How are we to recognize the apostles and prophets for today? Cronquist says our hearts will know:

> The knowledge of a person as a prophet or apostle of God must be a heart revelation. . . . I could come to you and tell you that I am an apostle, but that doesn't mean a thing. Someone else could tell you they are an apostle; that doesn't mean a thing, but I will only be an apostle to you when you have heard from God's Holy Spirit that I am an apostle of God, and if you believe I am a false prophet, to you I would be a false prophet whether I am or not. As a man thinks in his heart, so is he.[40]

Besides erroneously applying Proverbs 23:6-8 ("For as he thinketh in his heart so is he"), Cronquist gives us the same formula used by the cults to validate their apostles and prophets: the "inner witness." Mormons believe their apostles are from God on that basis, as do Jehovah's Witnesses, the Moonies, and Roman Catholics. Their basis for belief in their hierarchies is not upon the clear teaching of Scripture, but upon subjective reasoning and a willingness to accept the claim to authority on nothing more than that claim itself. They "know in their hearts" that their apostles are from God.

Scripture tells us that our hearts are deceitful above all things and desperately wicked (Jeremiah 17:9). We are predisposed to believe what we want to believe unless we submit to an objective standard of truth by which we can judge what is of God and what is not of God. The only standard given to us by God is His written Word—the Bible. And the tests for prophets are found in Deuteronomy 13:1-5, 18:22, and in Galatians 1:8.

Dominion theology employs the same rationale as the cults and, in effect, has become a cult within the Church proper. The reason it is difficult to recognize it as a cult is because it has not openly identified all of its leadership as yet. Its proponents are laying the groundwork for their ascendancy by conditioning the Church to accept the idea of apostles and prophets for today and by pushing forward to visibility those they want recognized first as "great leaders" within the Christian community.

In order to understand the error behind their claims to the offices of apostles and prophets, we should put Ephesians 2:20 within the context it was written:

> *Wherefore remember, that ye being time past Gentiles in the flesh, who are called Uncircumcision by that which is called Circumcision in the flesh made by hands;*
> *That at that time ye were without Christ, being aliens from the commonwealth of Israel, and strangers from the covenants of promise, having no hope, and without God in the world:*
> *But now in Christ Jesus ye who sometimes were far off are made nigh by the blood of Christ.*
> *For he is our peace, who hath made both one, and hath broken down the middle wall of partition between us;*
> *Having abolished in his flesh the enmity, even the law of commandments contained in ordinances; for to make in himself of twain one new man, so making peace;*
> *And that he might reconcile both unto God in one body by the cross, having slain the enmity thereby:*
> *And came and preached peace to you which were afar off, and to them that were nigh.*
> *For through him we both have access by one Spirit unto the Father.*
> *Now therefore ye are no more strangers and foreigners but fellow-citizens with the saints, and of the household of God;*
> *And are built upon the foundation of the apostles and prophets, Jesus Christ himself being the chief cornerstone;*
> *In whom all the building fitly framed together groweth unto an holy temple in the Lord:*
> *In whom ye also are builded together for an habitation of God through the Spirit.* (Ephesians 2:11-22)

Seeing Ephesians 2:20 taken out of context, one might fall prey to the teaching that the "five-fold ministries" as described in Ephesians 4:11 comprise the foundation of the Church. But let's examine exactly what Paul was saying.

In the first place, it is not the so-called "five-fold ministries" to which Paul assigned the status of "foundation," but rather only the offices of the apostles and prophets. Because these offices are mentioned in Ephesians 4:11 along with those of evangelists and pastor-teachers (the latter being one, not two distinct offices), doesn't necessarily mean that the evangelists and pastor-teachers comprise part of the foundation.

In the second place, if we put Ephesians 2:20 in the context of the entire thought expressed in verses 11 through 22, we see that Paul was specifically addressing the Gentiles at Ephesus regarding their being joined in one body with the Jews through whom came the revelation of God's truth. Having been grafted into the true faith, which is the continuation of God's revelation through the prophets who preceded Christ, not something distinct from it, the Gentile believers were built upon the foundation of the apostles (New Testament) and prophets (Old Testament) combined. In other words, the teachings of the apostles and prophets, the Spirit and the Law, comprise the foundation upon which the believing Gentiles (the Uncircumcision) are joined with the believing Jews (the Circumcision). As the cornerstone of that foundation of teachings, Jesus is the element that holds all truth together, and to whom we look for guidance through the Holy Spirit.

It is also valid, however, to say that what Paul was referring to in Ephesians 2:20 was the foundation of the apostles and prophets in the Church. This might be borne out by applying Ephesians 3:2-6:

> . . . by revelation he made known unto me the mystery; (as I wrote afore in few words,
>
> Whereby, when ye read, ye may understand my knowledge in the mystery of Christ)
>
> Which in other ages was not made known unto the sons of men, as it is now revealed unto his holy apostles and prophets by the Spirit;
>
> That the Gentiles should be fellow-heirs, and of the same body and partakers of his promise in Christ by the gospel.

This Scripture indicates that there were apostles and prophets in the Church. This was necessary for the transition of authority from the priests to the apostles, who had a unique anointing that testified to their positions as the new order of leadership for the Jewish believers. The signs and wonders that accompanied the apostles were used by God to demostrate the transferral of spiritual authority from the priests of Israel to the apostles of the Church. They also testified to the Gentiles that the God of the Jews is the only true God, and for Him they must abandon their allegiances to their false gods.

Why Be Concerned?

There are those who wonder why we should be so concerned if some people claim to have an apostolic or prophetic ministry. We must understand that such a claim places these people in the same category as the apostles who established the Church in the Faith; they would have the same authority over the universal Church.

The office of apostle is one which brings discipline for the local churches and establishes doctrine. According to II Corinthians 12:12, the marks of an apostle are signs, wonders, and mighty deeds (miracles). But not these only. For an apostle teaches the Word of God in truth. In fact, the apostles defined the Faith for the whole Church, not only at its inception, but for its entire history. There is no one authorized to define the Faith today, since it was already defined by the apostles of Jesus Christ and was established by inspiration of the Holy Spirit in God's written Word.

Those who insist that they are apostles must validate their claim through the working of miracles in the same way that the apostles of Jesus did. There can be no failings. Everyone who comes to them for healing must be healed. They must operate fully under the anointing of the Holy Spirit. And their doctrine must be sound.

Where Are They?

The question is, who today—or at any time since the last of the first-century apostles died—has demonstrated through *unfailing* miracles that he is an apostle? The "healers" that came out of the Latter Rain Movement have not been unfailing in the miracles they claim to have performed. And certainly their doctrines are fraught with sufficient error to disqualify them even if their claims of miraculous healings were true.

Those who disagree point out that Paul left Trophimus sick at Miletum (II Timothy 4:20). But there is no indication that Paul attempted to minister healing to Trophimus; being sensitive to the Holy Spirit, Paul most likely knew that he was not to minister healing in that instance, and perhaps did no more than pray for the Father's will to be done. At best, this verse proves nothing either way. It neither proves that Paul failed, nor does it prove that he did not pray or attempt to minister healing. Lacking a Scripture to prove conclusively a failure, one cannot justify his own failure.

That there are exhorters who speak by the power of the Holy Spirit in specific instances I would not deny. By the same token I would not deny that God still works miracles through the ministry of His servants. Nor would I deny that there are missionaries who plant churches and oversee them until they mature to sufficiency in self-government. But these would not be called apostles, for the specific reason that the ministry of the apostles went beyond these duties to that of once and for all defining the Faith and establishing the doctrines and practices for the universal Church.

When the written Scriptures were completed the Church was equipped with all it needed in the way of revelational truth; we had the apostolic testimony of Jesus; we had the apostles' instructions that defined the Faith for the Church. The Scriptures instruct every succeeding generation on how to live in obedience to the Faith. Everything we need for living in accordance with His will is already provided in the Scriptures.

*All Scripture is given by inspiration of God, and is profitable for
doctrine, for reproof, for correction, for instruction in righteousness:
That the man of God may be perfect, throughly furnished unto
all good works.* (II Timothy 3:16-17)

Now, today's alleged apostles and prophets are careful to
stress that there are no new revelations, that Scripture is the final
authority, and that any word that does not agree with Scripture
must be rejected. But this disclaimer is more theory than practice.
This is evidenced by their insistence that no one should challenge
them or question their validity. And while they may not bring new
revelations in every instance, at best they bring new interpretations
of Scripture based upon alleged revelation knowledge. For the
most part, their claims are extra-biblical if not unbiblical.

There is also a distinction made between the apostles commissioned by Jesus personally, and the latter-day apostles. It is admitted that the former had a unique office which cannot be filled
today; but in the same breath it is stated that the latter-day apostles
will be *greater* than the original apostles.

If, in fact, there is any validity to the office of apostle today, in
a limited sense it may be applied to missionaries who plant churches and oversee them until they have come to maturity. But these
are not apostles to the Church as a whole. In the same limited sense,
any believer who speaks an exhortation, a rebuke, or an encourage-
ment under God's anointing, may be said to prophesy; but they are
not the same as the prophets of old, whom the latter-day prophets
claim they will one day eclipse in power.

Recognizing False Apostles And Prophets

Those who held the office of prophet prior to the Lord's
appearing had a specific role: to hear the Word of the Lord for the
people of Israel. The average Israelite did not have the Holy Spirit
until the Lord ascended and bestowed the Holy Spirit upon all
believing flesh. Those who had the mantle of prophet prior to that
time did not lose it, but were used by the Lord to validate the new
move among the Jews. There is no evidence of apostles or prophets
arising in the churches since then.

For those who may doubt this, I offer a guideline for them to
recognize false apostles and prophets.

Not For Sale

**A true apostle or prophet would not sell his prophecies or
services.** God's Word instructs us to buy the truth and sell it not
(Proverbs 23:23). Given today's expansive nature of the Church, it
may be necessary to sell books through retail outlets in order to get
a teaching out; but generally, a true apostle or prophet will not

place price tags on his word, and will not require any remuneration for his ministry.

If a person puts a price tag on what he calls a revealed word or an indispensable teaching, you can be sure he is not from the Lord. Today's alleged apostles and prophets sell their prophecies in the form of publications and audio or video tapes that they claim are "required" if you are to enter into God's move.

But what about Elijah who asked the widow for a cake before ministering to her? The difference in this *unique* instance is that Elijah gave her in return far more material goods than she gave him. Do today's professed apostles and prophets do this? Rather, they keep everyone scurrying to their conferences. They sell an endless array of books and tapes through which they dangle before the people a carrot of future promises of power and perfection.

What He Says Is What You Get

A true apostle or prophet would always be accurate when he claims to speak in the name of the Lord; just as importantly, he would never defend his errors or allow the people to follow anyone who is in error. But error is of little concern to today's alleged apostles and prophets.

Errors on the part of today's professed apostles and prophets are justified by pointing to Jonah's prophecy to Nineveh; he did not tell them that, if they repented, their destruction would be withheld. But every prophetic warning of God's judgment implies allowance for repentance. It need not be stated. Otherwise He would not let the people know how much time they had.

Should a prophet err for any reason, he would not justify his error, but would repent in sackcloth and ashes for betraying the sacred trust of God's people.

Calling Those Things That Are

A true apostle or prophet would call out the false ones for what they are. Not only have today's alleged apostles and prophets proven themselves in error, they criticize those who expose error in the Church, calling them anti-Christ and of the Jezebel spirit. To them doctrine is divisive.

Today's alleged prophets rarely prophesy future events apart from what Scripture has already prophesied, and when they do, they are woefully inaccurate. There are certainly none that are universally known throughout the Church who meet the biblical criteria. Also, a true prophet will not give prophecies to everyone who asks for them; he will be selective according to God's leading

Because of today's tendency toward mysticism, the gift of prophecy is greatly misunderstood. It has taken on the aura of one given to receiving "new revelations" from God. But it is not as mystical as it is often portrayed. It more often manifests itself as an exhortation based upon the revealed written Scriptures to bring God's word to a specific need in a congregation.

But this does not mean that those who speak prophetically are prophets to the whole Church. It merely demonstrates that particular gift of the Spirit for a specific instance.

As long as no one establishes conditions for the test there can be no claim to the office of prophet. Since the days of the apostles (who were also prophets) no one has established those conditions. Nor have those who claim that office today provided the conditions. So their claim to the office of prophet is invalid. Likewise, then, their teaching that there is a restoration of that office is invalid.

By taking a single Scripture and building a doctrine so serious in its consequences, those who teach the "five-fold ministries" doctrine act contrary to basic principles of biblical exegesis. This error is compounded by equating today's teachers with the early apostles. This opens the Church to their new revelations, many of which are not based on God's Word, but are totally subjective.

In view of the shambles of today's alleged apostolic and prophetic ministries, there is no other alternative than to conclude that the offices of apostle and prophet are not for today's Church. This conclusion is further strengthened by the fact that the teaching of apostolic authority beyond that of the apostles named in Scripture originated in the Roman Catholic Church as justification for its own dominion mandate The belief in latter-day apostles and prophets is an outgrowth of the aberrant beliefs of people who have demonstrated consistent error in their doctrines and practices, and is basic to every aberrant "Christian" cult. It is not supported by any clear teaching of Scripture.

4
Who Are
The Apostles And Prophets?

Since the late seventies and early eighties especially, there have been increasing references within the dominion camp identifying specific people as "apostles" or "prophets," and many leaders are supportive of each other in those roles. It is said that the decade of the eighties revealed the prophetic ministries (which will continue to increase), and the nineties will reveal the apostles. As a result, many of the alleged prophets have been made known, but as of this writing there have been few apostles identified, and then generally in vague terms. For instance, certain men, have been designated apostles over certain types of ministries (e.g., Larry Lea as apostle of prayer; Oral Roberts as apostle of healing, etc.).

Although some are more visible than others, these leaders are showing up on the same platforms in varying numbers and orders. They are on a constant circuit, conducting leadership conferences for pastors and teachers from around the world, and spiritual warfare rallies for anyone and everyone they can reach.

Leadership Conferences

At leadership conferences pastors and teachers are instructed in the latest methods on church growth through the utilizing of proven methodologies: 1) spiritual warfare against evil territorial spirits; 2) psychological testing for gifts among congregants; 3) covenants requiring congregants to follow their pastor's vision; 4) visualization and other meditative exercises; 5) formula prayer (Larry Lea and Dick Eastman are the leaders in this area); and other approaches related to church ministry and administration.

Armed with that knowledge, the pastors take what they've learned and implement it in their congregations in order to teach the people how to take dominion over their cities, how to institute proper worship and praise in order to move God and to receive power, how to work miracles, signs, and wonders, how to bind the spirits allegedly controlling the four directions—North, South, East and West—and other dominion-oriented exercises.

All these are conducted with the intention of waging spiritual warfare over evil territorial spirits that allegedly keep cities, states and nations under spiritual bondage. These spirits are believed to be responsible for all the evils that plague civilization, from illicit drugs to abortion, to satanic rituals, to organized crime.

Larry Lea, pastor of Church on the Rock in Rockwall, Texas, is generally recognized among Charismatic Dominionists as the leading apostle of prayer. His teachings treat the Lord's Prayer as a formula for spiritual warfare with special emphasis on calling God's Kingdom to earth as it is in heaven. This formula has been adopted by thousands of pastors and teachers as a means of establishing dominion over their cities.

But the dominionist prayer is not prayer alone; it involves time out to rail against the devil and command evil spirits to depart from one's city, county, state, and nation. Dick Eastman's teachings on prayer are designed to "change the world."

Because dominionists lack understanding of the method by which the Lord is dealing with the world, they assume that if enough Christians will pray for the world, it (or at least a significant portion of it) will be saved. Yet Jesus himself, in His final hours, did not pray for the world, but only for those the Father had given Him (John 17:9). It takes discernment to pray according to the Lord's will as much as it does to wage spiritual warfare according to His will. In fact, the two cannot be separated. Prayer according to the Lord's will is an integral part of proper spiritual warfare.

Spiritual Warfare Rallies

In the process of deceiving the people into thinking that spiritual warfare consists of railing against spirits, dominionist preachers blow into cities boasting that they are going to take those cities for God by holding pep rallies designed to scare the devil away. Their promise is that whole cities will turn to God, crime will decrease, anti-social behavior will be abated, and godliness will become fashionable. They neglect the fact that God uses evil spirits to accomplish His purposes in the earth (I Samuel 16:14-23; 18:10; 19:9; I Kings 22:22-23; II Chronicles 18:21-22).

Focusing on the external forces for man's evil is very exciting and works people into a frenzy, but the results have proven inconsequential. After barking at the devil for several hours, the apostles of prayer (or whatever) blow out of town on their way to some other locale and everybody goes home feeling self-satisfied that they told that old devil off!

Primed by zealous teachers who promise victory over Satan, Christians lacking even the rudiments of spiritual preparation are propagandized at seminars and urged to "take their cities," or to "take back what Satan has stolen." These pep rallies leave them no more prepared for warfare against Satan than spectators at a football game are prepared to put on pads and butt heads with 280-pound linemen. After it's all over, a let-down settles in and they continue from seminar to seminar and rally to rally seeking the spiritual high that eludes them without the hoopla.

And in every town in which these pep rallies are held, the evils not only remain, they continue to increase at the same steady rate.

Yet the alleged apostles and prophets are gaining greater impetus, and have formed alliances to propagate their heresies. We'll look at some of those who are acting as apostles and prophets to the Church at large through their conducting of broad-based seminars designed to influence pastors and church leaders.

Although not all of these claim to be apostles or prophets, it must be understood that the only scriptural office that supersedes local authority is that of apostle, and possibly prophet. Those who claim to bring words of revelation from the Lord to local church leaders, therefore, are assuming those offices whether or not they overtly claim to hold them.

While I don't wish to label everyone who has contact with dominionists a fellow traveler, it's obvious that those who are asked to teach on the same platform would share similar views. Otherwise their appearing together would be billed as a "debate" or a "dialogue." And while they may not agree on every issue, there must be sufficient agreement in order to be supportive of one another. So those who are supportive of dominionists and/or hold to important dominionist philosophy are well known among their peers. To seek unity with them without challenging their error leaves one's own beliefs open to question. Those who defend heretics, even if they do not believe in their teachings, are guilty of lending credibility to their heresies, and will be held accountable to God for the souls that are destroyed as a result. It's up to those who know the truth to defend the Church against false teachers whatever the cost to unity or to personal benefit.

CHARISMATIC BIBLE MINISTRIES

Charismatic Bible Ministries, founded in 1986 by Oral Roberts, is an important organization conducting leadership conferences. CBM is a coalition of charismatic leaders, many of whom espouse dominion tenets. The original officers and trustees of CBM were:

Since its founding, some have left the organization, others
have joined. I cannot stress enough the fact that not everyone
involved in CBM has openly advocated dominion theology. Of
significance, however, is the fact that a vast majority of the founding trustees openly profess belief in major tenets of dominion
theology, as do the vast majority of the overall members. In addi-

tion, some among them espouse other questionable doctrines such as the "Jesus died spiritually" heresy which, when carried to its logical conclusion, denies the blood of Christ as sufficient for atonement for our sins.

Several members of Charismatic Bible Ministries have been approached with information regarding the heretical teachings of many in this organization, but none have acknowledged the need to take a stand for sound doctrine. Unity at the expense of truth is indeed the mindset of many leaders in the Church today, despite their denials. In fact, the slogan for Charismatic Bible Ministries is "Love and Unity through Signs and Wonders."

This slogan is a good example of how so many of today's leaders have things backwards. Love and unity are not produced through signs and wonders; if anything, signs and wonders are the product of love and unity in the Spirit, based on the truth of God's Word. When people look to signs and wonders to produce love and unity, they will find themselves united with everything that appears miraculous regardless of the source. If, on the other hand, we leave the signs and wonders to God's volition, and concentrate on loving one another and uniting with one another in truth, we will receive all we need from the Father. And if He perceives that signs and wonders are needed in any given instance, they will follow.

THE KANSAS CITY CONNECTION

As strong advocates of apostolic and prophetic ministries, Kansas City Fellowship and its parachurch outreach, Grace Ministries, virtually exploded onto the international Christian scene in the late eighties. This is due in part to exposure in *Charisma and Christian Life*, and their endorsement by prominent leaders such as James Robison, Dennis Peacocke, Art Katz, and others.

In The Beginning

In June 1982 a man named Augustine claimed to hear the audible voice of God instruct him to tell the young pastor of a small church in St. Louis, Missouri, that, by the Spirit of Truth, he would prophesy on the condition of the congregation. That young pastor, Mike Bickle, was impressed by Augustine's seeming accuracy in describing the spiritual condition of the church, and he accepted Augustine as one sent by God to give him direction.

Mike Bickle claims that while in Cairo, Egypt, in September, 1982, he heard a voice tell him, "I am inviting you to raise up a work that will touch the ends of the earth. I have invited many people to do this thing, and many people have said yes, but very few have done my will."[2]

On December 5, 1982, Kansas City Fellowship held its first service and within seven years grew from a handful to over 3,000 members in six congregations.[3]

Grace Ministries

In 1986 the leaders of Kansas City Fellowship formed Grace Ministries, a "ministry team of men committed to seeing the church fully restored to the glory described in God's Word."[4]

Grace Ministries is a parachurch organization that represents several men who engage in itinerant, allegedly prophetic ministries. Although the majority of the team consists of those who started and are leading Kansas City Fellowship, it is organizationally distinct from the church. Some team members are pastors of churches in other cities. Several travel throughout the United States and abroad speaking at conferences and in churches.[5]

During the late 1980s Grace Ministries developed cooperative efforts with other movements, including the Vineyard churches. They call this cooperative effort "cross-pollination."[6] This is the same term that was used by the Council in their efforts to build a coalition of Shepherding-Discipleship communities. Is this mere coincidence?

In May 1990 Kansas City Fellowship and Grace Ministries placed themselves under the headship of John Wimber, and all the affiliated churches subsequently became Vineyards.[7]

Apostolic Teams

According to Grace Ministries, "An apostolic team is a team of ministries joined by the Holy Spirit to plant churches. This team is comprised of mature and proven men with apostolic and prophetic ministries in addition to including evangelists, pastors and teachers. . . . An apostolic team is led by one with a proven apostolic ministry evidenced by successful church planting endeavors with abundant signs and wonders."[8]

Shiloh Ministries

Shiloh Ministries is a major facet of Grace Ministries that designates the prophetic outreach. It is a piece of land where various prophets can live together and share their revelations. It is believed that this will "release a greater prophetic understanding of God's purposes as they submit one to another."[9]

Prophets based at Shiloh will hold seminars and conferences across the nation. John Wimber is credited for playing a key role as a counselor in helping the team members establish some of Shiloh's basic principles and practices. He and Vineyard Ministries International were the major financial contributors to the Shiloh project even before GM/KCF came under Wimber's authority.[10]

Another major influence in the Shiloh project—in fact, in the entire Grace Ministries/Kansas City Fellowship outreach—is Paul Cain, who claims to be a former associate of William Branham. Cain is said to have had several visitations from the Lord about Shiloh alone (in addition to "hundreds" of such visitations on other matters) in which he was given specific details about Shiloh. Cain's dominance over Grace Ministries is evident:

> Grace Ministries team leaders have recognized Paul as having the senior prophetic authority over Shiloh and those in prophetic ministry who are based there.[11]

Ministerial Teams

At the time of this writing, Grace Ministries' ministerial team consists of Paul Cain, Bob Jones, John Paul Jackson, David Parker, Jim Goll, Francis Frangipane, and Reuven Doron.

These men provide service to Kansas City Fellowship, but are not necessarily on its staff, or even membership rolls. Though they have come to be recognized as prophets by some, Mike Bickle stated that he does not recognize them as full-fledged prophets:

> There's no one in our midst that we give the title "prophet." The only one I would feel comfortable of giving that office would be Paul Cain, but he refuses to accept it. So I'd say both of them—apostle and prophet—I believe that in God's purpose they exist, but we're very hesitant to designate somebody as being one at this point in time. But I believe that will be recognized in the future, but it will be much more widespread.
>
> I don't think that the men themselves should go very heavy on calling themselves that; we definitely don't call the other prophetic guys prophets. I don't feel they have the stature of a prophet yet; I think they have a prophetic ministry, but I don't think they're actually at the level of a prophet.
>
> I believe that people can have a prophetic ministry, meaning they move in the revelation gifts and they have insight into things without being a full-scale New Testament prophet.[12]

Despite his denials, there are many examples of Mike Bickle calling these men prophets. In one statement to Bob Jones, after hearing Jones' claim to have heard from the Angel of the Lord, Bickle exclaimed, "Truly, you are a prophet of the Lord!"[13] In addition, John Wimber, under whose authority Bickle has placed himself, consistently referred to these men as prophets until such a cry of protest arose from those who have seen the error in their claims. For a time, at least, Wimber backed down and stated that they merely have a "prophetic ministry."

This is a fallacy. The prophetic ministry cannot be separated from the office of a prophet. To some degree, every believer has a "prophetic ministry," because we all may receive a word from the Lord, usually a Scripture to reprove, rebuke, exhort, or encourage one another. But this is not what these men practice; they claim a prophetic ministry similar to that of Old Testament prophets: revealed knowledge gained from direct, face-to-face encounters with God; they give directive prophecies to individuals, entire congregations, and to the Church at large. They want the glory of a prophet, but not the responsibility.

In spite of Bickle's and Wimber's denials, one of their leaders, John Paul Jackson, is recommended as a prophet by Royal Cronquist, a Manifest Sons of God apostle, and Francis Frangipane was an apostle of the Walk, under John Robert Stephens.

It would take volumes to detail the roles of each person involved at GM/KCF, so we will concern ourselves primarily with Paul Cain and Bob Jones, since they have received the greatest notoriety. And I will not refrain from referring to them as "prophets" on occasion; if they are going to act like prophets they must be willing to bear the scrutiny of prophets. In another section we will address John Wimber and the Vineyard movement.

Paul Cain

Paul Cain was born in 1929 at Garland, Texas, a small farming community about 20 miles from downtown Dallas. He reports that, just prior to his birth, his mother, Anna, was terminally ill from four major diseases: cancer of the breasts, tuberculosis, heart disease, and three malignant tumors that prevented her from being able to have a normal delivery. While on the verge of death, one whom she believed to be the Angel of the Lord appeared to her.

> The angel put His hand on her shoulder and said, "Daughter, be of good cheer, be not afraid, you shall live and not die, the fruit of your womb shall be a male child. Name him Paul. He shall preach My gospel as did apostle Paul of old."[14]

At the age of eight, the entity Cain calls "the Angel of the Lord" visited him for the first time.

> The Angel of the Lord said to Paul, "I want you to preach my gospel as did Paul of old. Open your mouth and I will fill it. You will preach the gospel by binding the sickness and the infirmities of God's people."[15]

Cain believes that this Angel of the Lord is Jesus, but he isn't absolutely sure:

> I heard an audible voice and, of course, often the Angel of the Lord—it might have been the Lord Jesus Christ—but anyway when he speaks it's rather awesome.[16]

In 1947, at age 18, Cain began to hold "healing meetings" in his native Garland. He was the youngest of many who built their ministries during the "healing revival" period that lasted from 1947 to 1958. His contemporaries included Oral Roberts, William Branham, O.L. Jaggers, A.A. Allen, T.L. Osborn, Jack Coe, and Franklin Hall. Cain admits that he suffered the same greed and pride that he says characterized his contemporaries. He says that it was because he succumbed to these weaknesses that God caused him to lose everything including his health.

> In the midst of Paul's despair and repentance, God told him that if he kept himself from corruption and remained content with living a humble life marked by Scripture study and prayer, one day he would be allowed to stand before a new breed of men and women leaders. These would be marked by simplicity, purity and remarkable manifestations of power.[17]

The new breed of which Cain speaks is marked by the absence of any recognizable leaders—a "faceless generation" of hundreds of thousands of believers manifesting signs and wonders greater than those of Jesus or the apostles.

In April 1987 Cain met with the leadership of Kansas City Fellowship and they received him as a father. Grace Ministry's other major prophet, Bob Jones, said that Cain's ministry is called by God "the terror of the Lord," or "the jealousy of God." He called Cain "the most anointed prophet that's in the world today."[18] Cain, in turn, has called William Branham "the greatest prophet who ever lived." This would make Branham greater than Elijah, Elisha, Jeremiah, Daniel, David, and John the Baptist, just to name a few.

Considering the occult manifestations and false doctrines that characterized Branham's work, one must question whether Cain himself understands truth. This also calls into question Jones' claims about Cain.

Paul Cain has prophesied a day when sporting events throughout the world will be cancelled because the stadiums will be used for revival meetings. He says the Lord gave him this vision around the late fifties or early sixties, and it has been repeated more than 100 times since then. This spectacular happening will see millions brought to Christ in a short period of time. The catalyst for this great revival will be the healing, signs, and wonders that will follow hundreds of thousands—perhaps millions—of prophets and apostles released through the major streams of the prophetic ministry of which GM/KCF is a part. Television cameras will record resurrections and miracle healings.[19]

Cain likens those who will perform these wonders to Joel's army, spoken of in Joel 2, which destroys everything in its path and has immunity from death. This army, says Cain, will go forth to conquer the earth for Christ. This, you will recall, is Franklin Hall's interpretation.

Cain also claims to have regular visitations with the Lord—sometimes on earth, sometimes in heaven. He claims to live a celibate life in obedience to God's special call upon him.

Besides his relationship with GM/KCF, Cain has developed a very close relationship with John Wimber:

> Paul has made a special commitment to travel with John and to supporting the vision that God is currently unfolding to him. The Lord told Paul and Bob Jones that this was a priority of the Spirit—for Paul to make a commitment to John Wimber.[20]

According to the testimony of some, many of Paul Cain's predictions have proven astoundingly accurate, particularly in regard to signs and wonders in the heavens and in the earth.

Jack Deere, a Vineyard pastor, states that in January 1989 Cain told him an earthquake would occur on the day Paul arrived for the first time to meet John Wimber at the Vineyard church in Anaheim, California. Another would occur elsewhere in the world the day after he left Anaheim. According to Deere, Cain said the earthquake would be a confirmation that the Lord had a strategic purpose for the Vineyard movement.

A relatively minor earthquake common to Southern California shook Pasadena the day Cain arrived. The day after it is said he left Anaheim, the Soviet-Armenian earthquake occurred.[21]

Blowing Fuses

Other phenomena akin to occult spiritual activity has followed Cain. According to Mike Bickle, Cain, while speaking at KCF's Olathe Worship Center in 1988, called out by revelation seven people and gave astonishingly accurate "words of knowledge." There was a tremendous surge of electrical power that caused the circuits to be blown and the alarm system to go off. Fire trucks arrived, and the firemen were surprised not to find a fire in progress. It is reported that the firemen said, "All the alarms at the station were going haywire. There must be a fire somewhere here."[22]

If this sounds like Franklin Hall's Holy Ghost Fire and Smoke meetings, it's not surprising considering the spiritual link Cain has to Hall through Branham.

There is an account of another power surge at the hands of Cain during a spiritual warfare conference in Anaheim, California, in February 1988:

> On the first occasion in Anaheim, an expensive video camera was short circuited. This was particularly unusual because the camera was battery powered. It was not plugged into any outlet.
> The following night, the telephone system was blown-out [*sic*]. This was notable because no one was on the phone at the time.[23]

One must wonder if the Holy Spirit is a clumsy, out of control source of electrical energy. Such happenings are not dissimilar to those that occur during UFO sightings or poltergeist activity. For that matter, it is not unusual for electronic equipment to experience such problems. But if someone who claims to have a prophetic anointing happens to be preaching at the time, it is almost certain that someone will draw the conclusion that the Spirit of God is manifesting Himself.

But it does make for good press, and everybody likes a light show.

Bob Jones

There are not many of whom it can be said, "he seems to walk with the Lord both day and night, and the supernatural is an everyday occurrence" to him.[24] This is Grace Ministries' view of Bob Jones.

Jones' testimony is as remarkable as Paul Cain's in its plethora of alleged supernatural experiences, face-to-face talks with God, miracles, healings, and the like.

Mike Bickle relates the degree of supernatural visitations Jones allegedly receives nightly:

> You know, I'm going to tell you something about Bob.
> Ever since that time in '74 when he was filled with the Holy Spirit he began to see the technicolor visions and the Lord began to visit him. Since that time he has seen many, many times, five, ten visions and dreams a night. And when I first met him, I couldn't hardly comprehend that.
> I said, "Five or ten a night!"
> He said, "Oh, yes, all the time. Sometimes more, sometimes three or four."[25]

Jones claims he has no trouble talking to angels or rebuking devils. He relates his concern about the rise of abortion and homosexuality, and a conversation he had with a devil:

> He told me the next time that I prophesied and told anybody about it, he would kill me. He said, 'If you knock that off we'll move back into all the signs and wonders you want to. You can heal people and you can prophesy day and night if you want to, if you leave these two subjects alone.[26]

What a revelation: the devils will move people in signs and wonders if they will avoid certain subjects. If this is true, then who's to say that the signs and wonders attributed to these prophetic voices really aren't of the devil? There are many reports of phenomena similar to the kinds found in occultism: heat in one's hands when the spirit of healing comes over them; touching someone to feel the same pain they do in order to diagnose sickness; predicting future events concerning famous personalities. None of these are recorded in Scripture as the pattern of the Holy Spirit's work. But they do manifest themselves among healers in the occult sciences.

Occult Influences

Jones claims a special gift from God which demonstrates that the people's prayers are being heard by the Father (whom he calls "Papa"), particularly in the area of healing:

> I was over there with Jim awhile ago. My hands turned blue, and then they turned purple. And when that happens that means you've got some incense that's gone up. You've got some intercession that's gone up that Papa's saying yes to. There's some prayers that's gone on here that the answer is yes. . . .
>
> When you've got this kind of anointing some of you are already entering that secret place of the Most High. You're already bowing down to that altar of incense. Your tears are falling on those coals and they're coming up before Papa. Papa's saying, "Come with more. Believe for more." Because when my hands turn purple it means you're getting through to the Royalty; you're getting through to the top. It's yea and amen, and that's what He's calling you into: that holy place of divine health. The Holy of Holies which your children are called to enter in can crash that threshold. It's called the place of divine health. . . . That's what the children are entering into: they'll have the Spirit without measure, they'll walk through walls; they'll be translated—everything that was ever in the Scripture.[27]

This peculiar phenomenon is not found in the annals of God's healing power at work. But Alice Bailey, a premier spokesperson for the New Age Movement, described violet (or purple) light as a catalyst for bringing about healing:

> [There are] four groups of angels that are bands of servers who are pledged to the service of the Christ [the New Age Christ, not Jesus], and their work is to contact man and to teach them along certain lines. . . .
> They will give instruction in the effect of colour in the healing of disease and particularly the efficiency of violet light in lessening human ills and in curing those physical plane sicknesses which originate in the etheric body.[28]

Bailey was describing the manifestation of the healing properties of the healthy human aura (the energy field which emanates from the body) ministering to the infirm human aura. This is employed in occult healing practices through the laying on of hands. Another technique is to simply wave or hold one's hands above an afflicted area, touching aura to aura. This has been a method employed to a large extent by the Vineyard movement, although they would deny that they have adopted any New Age beliefs.

Bailey's angels are the spiritual hierarchy of demon spirits masquerading as ascended masters guiding man's evolution toward godhood. It should be mentioned that much occult healing, even in the New Age Movement, is done in the name of Jesus.

Jones also states that his alleged healing power came upon him when he was struck by lightning:

> It was about '76. A bolt of lightning. I was inside—I didn't have my wires grounded in the basement down there, and I grabbed ahold of the refrigerator, and lightning hit the wires outside, and a great blue flame came in. And a ball of fire danced all over that basement, and didn't hurt me. But from that time forth my hands worked funny. And a lot of people have had a lot of good laughs about it. But a lot of people have got healed by it, too. And miracles and everything else, and got anointed by it.
> Anytime God is going to start a fire, He starts it with lightning. And you can take a little of that fire and impart it wherever it is needed. And it will start a God's fire.[29]

Such manifestations have no precedent in Scripture. They leave the impression that the Holy Spirit is some impersonal electrical force—a concept closer to that held by occult healing practitioners.

Faith Not Required

Concerning Jones' claim that his purple hand is evidence that the believer's prayers are being heard by "Papa," Jesus already gave ample testimony in His Word that the Father hears those who are His. But it takes faith to believe that His Word is true. If there is one characteristic of trusting in signs and wonders it is that faith is not necessarily required. To this even the prophetic voices admit:

> There will be some new wonders coming to the church. We had some of these just recently, where Bob Jones and I heard angels singing twice in a meeting. This didn't even take any faith, it was so loud and so clear; it was like the choir singing.
>
> Another time we had the odor of incense fill a meeting for about fifteen minutes. It was so intense that you couldn't help but smell it. I mean, it was not one of those instances where you think you get a "whiff," but He gave it as a witness that He was receiving the intercession from these people—the prayers and their intercession. He had said He would come with a sign: that we would smell the incense. It came so powerfully faith was hardly needed.
>
> And we saw the wind of the Spirit blow so hard at a meeting you could see people's hair blowing! . . .
>
> So He is coming a whole lot more dramatically. As one brother said, "This hardly takes any faith, it is so obvious."[30]

Those who follow signs and wonders are so taken by what they perceive is evidence of God at work that they leave themselves open to deception. The "faith" that results from such special effects is established on sandy ground. When those to whom they look for spiritual guidance fall, they, too, will fall. When persecution comes, they will deny the Lord they claim to follow.

The Lord requires faith. More blessed are those who believe without seeing (John 20:29). Faith is the foundation upon which rests every victory we have in our spiritual walk. Without faith it is impossible to please God (Hebrews 11:6).

Scripture and history prove that signs and wonders do not instill faith. Just the opposite—lack of faith—prompts the desire for signs and wonders. Those who are strong in faith do not need signs and wonders to know that the Father is caring for them, or to be further convinced of the reality of God's power. We do not need signs and wonders to prove that He exists or that He hears our petitions. Faith comes by hearing the word about Christ (Romans 10:17). Without seeing any evidence of supernatural manifestations, we believe because God has granted us grace to believe based upon the testimony of His Word.

If we look at the people who have had supernatural experiences, we'll find that, in many cases, when the signs and wonders cease, their faith ceases. It was not true faith, but rather mere belief in what they could not deny seeing. They believed because they saw, but they did not have faith.

We marvel at the degree of unbelief that the children of Israel exhibited in spite of awesome signs and wonders done on their behalf in delivering them from Egypt and guiding them through the wilderness.

The Old Testament prophets performed miracles in the sight of kings, priests, and the people at large. Yet rather than instill faith, they were more often put to death.

Jesus, after performing miracles of a quality and quantity unheard of prior to His sojourn on earth, was crucified when the belief system the people held was challenged by the evidence of His divine nature. The masses followed Him for the temporal benefit they realized through His signs and wonders, but when push came to shove, everyone including His closest disciples abandoned Him.

Even the miracles performed by the apostles did not initiate faith. They merely attested to the validity of the apostle's office and affirmed the truth of their message about Christ. But *it was the preaching of the Gospel* that brought faith.

The Sign Of Unbelief

Just as in Jesus' day, the cry today is, "show us a sign." Jesus would not yield the sacred power in order to convince people that He was from God. Nor does He work through His people in that manner today. It is significant that genuine signs and wonders are reported more among evangelists witnessing to those who have never heard of Jesus; this indicates that, today, the primary purpose of signs and wonders is the same as it was in the first century: to convince those who worship false gods that Jesus is the True God who is greater than their gods.

Signs and wonders are not given to instill faith in those who already have the evidence of the Scriptures but feel they need more proof. They may be used by God to get people's attention, such as it is recorded in Acts 8:6, but faith always comes by the Word of God being preached with or without signs and wonders.

Although here in the West we have His written Word to testify of Him, to many that isn't enough. Even church people won't believe unless they see a sign. But the fact is, that even if they were shown a sign, they still would not believe.

No, we do not need signs and wonders to instill faith. If God grants signs and wonders—a healing, a miracle—we may be bolstered in our faith. But no genuine faith will be initiated through signs and wonders.

Other Alleged Prophecies

Some prophetic words attributed to Jones are the kidnapping of Patty Hearst, the assassination of Egyptian president Anwar Sadat, the assassination attempt on President Ronald Reagan, and the eruption of Mt. St. Helen's. Of course, all of these we have learned of after the fact; there is no hard evidence to support these claims.

One of Jones' more spectacular predictions, attested by Mike Bickle and others at GM/KCF, was the appearance in March 1983 of a comet unknown by the scientific community to exist. This comet allegedly was a sign from God to Kansas City Fellowship that He was affirming their direction; it also cemented in their minds the belief that Jones has a genuine prophetic ministry. But, again, there is no hard evidence to support this claim. It was allegedly made in private.

Failed Prophecies

In spite of their constant boasting of successful prophecies, the records of both Cain and Jones, as well as all the prophets at Kansas City Fellowship, fall short more often than not. According to the testimonies of former adherents to Kansas City Fellowship, some of the failed prophecies have resulted in dire consequences for those who placed their trust in them:

> Personal prophecy was used a lot and often didn't come to pass. When a prophecy was not fulfilled, the recipient was blamed (you didn't pray it into being, etc.). The "victims" were often the most vulnerable people in the church—single women, the sick, the very people that needed the covering and the protection of the church. One woman (going through a divorce) was prophesied to, that the Lord would not allow her divorce to become final and that she would not lose custody of her daughter. Her divorce became final and she did lose custody of her daughter. Often prophecies came with specific dates by which they would be fulfilled. The accuracy rate of the prophecies given were very low and there was no public accountability for these false (or at the very least, incorrect) publicly proclaimed prophecies.[31]

Our first experience with a false prophecy being made was when Tim Golden was killed in a car wreck. It was prophesied that he would have a worldwide ministry and would be known around the world. A few weeks later he was killed in a car accident. At a church dinner, the sound man who taped the prophecies shared with my husband and I that he had to edit those tapes before a memorial that was given.[32]

One bizarre prophecy confirmed the concept of vicarious sacrifices provided by someone other than Jesus:

> The wife of the worship leader of all KCF churches comes to practice telling us that she has lost her baby (she was only 3 or 4 months along)—that she was bleeding heavily, so they called Bob Jones and John Paul [Jackson] over to pray for her. Bob Jones prophesied that God has martyred her baby and that for every drop of blood the baby lost, a soul will be saved in Wichita.[33]

On one occasion at least, John Paul Jackson urged people to practice instant obedience to the prophets, and threatened financial ruin if they didn't heed their warnings:

> The dollar is going to fall; it's going to literally plummet. . . . The day will come when you'll need to be listening to the Lord because you'll need to take the money out of the bank . . . get your money out of the stock market because it will fall like a ton of bricks. It will collapse. . . .
> Now you're saying to yourself, "When will we know when we should do this?" The Lord will tell you. That's why He put prophets in the church. And He'll say there'll be a prophet come through, or Bob or somebody will say, "I had a dream; I had a vision; the Lord just told me that next week—next Friday the banks are gonna collapse and you need to get your funds out right now and you need to invest in such and such and such and such." And do it. And do it.
> He'll say, "You need to sell your company." He'll say, "Brother, you need to sell your company this month because, because if you wait, you won't be able to sell it . . . if you wait you gonna get a terrible price and your company will go bankrupt." Listen. Listen, because the day is going to come when you're gonna have to act instant. That's what Ephesians is talking about also when it says (to) be instant in season and out of season. That means obedient. Be obedient. Be obedient.[34]

What Jackson encourages—indeed, what the very concept of regular directive prophecy encourages—is a priesthood that keeps the average person at its mercy. The Lord often directs the average believer through circumstances and other means without the benefit of priests who call themselves prophets. In view of the terribly inaccurate nature of these men's predictions, such directive prophecy that demands instant obedience is dangerous. Coupled with the fact that they misapply Scripture to prove their case, the danger is all the more evident. Jackson was wrong on two points in citing Ephesians as meaning to be ready to obey the prophets instantly: 1) Ephesians has no such command. II Timothy 4:2 is the only verse that says, "be instant in season, out of season"; 2) Paul was instructing Timothy to "Preach the word; be instant in season, out of season; reprove, rebuke, exhort with all longsuffering and doctrine." It would be foolish to trust a "prophet" who cannot accurately cite the Scriptures.

In Defense Of Error

Those who defend the inaccuracies of today's alleged prophets point to the imperfections of biblical prophets as evidence that perfection is not a requirement. But the biblical prophets' imperfections were related to their personal failings, not to their prophecies when speaking in the name of the Lord.

Faced with that, the excuse for error falls upon a single Scripture that seems to indicate that a New Testament prophet failed to be accurate. It is pointed out that Agabus told Paul that the Jews would bind him and hand him over to the Gentiles if he went to Jerusalem (Acts 21:10-11). But it was the Romans who bound Paul with chains, not the Jews (Acts 21:33).

We must concede that the details of the prophecy seemed not be have been fulfilled perfectly. The fact is that the Jews first laid hold of Paul and created such a stir that the Roman captain had to rescue him; he also bound him until he could get to the cause of the disturbance. That was the beginning of Paul's captivity as he sought to take his case before the Roman courts and, ultimately, to Caesar.

But although the Jews did not physically bind Paul, their accusations bound him. The Roman captain was the cause of Paul's being bound just as Pontius Pilate was the cause of Jesus' crucifixion; *but the guilt fell upon the Jews in both cases.*

Certainly the technicality of Paul's being bound in such a manner cannot be compared to consistent, blatantly false prophecies such as characterize today's alleged prophets. And there is not a single person today who can say he meets the criteria necessary to call himself a prophet in the biblical sense.

But, again, this does not negate the prophetic gift given on occasion for the purpose of edification, exhortation, and rebuke. Nor should we forget that there are two types of prophecy: 1) *foretelling,* which is a revealed word of knowlege, *sometimes* speaking of a future event to transpire; 2) *forthtelling,* which is a word of knowledge or teaching based on Scripture for the purpose of ministry to the Church. But there is no scriptural basis for the belief that prophets exist today for the Church at large. In any case, all that is claimed to be prophecy must be tested by Scripture.

TESTING THE PROPHETS

Kansas City Fellowship aside, there are many alleged prophets (or prophetic voices) appearing on the Christian scene, not all of whom are associated with GM/KCF. None have proven themselves 100% accurate in their prophetic words. Granted that many are not considered by themselves or by others as prophets in the truest sense of the word; but because they attach a disclaimer to their ministries does not alleviate the problem of their being looked to for prophetic guidance. Responsibility requires that they not be placed before the Body of Christ as having anything more than a teaching which can be tested by Scripture.

In view of the dangers present in claiming a prophetic voice, would it not be reasonable to expect these men to be 100% accurate in their predictions as well as 100% successful in their healing attempts, not to mention 100% accurate in their application of God's Word? But as we examine these prophetic voices we find that not only do none of them meet the scriptural criteria, they justify their errors on the basis that they are just learning how to move in the prophetic ministry. In fact, they state that 100% accuracy can be detrimental.

Rick Joyner's account of a message Bob Jones says the Lord gave him confirms this:

> Bob was told that the general level of prophetic revelation in the church was about 65% accurate at this time. Some are only about 10% accurate, a very few of the most mature prophets are approaching 85 to 95% accuracy. Prophecy is increasing in purity, but there is still a long way to go for those who walk in this ministry. This is actually grace for the church now, because 100% accuracy in this ministry will bring a level of accountability to the church which she is too immature to bear at this time; it would result in too many "Ananias and Sapphiras."[35]

This is scary business. To think that God's grace allows such a magnitude of error proclaimed by His spokespersons leaves the Body of Christ in a state of confusion. The statistics Jones gives are no better than those of psychics and prognosticators in the occult arena. This also suggests that God isn't in control of these people sufficiently that we should place any trust in them. Yet they are demanding that we trust them if we do not want to miss God's move in these last days.

I would ask those inclined to follow these men: would you fly on an airline whose planes crashed 35% of the time?

According to the GM/KCF leadership, no one can expect perfection from their prophets until they have matured to the status of a manifested son of God. Therefore, we are not to judge them by their lifestyles or by their errors, but by the good fruit they produce. Mike Bickle states:

> Proverbs 14:4 encourages us to be patient with sincere ministries, though they might be immature, because they will bear more fruit in due season as they grow up. If we kill them off with criticism and impatience before they flower, then we have gained nothing. . . .
>
> Some people prefer a ministry that is mess and risk free. But this approach hinders their ability to raise up and send out young ministries. Some men have been in the ministry for many years and have never seen one prophet grow to maturity under their ministry.
>
> Maybe God never sent them one to help nurture and raise up to maturity. Maybe God did send them one but their critical and impatient spirit could not bear with the inevitable mess that young prophets make.[36]

Using Proverbs 14:4 to suggest that prophets learn their trade through trial and error because oxen make messes demonstrates a lack of understanding. The use of allegory to support so consequential a doctrine is not only irresponsible, it's dangerous. And notice that, here again, Bickle called them "prophets."

The messes these people make may be good for the prophets, but they wreak havoc in the Body of Christ. We're not concerned about the mess these "prophets" make of themselves; it's the mess they make of other's lives that causes concern. Are people so desirous of signs and wonders that they will accept them without testing them by the Word of God that sets the standard for a true prophet of God: 100% accuracy *and* absolute conformity to the Scriptures? GM/KCF doesn't hold up to that litmus:

> In our zeal to judge prophets, we must be certain we aren't being influenced too strongly by the past mistakes of other ministries. We must judge by the Holy Spirit's revelation and not by fear of man's past failures.[37]

This is a rather subjective test, dependent upon one's impression of what he thinks is of the Holy Spirit. But the Scriptures offer a more sure word of prophecy, and they already give us the parameters for testing prophets. GM/KCF has discarded those parameters for the sake of not bruising "immature" prophets. This leaves the Body of Christ at the mercy of these prophets' growing pains. Yet if they wish to be absolutely true to the Word of God upon which they claim to base the validity of their prophetic ministries, they would stone those prophets whose predictions failed. Given society's lack of support for such action, they would at least stop promoting those whose predictions are not 100% accurate.

We're not dealing with a small matter. If God is in control, it should be so evident that the person could not speak a prophetic word in error. But if man is in control, then there will be many messes made of people's lives. This is of more importance than worrying about the bruised psyches of someone who uses the Body of Christ as a source of guinea pigs for his prophetic experiments.

Mike Bickle recognizes that most of what passes as prophecy is of the flesh. But he leaves the impression that it doesn't matter how many times someone is wrong:

> Now, obviously, probably about 80% of what's in the Body of Christ that's called prophecy is fleshiness. And so we're in a day when we're in such an immature stage of this. So much of what is called prophecy is not truly prophecy. So we realize that; so what's our reaction to that? We don't throw out the baby with the bath water. We say, "Lord, we don't throw out prophecy. We ask You to mature it." We don't take it as serious in the early days as we will in the days to come.
>
> But there have been some real diamonds in the rough that have been given to us. And so, though we want to grow in prophecy, we don't believe everything that's said. We've been given 10,000 prophecies, and I believe there's only a small number that I've really cherished in my heart as from the Lord.
>
> So do we get mad at the people that gave the other ones? No. We just let them go; just sit on the shelf, and let them just go on down the river.
>
> But I tell you, because there's immaturity in that gift does not mean the gift is invalid. Because there's show people—because there's proud men and women—we don't throw the gift; we ask God to perfect it.
>
> We with patience and humility say, "Lord, do something more pure." And He says, "Wait till the nineties; wait till the year 2000; wait till 2010. You think the gift of prophecy's flowing—I *will* purify it because I said I would give it to my people."
>
> So we don't want to be in a place we just believe everything that comes along. But we don't want to be in the place of the cynic and sit in the seat of the scoffer either.

God's saying, "I'm trying to give something to my people. They must in humility and in patience allow this gift to mature in your midst."[38] (Bickle's emphasis)

Scripture doesn't allow for a maturing period when it comes to prophecy. If Bickle is correct in that the majority of prophetic words are of the flesh, how is one to know the genuine from the fake? Of course, they would say, we're to be led by the Holy Spirit. But if the *prophet* doesn't know if his words are of the Lord, how can he expect the *people* to exercise any better discernment?

While speaking of humility and patience, what the prophets are really saying is that they are immune from the consequences of their own errors. They don't seem to care that the people will have to bear the brunt of those consequences for trusting them. This is nothing less than religious tyranny.

Ungodliness Overlooked

When the Scriptures tell us to judge the prophets by their fruit, it means their holy living and conformity to God's Word for themselves and those they teach. It does not mean the number of spectacular events that transpire in their lives. Nor does it rest on how many people are blessed by them; many are blessed by New Age practitioners. Pharaoh's magicians had "fruit," if we judge by spectacular events. Yet today's prophets tell us not to judge the ungodly lives of the prophets, but to believe in them because of the "fruit" of their ministries. This attitude is reflected by Paul Cain:

> Now I know which is perfect is come, [*sic*] that which is imperfect must be done away. But anyone knows that which is perfect has not come. And we don't have the full revelation—we haven't grown up in the stature of Christ as we should. And there is no manifestation on a wholesale basis of the sons of God. And I'm not afraid to mention that even though I get shot down everywhere I go every time I mention the manifestation of the sons of God. I'm not afraid to mention any biblical, scriptural terminology.
>
> If divine healing's in the Bible I'm going to preach it. I don't care if the preacher runs off with the piano player or if he runs off with the bag of money, or the bag, or anything else—I don't care what he does, I'm going to keep on preaching Bible healing. . . . So I want you to know no matter who falls, or what, God is going to pull this thing off, Glory to God![39]

The issue isn't the validity of God's power—any true believer will acknowledge that God can and will do anything He chooses to do through whatever vessel He chooses to use. The issue is whether we should accept the validity of someone who claims to speak for God on the basis of alleged signs and wonders. If we judge them worthy on that basis, we may easily be led into error.

Manifest Sons of God Theology

Cain's defense for using biblical terminology corrupted by the Manifest Sons of God might be acceptable were he and the other prophets with whom he associates not steeped in Manifest Sons of God theology.

To illustrate, the scriptural reference to the manifestation of the sons of God speaks of the resurrection of the saints and the translation unto immortality of believers living at the time of the Lord's return to catch the Church up to heaven. The Manifest Sons of God interpretation is that certain overcomers will attain immortalization after coming to perfection under the authority of the latter-day apostles and prophets. They will be able to move in and out of the supernatural and natural realms, even walking through walls. This is Paul Cain's interpretation:

> So my point is, that there will be a manifestation of the sons and daughters of God. And it won't be this baloney that we've heard of in the past; I mean, there's been a few people tried to walk through a wall like this over here and knocked their brain loose, but that's not what I'm talking about. I'm talking about a true manifested son of God: if anyone walks through this wall over here, they're not going to tell you about it—I mean, they're just going to do it. And sons of God don't tell you they're sons of God, they'll just show you! Amen![40]

Cain's seeming complaint against the Manifest Sons of God is not that they were incorrect in their belief in immortalization now, but that they tried to move into it prematurely. His closing remark reveals that he believes the same way—he just recognizes that the time has not yet come.

There are Manifest Sons of God influences found in Bob Jones' beliefs also:

> The last day church is being birthed now out of the old church, and the old leadership is coming to an end, and the new young leadership is being raised up to reign over an end-time church that will bring forth the Bride. He's not even dealing with the Bride yet; he's got to get him a church right so he can get the fruit of the Bride: your children—my bank account—my grandchildren will be the Bride. You've got to have the church first in the right foundation. That's what he said, "Come back and touch those that'll be the right foundations."[41]

According to Jones, Jesus told him this end-time church will be immortal, and certain souls are being reserved in heaven for the end time army of God. Notice that Jones calls children his "bank account." The significance is seen in the following statement:

> I went and I seen the Lord, and it was like He was looking at little yellow things—little round, yellow things like a spirit of God itself. And there were billions of them. And it was like Him and all the angels were looking through these and every once in awhile they'd say, "Hey, here's an end-time one; get it down here on the end. Here's another good one."
>
> I said, "What are you doing?"
>
> He said, "Oh, we're collecting those who are foreknown and predestinated for the end-times, for you see, they'll be the best of all the seed that's ever been. And we're looking through the seeds and this'll be your grandkids. This will be the end generation that is foreknown and predestinated to inherit all things. And these will be like grandchildren to you—even those that you minister to won't be this generation; their children will be.
>
> "You are to write into their minds, as they write into the children's minds. You're to bring them to a place to allow My Spirit to rule in their life where they can begin to set the Church on the proper foundations, as they will. They'll birth the Church, but their children will attain levels of the Holy Spirit that they will not.
>
> "Although their parents will reign over them and be the leaders of the last-day church, their children will possess the Spirit without measure. For they are the best of all the generations that have ever been upon the face of the earth. And the best of all generations are those elected seeds that will glorify Christ in the last days.
>
> "That's the purpose so that Jesus in the last days has the seeds that will glorify Him above any generation that has ever been upon the face of the earth. They will move into things of the supernatural that no one has ever moved in before. Every miracle, sign and wonder that has ever been in the Bible, they'll move in it consistently. They'll move in the power that Christ did. Every sign and wonder that's ever been will be many times in the last days. They themselves will be that generation that's raised up to put death itself underneath their feet and to glorify Christ in every way.
>
> "And the Church that is raising up in the government will be the head and the covering for them. So that that glorious Church might be revealed in the last days because the Lord Jesus is worthy to be lifted up by a Church that has reached the full maturity of the God-man!"[42]

If Jones is correct, we can forget about looking for the Lord's soon return. This fits well the Lord's prophecy that He would return at an hour when we least expect Him. It also fits the Manifest Sons of God theology that envisions an immortal company of "overcomers" who will "put death under their feet" and rule the earth through supernatural power before Jesus returns.

Jones' "little, round yellow things" imply preexistence of the soul, a doctrine upon which to base unity with the Mormons. Such unity may be forthcoming, at least with the Reorganized Church of Jesus Christ of Latter-day Saints (RLDS):

> I'd been told a long time ago that there would be a great wave among the RLDS people. There's some real excitement there. There's some tremendous excitement there, and I know that in the East there'll be a release this year (1989). The angels are there; they are doing warfare there; they are pushing back darkness, getting ready to release.[43]

As far as immortalization is concerned, it's coming, says Jones, but it is reserved for the Melchizedek Priesthood:

> And the Lord spoke and said, "Bob, the white horse is coming and that will be the Christian group that I'm going to use. Incorruptible flesh will they have, and the lightning in their hands will be the hiding place of their power."[44]

> First He will bring the five-fold, but there is a ministry after the five-fold called the Ministry of Perfection: the Melchizedek Priesthood. You that are here now, you'll be moving into the five-fold ministries, but your children will be moving into the ministries of perfection. Coming to that characteristic, coming into that divine nature of Jesus Christ.[45]

This reference to taking on the divine nature of Jesus Christ is pure Manifest Sons of God theology, and is alluded to in the teaching that the Second Coming of Christ is not the Second Coming of Jesus in the clouds, but the spirit of Christ coming into the Church. Linda Bonville, a "prophetic voice" loosely associated with Kansas City Fellowship espouses this view:

> Remember the time when He [Jesus] talked to the Pharisees and He said, "You're a whitewashed sepulchre"? He said, "You're full of dead men's bones." He says, "You look good on the outside, but your inside needs to be taken care of."
>
> I said, "Lord, how do you get the inside taken care of?" And this is the answer He gave me: He comes in Himself and cleanses us out from the inside outward. And that's what He

does in His Second Coming. . . . Now, the disciples came to Jesus and they wanted to know when He would return the second time. Remember him going and asking the question? And Jesus said, "It's not for me to tell you." He says, "Only the Father knows."

Now this is true. Only the Father knows when He'll send the Son of Man back to any individual person. And it's different for different people. I went through it in 1983; some people went through it in '84; some people went through it in '85; some went through it in '86; some are just now coming into it.

All the Word has already happened. It's a matter of our faith—receiving for ourselves what's already been done as the Spirit of God reveals it to us. . . . the whole Word of God has been done in and through people since 2,000 years ago—since His first coming. It's been made available. We just have to enter in at the time that the Father says it's your turn and sends the Son to you, or you hear the message and you say, "I want the Second Coming of the Lord for me now."[46]

This may sound strange to those unfamiliar with Manifest Sons of God teachings. But it stems from the belief that the Church is Christ in the sense that Jesus is the head, and the Church is the body. The Second Coming of Christ, therefore, is through the Church, not Jesus returning in the flesh; we should not wait for Him to return in order to set the world in order, but we are to take His authority over the world and the spiritual realm now. This concept reduces Jesus to just one part of a greater whole.

The biblical picture of the Church as the Body of Christ was not meant to elevate the Church, but to elevate Jesus. It depicts Jesus as our authority and establishes us under His headship.

Bonville credits Dick Eastman's "Change the World School of Prayer" with giving her understanding of the need to pray for one hour per day. Eastman's prayer model is similar to that of Larry Lea's in its dominionist purpose to establish authority over the nations. Bonville's earlier affiliation with one of Larry Lea's satellite churches in Harrisonville, Missouri helped solidify her mystical approach to prayer. She suggests that by employing certain methods of concentration we can affect the lives of others:

> When you're doing spiritual warfare on your knees, by His Spirit, you've got to send the Name, and the Spirit and the Word together.
> You direct it like an arrow. When you're doing spiritual warfare or you're praying for somebody, you need to send the name of Jesus, you need to send His seed, which is the Word, you need it to go by His Spirit and do the work, and you need to shoot it like an arrow. That's why you pray for people by

name. Because as you are praying the Word and you are sending it directly to a particular person, it will go right into the soul
of the person you're praying for. If you direct it that way; if you
speak it as such.[47]

What Bonville proposes is to use the Spirit of God to effect
one's purpose, while qualifying it with the idea that it must, of
course, be done according to God's will. But this is really a form of
witchcraft: the invocation of spirits to do one's bidding. Because
one calls the spirit the Holy Spirit, and claims to be serving God,
doesn't make it any less witchcraft. And does it not stand to reason
that the same "Name, Word, and Spirit" can be shot like an arrow
to destroy one's enemies? Prophets have the power to speak evil
over someone as well as good.

Judgment On Dissenters

As much as the vanguard for this new breed speak about love
and unity, humility and Christlikeness, they appear to look forward to the day when, they say, those who will not follow this new
wave of God's move will be dealt with severely:

> Don't speak a word against signs and wonders and the
> prophetic ministry in these last days or God's zeal will chasten
> you![48]

This is not an idle threat. There have been many "prophetic"
voices that have warned not only of chastening, but of death to
those who will not bend to the ministry of the latter-day apostles
and prophets. The Grace Ministries threats are still somewhat
veiled, but knowledge of the philosophy behind the restoration of
apostles and prophets can lift that veil:

> But never forget this is *My* Wind, saith the Lord. With
> tornado force it will come and appear to leave devastation, but
> the Word of the Lord comes and says, "Turn your face into the
> Wind and let it blow." For only that which is not of Me shall be
> devastated. You must see this as necessary.[49]

> Some pastors and leaders who continue to resist this tide
> of unity will be removed from their place. Some will be so
> hardened they will become opposers and resist God to the
> end.[50]

> This is the year when the Lord starts to bring down the
> spirit of Jezebel. He will begin by calling her to repentance.
> Those who have become vessels for this spirit, and who do not

repent, will be displayed as so insane that even the most immature Christians will quickly discern their sickness.[51]

The "Jezebel spirit" is the name that the movement applies to
so-called "heresy hunters"—those who warn the Body of Christ
about the deceptions that threaten the purity of the Faith. Those
who do this are accused of practicing witchcraft:

> The source of witchcraft against us may not be the obvious
> satanic cults or New Age operatives. It can come from well
> meaning, though deceived, Christians who are in fact praying
> against us instead of for us.[52]

These charges indicate that the leaders of this movement have
judged those who challenge them, even on clearly scriptural
grounds, of practicing witchcraft. Their purpose is to instill fear in
the hearts of those who would oppose them.

Unity

In order for God to work through the latter-day apostles and
prophets, it will be necessary to achieve unity. Particularly, Jones
says that the Lord told him the Body of Christ must be united
around the principles of his movement:

> He said, "There has to be a bunch of full-time leaders
> joined and the lay-leaders have got to be ready, and a lot of them
> are going to be released after that time of visitation. And they
> have to be unified; they have to have affection for one another;
> they have to be grounded in unity around the principles that
> God has given us, and we have to be in divine order with our
> place in the structure of God's divine order.[53]

If, in order to enter into God's work, it is necessary to be in
unity with the principles that God has given to GM/KCF, where
will that leave those who, for scriptural reasons, do not accept their
ministry? Will we be judged unworthy, not because we reject Jesus,
but because we reject the latter-day apostles and prophets?

Eventually, it may dawn on people that unity is not found in
uniformity of thought, but in the fellowship of the Spirit, based on
sound doctrine which, in turn, is predicated upon the clear teaching of Scripture. This is why Paul exhorts us to "mark them which
cause divisions and offenses contrary to the doctrine which ye have
learned; and avoid them" (Romans 16:17).

The false prophets call for unity based not on Scriptural
doctrine, but on their claims for authority; then they accuse of
causing division those who do not accept their claim for authority.

Those who insist on fellowship based on sound doctrine are labeled legalists, while the false prophets are the ones imposing unscriptural demands upon those who follow them. They are placing on a par with Scripture, the teaching authority of their priesthood. This is an inheritance of the Roman Catholic Church's doctrine of Magisterium.

Churches Targeted

Even before becoming a Vineyard church, Kansas City Fellowship demonstrated a like tendency with the Vineyard movement to infiltrate and split or take over existing churches. It has been a tactic of the Vineyard movement to glean from existing congregations those who would follow John Wimber's doctrines of signs and wonders. The same tactic had been employed by KCF on behalf of its leadership prior to its being swallowed up by Vineyard.

The result has been that churches have split, and even entire congregations have been swayed into their camp through means that some call infiltration and subversion. This is what accounts for the seemingly phenomenal growth of both KCF and the Vineyard movement.

Since they are now working together, it is natural that Bob Jones would place the Vineyard Ministry in the forefront of the "new move of God," along with Grace Ministries.

As much as KCF desires unity under its terms, they have alienated many churches because of their attempts to establish KCF as the headquarters for the church in Kansas City. One major principle of the GM/KCF movement has been that there is to be only one eldership in each city. Denominationalism and independent local congregations must fall by the wayside. It was not the suggestion of offering leadership that caused the alienation, but KCF's method of operation to bring it about.

One example of KCF's method was offered by Ernest Gruen, pastor of Full Faith Church of Love in Kansas City. Pastor Gruen stated that KCF worked aggressively to take over existing churches. Among Gruen's accusations were the use of threats that bad things happen to people who touch the leadership of KCF.

Before being chastized for their actions, a practice of Kansas City Fellowship, was to prophesy evil upon churches that did not disband according to the instructions of the prophets, in order that a "one-city-one-eldership" prophecy would become a reality:

> On June 22, 1986, three prophets from Kansas City Fellowship were invited to our church. Among other things, they each prophesied that the Lord had told them that our church was to disband, that we had no right to challenge the prophecy, and

that if we failed to heed the prophecy, "Ichabod" (the glory has departed) would be written above our door! As a result of the prophecy many people left our church. Those of us who doubted the prophecy prayed and sought the Lord's will about what we should do. We believe that the Lord wanted us to stay and form a new fellowship, which we did.[54]

> John Paul came and prophesied . . . "CCF will collapse unless it comes under Mike's anointing." Two things bother me: We have done fine for four years; there should be nothing to fear. . . . "Mike's anointing"—I want Jesus' anointing.[55]

These are just two of many such directive prophecies that typify not only the prophets from Kansas City Fellowship, but virtually all the "prophetic voices" allegedly bringing new revelations to the churches today. Because of the uproar caused by their way of dealing with other churches, GM/KCF eventually backed down from demanding one eldership for their city.

Under John Wimber's direction, Mike Bickle publicly recanted his elitism at a KCF prophecy conference in June 1990, and apologized to Ernie Gruen for his statements. In the interest of unity, Gruen decided that he would no longer distribute his exposé of the GM/KCF errors; but at the time of this writing he has not acknowledged any error on his part in producing his exposé.

Additionally, Wimber and a team of Vineyard seminarians examined GM/KCF's practices and concluded that Bob Jones had made some "unwise, but not unbiblical" statements, and needed to be disciplined; but they affirmed that GM/KCF's practices are sound and biblical.[56]

While these tactics managed to give an appearance of contriteness on Wimber's and GM/KCF's part, they did not deal with the central problems: unbiblical and extra-biblical revelations, the teaching that there are latter-day apostles and prophets who are to be followed in order to remain in God's stream of revelation, and the continuation of unscriptural practices. Nor have they repented of the unbiblical shepherding practices that have characterized their movement.

As far as Wimber's pronouncement on Jones' statements being unwise but not unbiblical is concerned, "unwise" *is* "unbiblical." What was unwise, evidently, was Jones being so open about what he believes. Of all the bizarre statements Jones has made, it's inconceivable that Wimber couldn't find any that were unbiblical. The same can be said of many teachings and activities at GM/KCF. But, then, how is Wimber to judge what is unbiblical when the history and methodologies of the Vineyard movement itself are considered?

JOHN WIMBER & THE VINEYARD

John Wimber, apostle of the Vineyard churches, believes that signs and wonders are the means to world evangelization—what he calls "power evangelism." It is his contention that the church should be doing "the stuff"—that is, the things that he says the first-century Church did en masse: healing the sick, raising the dead, and saving souls by the thousands as a result. A careful study of Scripture reveals that such miraculous events were rare outside the ministry of the apostles.

In 1975 Wimber left the pastorate of a conservative Quaker church in Yorba Linda, California, and became a lecturer on church growth with the Fuller Evangelistic Association at Fuller Theological Seminary in Pasadena, California.

Fuller's influence was to have a profound effect on Wimber through its professors, particularly George Eldon Ladd:

> From George Eldon Ladd, Wimber gained his understanding and emphasis on the kingdom of God. For Ladd, the kingdom of the world was under the dominion of Satan, afflicted with natural catastrophes, [sic] bondage to sin, sickness, demons and death. Jesus, however, came proclaiming the kingdom of God, rebuking storms, healing the sick, casting out demons and raising the dead. Jesus' followers are to follow in his footsteps, performing the same works and proclaiming the presence of the kingdom.[57]

Encounters with students from third world countries who reported of healings and other miracles, convinced Wimber that the reason miracles did not happen in North America was because they are not expected here; our materialistic, scientific culture just does not allow for it. This, however, does not explain why they do not always happen even when they *are* expected, not only in North America, but in other parts of the world as well.

Out of Wimber's Quaker congregation, a few leaders began meeting together in October 1976, for the purpose of encouraging one another. Wimber began attending in January 1977. As the group grew from twelve to 125, those attending were asked to leave the church. On May 8, 1977, the group began meeting as a Calvary Chapel under the auspices of Chuck Smith's church in Costa Mesa, California. But Wimber's religious philosophy was eventually found incompatible with Chuck Smith's conservative evangelical approach to ministry. So Wimber made the break from Calvary Chapel and joined with Kenn Gulliksen's Vineyard movement which at the time numbered seven churches. Gulliksen eventually turned over control of the Vineyard churches to Wimber and went to plant another church in Boston, Massachusetts.

Perhaps the biggest influence in Wimber's philosophy is Dr. C. Peter Wagner, whose teachings on church growth have become popular among many pastors of all persuasions. Wagner was impressed by the growth of Pentecostal and charismatic churches, and his reciprocal admiration for Wimber's power evangelism philosophy resulted in his applying to it the term "third wave."

Stealing The Sheep

In 1983 Wimber moved his congregation to Anaheim, California, and by 1985 it had grown to some 5,000 members. Another 120 Vineyard congregations had been added, but not without expense to many congregations who lost members to them.

Wimber's approach to church growth has been to offer seminars on signs and wonders to other churches, and then to set up Vineyards in those churches' areas. James R. Coggins and Paul G. Hiebert, cite one example of this tactic:

> Wimber directs his appeal to Christians, advertises in other churches and asks for the cooperation of other churches in supporting his seminars. When the Vineyard movement moved into southern British Columbia, for instance, it did so with the qualified support of some other denominations. One pastor with some charismatic leanings reported that he had promoted a "signs and wonders" seminar in his congregation. It was advertised as a nondenominational ministry designed to bring revival to the churches, much like a Billy Graham crusade—and he had encouraged some of his members to attend. After a second seminar, the movement started setting up Vineyard churches in the area and attracting those who had been blessed by the seminars. The pastor felt betrayed. Rather than bring revival to his congregation as had been promised, the seminars brought division. The interdenominational seminars had seemed a ploy to start a new denomination.[58]

These tactics account for the seemingly phenomenal growth of the Vineyard movement in such a short time. Most Vineyards have been built on the foundations lain by other pastors.

Wimber's outlook seems to be somewhat stoic about these methods of promoting growth. Division of other churches is helpful to the signs and wonders movement wrought through his apostleship.

Wimber has subsequently invaded other countries with his signs and wonders teachings, reaching into Canada, Ireland, the United Kingdom, Sweden, Germany, South Africa, new Zealand and Australia.[59]

Healing Methodologies

Wimber's approach to healing does not consist merely of prayer or even of the laying on of hands and anointing with oil by the elders. He has incorporated Jungian psychology and, especially, Agnes Sanford's inner healing techniques. (Sanford's pantheistic philosophy is well-documented in the Media Spotlight special report, "Inner Healing: A Biblical Analysis.")

Abraham Friesen, professor of history at the University of California in Santa Barbara, points out how experience takes precedence over Scripture in Wimber's philosophy:

> From the basis of experience, Wimber can dabble in Jungian psychology—which itself has mystical roots. He can accept such practices as "visualization," the "healing of memories" and other extra-biblical ideas and practices. He can claim to have discovered the methods by which God's power can be manipulated. In recommending the Linn brothers, the most prominent members of the inner healing movement, Wimber writes, "Father Dennis and Matthew Linn . . . are Jesuit priests who have written books which deal with physical, psychological and spiritual wholeness. They are highly trained in psychology and combine the best insights in this field with theological understanding, shaped by charismatic experience." Not a word about scripture.[60]

Wimber's question, "When are we going to see a generation [which] doesn't try to understand this book [the Bible] but just believes it?" has raised the concern of Bible scholars, among them Friesen:

> With this anti-intellectualism comes a type of spiritual arrogance that ill becomes the Christian. If one claims to possess the Holy Spirit and has been inspired by him, and that infallibly, then anyone who disagrees with such a person must at best be a lesser Christian, at worst a servant of the devil. The diligent and careful study of the scripture, by which we might hope to reconcile our differences is scuttled.[61]

As well, Friesen states that, what Wimber really means is, "When are we going to see a generation that believes *my* interpretation?"[62]

No Qualifications Needed

Perhaps the underlying reason for the disillusionment that has settled in the lives of many Vineyard adherents and which has left a wake of broken lives and few genuine spiritual benefits, can be seen in the fact that the Vineyard healing techniques are taught to anyone who wants to learn them, regardless of spiritual maturity. One method of ministry is to have everyone in the congregation lay hands on one another and pray for or rebuke an illness or other problem area. This haphazard approach is dangerous; one cannot know of a certainty what the spiritual condition is of one who lays hands on him. There are many occultists who look for just such opportunities to draw Christians into their web of deceit. And how can one know if the stranger next to him, whose hands he has lain on him, might not be demonized?

Inner healing techniques predicated upon Jungian psychology are also part of the Vineyard modus operandi.

When my wife and I attended a Vineyard church for over a year in 1983-1984, I voiced this concern to some of the pastors. But my concerns fell on deaf ears. So hungry are those who follow after signs and wonders that they lose perspective of the real battle going on in the spirit realm—a battle for which they are ill equipped without discernment and a sense of responsibility to Scripture above experience.

Scandals

Eventually, Wimber had to face the fact that scandals were plaguing the Vineyard leadership. Admissions of adultery, lying, drunkenness, revelry, and licentiousness of all types among the pastors of the Vineyard have raised questions as to whether or not God is in their midst. Wimber has stated that even he has felt far from God for several years.[63]

It appears as if, in view of these facts, Wimber underwent a good deal of soul searching. He called for his pastors to begin to care for the sheep, and no longer to abuse them as they had in the past. At the same time, he accused all pastors of failing in their responsibilities to care for their flocks.

Yet it appears that, in his concern over the past abuses, he has left himself and the flocks under his care open to deception. After hearing from the KCF leadership that God had chosen him to be a "David" and to take a position of strong leadership over the KCF churches, he accepted their words as evidence that God really had chosen him to do great things, particularly in the area of signs and wonders. This also allowed the Vineyard to grow considerably in one leap, not only in numbers, but in notoriety.

A New Breed Of Prophets

Wimber has become a believer in Paul Cain's new breed concept in spite of its Manifest Sons of God origins and its allusion to the overcomers' immortalization:

I think that what God is doing is raising up a new breed of leaders. And I believe that He's inviting us in this room to participate in that new breed.

Now that's a term you've become familiar with this week; it's been prophesied by Paul Cain, and I think it's a very important concept.[64]

And I believe the Church of Jesus Christ that we're part of—the larger body of Christ the world over—has been weighed and judged in this generation. And that instead of learning from our predecessors from the Latter-day Rain Movement, from any number of movements of God that have occurred in this century, we have allowed the enemy to come in and distract and take away the passion of God, and rob it out of our lives.[65]

Wimber also appears to have bought the lie that the Latter Rain Movement was of God in spite of overwhelming evidence that it was led by men who were strongly influenced by demonic presences and who propagated grossly unscriptural doctrines.

In the process of his new leadership over KCF, Wimber is making the KCF ministry team available to the entire Vineyard movement. At a Vineyard conference held in Denver in August 1989, Wimber voiced his desire that every Vineyard pastor present should allow the KCF prophets to minister to them:

Another issue that has come forth is, who are these prophets, anyway, and how much influence do they have in the movement, and in John Wimber's life? And do we now look to Kansas City for leadership, or do we continue to look to the Lord as we have in the past?

I think you'll find that the prophets are pretty nice people, by and large. I've come to know them and love them. We've invited several of them here, I think maybe five or six, that are from the Kansas City Fellowship. And then we have Paul Cain that lives in Dallas, and has quite a relationship with Kansas City for a number of years, but is not evidently, technically, considered a Kansas City prophet.

You'll hear from them some this week, although they won't be largely behind the scenes. They've already ministered significantly to folks here this weekend. And it's my hope that every one of you, if you've not today had the occasion of sitting down with one or two of them and having them minister to you, that that will happen before the week's over. Because I believe that in God's providence you'll be blessed, and you'll go home with your pockets full and your heart singing, if they do so.[66]

Wimber never did answer the original questions he himself raised. And chances are that he doesn't know the answers. But it would behoove all those associated with the Vineyard to consider carefully where they are headed.

There is every indication that the Vineyard movement, chasing after signs and wonders, has become caught up in a mystical mindset that will lead inevitably to the greater religious deception to which the vast majority of the world's populace will succumb.

Ecumenism

Wimber has consistently maintained an ecumenical spirit toward Roman Catholicism. He has appeared on the same platform with Roman Catholic clergy in ecumenical gatherings, and what he calls "internationally recognized Catholic leaders" were present at the Denver conference. Wimber wrote an article entitled, "Why I Love Mary" for the Catholic charismatic publication, *New Covenant*. While he restrained himself from applying unscriptural references to Mary, in view of the well-known veneration Roman Catholics bestow upon her as the "mother of God" and co-Redemptrix of our salvation, his actions cannot help but lend credibility to the doctrines of Mariology; at the least they leave Roman Catholics comfortable in the false doctrines of their church.

This will undoubtedly help the Vatican's designs for reunification, particularly should the pope and/or other visible Roman Catholic clergy and laity begin to truly perform signs and wonders.

Dissent Unwelcomed

Wimber has chosen to reject the voices of concern that have warned him of error in focusing on signs and wonders. He has stated emphatically that such voices are not welcome:

> I've determined in my heart, I'll never, ever, answer another spectator's questions the rest of my life. I'm not interested in their theories, their speculations, their criticisms, their confusions, or their comments. From this point forward I'm only going to dialogue with those people who are in the arena. And in the place of the touch of God.[67]

This is a terrible mistake; dissenting voices may not always be right, but when we decide not to listen to them at all, we have placed ourselves in a very precarious position. Just because Paul Cain has told Wimber the secrets of his heart and prophesied over him good things, has he forsaken the counsel of those who see through this error? What are the secrets of any pastor's heart, anyway? One may be 98% on target by telling any pastor that the desire of his heart is to serve God and minister effectively to the people under his care; to see holiness and caring grow in his congregation; to see God move with power among the people. Striving for humility, most are not even aware, or would not admit to themselves the proud secret of their heart: the desire to be chosen for great ministry, and to see their congregation achieve great things no matter what it costs it, and no matter what degree of control might be necessary to see the pastor succeed.

John Wimber has given to the Church some of the most beautiful and moving songs. They reflect, I believe, a heart that desires a close communion with God. But it appears as if, in that desire for close communion with God, the desire for mystical experiences has gotten the upper hand.

CHRISTIAN INTERNATIONAL-NETWORK OF PROPHETIC MINISTRIES

Another well-known group claiming apostolic and prophetic authority is Christian International-Network of Prophetic Ministries, founded by Bill Hamon, pastor of Christian International Church, and author of *The Eternal Church*. Writing in *Charisma and Christian Life* magazine about the rise of the alleged prophetic ministries, Paul Thigpen states:

> CI-NPM provides coherence and mutual support for 250 members, many of whom direct ministries with an emphasis on prophets and prophecy. Some are pastors of "prophetic churches"; others are traveling prophets; still others lead "schools of the Holy Spirit," in which Christians are trained to minister prophetically. A few of the ministries focus on "prophetic worship."
>
> CI-NPM sponsors a number of regular gatherings, including monthly seminars, Regional Prophets Conferences and the annual International Prophets Conference, which last October [1988] drew more than 800 attendees from around the world. Participants come together in these meetings for training and encouragement in prophetic ministry.
>
> According to Hamon, CI-NPM seeks "to help usher in prophets of God and facilitate the full restoration of prophetic ministry" to the church. "I believe God is currently bringing forth a company of prophets—literally thousands—who will help prepare the way for His second coming."
>
> Within that "company of prophets" are "prophetic churches"—congregations with an emphasis on personal prophecy. Life Center Ministries in Atlanta, for example, is a CI-NPM member ministry that began as a school of the Holy Spirit where believers gathered weekly to learn how to minister prophetically.[68]

Hamon unabashadly calls himself a prophet. His son-in-law, Glenn Miller, is also considered a prophet, as are Travis and Ann Thigpen, founders of Hosanna Victory Church and Gateway Ministries in Richmond, Virginia. Travis Thigpen is also ordained with Liberty Fellowship of Churches under "Apostle" Ken Sumrall.

MORE APOSTLES AND PROPHETS

There are other major organizations and independent churches, not necessarily affiliated with one another, that are in the forefront of the restoration of apostles and prophets, and/or espouse other dominion teachings. Some are headquarters for many smaller affiliated churches. Among these are:

Abundant Living Faith Center, El Paso, Texas
Apostolic Ministries International, Ephrata, Pennsylvania
Calvary Temple, Fort Wayne, Indian
Capitol Christian Center, Boise, Idaho
Carpenter's Home Church, Lakeland, Florida
Casey Treat Ministries, Seattle, Washington
Christ for the Nations, Dallas, Texas
Christian International Publishers, Phoenix, Arizona
Coalition on Revival (COR), Mountain View, California
Coral Ridge Presbyterian Church/Ministries, Ft. Lauderdale, Fl.
Covenant Women's Ministries, Pomona, California
Christ As Life Christian Center, McKinney, Texas
Christ Church, Northgate, Seattle, Washington
Christian Faith Center, Seattle, Washington
Church of the Crossroads, Mountainview, California
Church on the Rock, Rockwall, Texas
Church on the Way, Van Nuys, California
Crenshaw Christian Center, Los Angeles, California
Dick Mills Ministries, Hemet, California
Eagles Nest Christian Fellowship, Santa Ana, California
Ecclesia Temple, Visalia, California
Ed Dufresne Ministries, Tulsa, Oklahoma
Elim Bible Institute, Lima, New York
Ernest Leonard Ministries, Newark, New Jersey
Eugene Christian Fellowship, Eugene, Oregon
Evangel Temple, Washington, D.C.
Faith Fellowship Ministries, Edison, New Jersey
Fellowship of Covenant Ministries & Churches, Orlando, Fl.
Full Gospel Business Men's Fellowship, Costa Mesa, California
Gospel Lighthouse, Eureka, California
Gospel Tabernacle, Coudersport, Pennsylvania
Gospel Temple, Portland, Oregon

Happy Church, Denver, Colorado
Higher Dimensions Ministries, Tulsa, Oklahoma
His Image Ministries, Fort Worth, Texas
International Communion of Churches,
International Gospel Center, Tulsa, Oklahoma
Kenneth Copeland Ministries, Tulsa, Oklahoma
Kenneth Hagin Ministries, Tulsa, Oklahoma
Lakewood Church, Houston, Texas
Lesea Publishing, South Bend, Indiana
Maranatha Campus Ministries, Tulsa, Oklahoma
Maranatha Christian Churches (network)
Melodyland Christian Center, Anaheim, California
New Life, Inc., Chapel Hill, North Carolina
North American Renewal Services Committee, Oklahoma City
Northside Church of Christ, Seattle, Washington
Orlando Christian Center, Orlando, Florida
Rhema Bible Training Center, Tulsa, Oklahoma
Rock Church, Virginia Beach, Virginia
Shiloh Christian Fellowship, Oakland, California
Shiloh Training Institute, Hamilton, Montana
Stone Mountain Church, Laguna Hills, California
Strang Communications Co., Altamonte Springs, Florida
Strategic Christian Services, Santa Rosa, California
Sweetwater Church, Glendale, Arizona
Trinity Broadcasting Network, Irvine, California
Victory Christian Center, Tulsa, Oklahoma
Victory Christian Fellowship, New Castle, Delaware
Word of Faith World Outreach Center, Dallas, Texas
World Harvest Church, Columbus, Ohio
Zoe Ministries, Brooklyn, New York

These are by no means the only organizations we could cite. And some are more involved than others. For example, Jack Hayford's Church on the Way does not stress dominion teaching to the degree that Earl Paulk's Chapel Hill Harvester Church does. But Hayford has accepted some dominion doctrines, and continues to minister in association with more aberrant teachers, thus placing his church in this category. This has saddened many, myself included, who have in the past held his ministry in high regard.

It should be stressed that not everyone involved in these teachings would consider themselves dominionists; but they are not aware that the doctrine of present-day apostles and prophets cannot be separated from dominion theology, simply because it originated there, and is a vital aspect of that movement. So I would urge readers to recognize that there are many precious brethren involved in these ministries, some of whom are momentarily deceived; they will come out when their eyes are opened. We must be careful not to count them all as God's enemies.

AN ANALYSIS OF APOSTOLIC & PROPHETIC CLAIMS

It is not an easy thing to challenge men who claim to be endowed by God with supernatural power, particularly when it is impossible to disprove many of their claims. But it really isn't necessary to challenge their claims of supernatural power. We can readily acknowledge that their power may be genuine and still question whether or not it is from God. We have every right—even the duty—to question them. Let us consider point-by-point some factors that sway people into believing that the power they perceive in these men is from God.

Power In The Name Of Jesus

Because someone speaks in the name of Jesus and does all sorts of miracles does not mean he is approved by God:

> *Not every one that saith unto me, Lord, Lord, shall enter into the kingdom of heaven; but he that doeth the will of my Father which is in heaven.*
>
> *Many will say to me in that day, Lord, Lord, have we not prophesied in thy name? and in thy name have cast out devils? and in thy name done many wonderful works?*
>
> *And then will I profess unto them, I never knew you: depart from me, ye that work iniquity.* (Matthew 7:21-23)

This prophecy from the Lord came just after His warning about false prophets who "come to you in sheep's clothing, but inwardly they are ravening wolves" (v. 15).

It is not to signs and wonders that we should look, but to the overall integrity of the man who performs them. Integrity must include not only freedom from greed, lust, and avarice, but there must be adherence to sound doctrine. And works, no matter how good or how spectacular, are built on wood, hay and stubble if performed apart from the Father's will.

For those *who claim an apostolic or prophetic ministry*, conformity to the Father's will is demonstrated by freedom from error in prophecy (100% accuracy), when speaking in the name of the Lord. This applies even if the words are not overtly stated to be prophetic, but when such an impression is given that they may be taken as prophetic. It is also demonstrated by freedom from failure in performing healings, miracles, signs and wonders (100% success with everyone prayed for or touched with the purpose of healing).

Those who fail these tests are not led by the Holy Spirit—they are presumptuous:

> *But the prophet, which shall presume to speak a word in my name, which I have not commanded him to speak, or that shall speak in the name of other gods, even that prophet shall die.*
> *And if thou say in thine heart, How shall we know the word which the Lord hath not spoken?*
> *When a prophet speaketh in the name of the Lord, if the thing follow not, nor come to pass, that is the thing which the Lord hath not spoken, but the prophet hath spoken it presumptuously: thou shalt not be afraid of him.* (Deuteronomy 18:20-22)

With something as sacred as His own reputation, God does not allow for haphazard performance on the part of those who presume to speak on His behalf. There is no "maturing process" involved when it comes to the office of prophet or apostle.

The disclaimer that these men are not really prophets, but merely have a prophetic gift and are thus prone to error, is a cop-out. It absolves the person who claims to speak for God from any genuine accountability.

There is no provision in Scripture for anyone to make such a claim; when a man speaks as an oracle of God he is not allowed a single error.

This does not mean he will be sinless, but it does mean that every time he speaks in the name of the Lord it will come to pass.

Do not be swayed by those who claim to be apostles or prophets. They are not God's spokespersons, though they think they are hearing from God because of some alleged supernatural manifestation that gives them direction. A voice out of the ether is not necessarily God's voice. Let's not forget the apostle Paul's warning:

> *I marvel that ye are so soon removed from him that called you into the grace of Christ unto another gospel:*
> *Which is not another; but there be some that trouble you, and would pervert the gospel of Christ.*
> *But though we, or an angel from heaven, preach any other gospel unto you than that which we have preached unto you, let him be accursed.*
> *As we said before, so say I now again, If any man preach any other gospel unto you than that ye have received, let him be accursed.* (Galatians 1:6-9)

Paul did qualify the term, "another gospel," by stating that it is a perversion of the true gospel. That is, it centers on the person and work of Jesus, but adds or subtracts teachings that refocus people's thinking toward untruths. This is what alleged apostles and prophets are doing when they purpose to establish an elitism among the brethren—particularly an elitism based on inaccurate prophetic utterances.

A major problem with listening to alleged prophetic voices is that while listening to them we shut ourselves off from hearing the true word of the Lord spoken into our consciousness by the Holy Spirit; we allow the "prophet" to usurp our own standing before God by believing that he or she has an entrance to the Throne of Grace that we do not have. Yet God's Word promises us that we can *all* enter boldly (though humbly) before the Throne of Grace. If we allow anyone—"prophet," "apostle," or pastor to place himself between the Father and us, we undo God's grace in our lives. We will have recognized a priesthood that was never ordained by God. This isn't to say that we cannot or should not seek counsel from others; but counsel is not the same as directive prophecy.

Power In The Heavens

One "proof" offered for the validity of these men is their ability to predict signs in the heavens and in the earth which cannot be controlled by anyone but God:

> If it does exactly what the man says, then you know the word that he gave was sent from God.[69]

This sounds reasonable. But the fact is that natural disasters have been accurately predicted by psychics. Yet there is something of great importance in the implication that we can be assured that a word from a prophet is from God if he predicts an event in nature and it comes to pass. It is that Satan can control the elements also.

Pharaoh's magicians duplicated the miracles that Moses performed. Yet when God's purposes had been achieved in allowing the magicians to harden Pharaoh's heart by their ability to duplicate Moses' curses, He no longer allowed them to duplicate His work.

God allows Satan to work signs and wonders in nature in order to test the hearts of men. In the feverish clamoring after signs and wonders today, it is often forgotten that the False Prophet who will appear with anti-Christ to cause all the people to worship him will also exhibit great signs and wonders in the heavens and in the earth:

> *And I beheld another beast coming up out of the earth; and he had two horns like a lamb, and he spake as a dragon.*

> *And he exerciseth all the power of the first beast before him, and causeth the earth and them which dwell therein to worship the first beast, whose deadly wound was healed.*
>
> *And he doeth great wonders, so that he maketh fire come down from heaven on the earth in the sight of men,*
>
> *And deceiveth them that dwell on the earth by the means of those miracles which he had power to do in the sight of the beast; saying to them that dwell on the earth, that they should make an image to the beast, which had the wound by the sword, and did live.*
>
> *And he had power to give life unto the image of the beast, that the image of the beast should both speak, and cause that as many as would not worship the image of the beast should be killed.* (Revelation 13:11-15)

It is not only the False Prophet who will perform such signs and wonders; Jesus warned us of many false prophets who would arise at the time of the end to deceive, if it were possible, even the very elect:

> *For there shall arise false Christs, and false prophets, and shall shew signs and wonders; insomuch that, if it were possible, they shall deceive the very elect.* (Matthew 24:24)

This means that the signs and wonders will be done in the name of Jesus, and will be so great that only those who are truly of God will discern that the prophets and their signs and wonders are really of Satan. This also means they must occur within the Church's assemblies. They must be done in the name of Jesus. They must be of such magnitude that by their very nature they will confirm the validity of the false prophets in the eyes of the deceived.

The fact that a sign or wonder is performed in the heavens or in the earth is not sufficient in itself to follow the man who performs it, let alone merely predicts it.

Incredible Circumstances

One of the areas to which men like to point to validate their calling from God is the incredible circumstances that accompany their activities. For example, Mike Bickle's testimony of the founding of Kansas City Fellowship is replete with such circumstances, including the provision of $21,000 they needed to move into their new building. But such occurrences are common not only in the Body of Christ, but even from New Agers who speak glowingly of the cosmic forces that work in their favor through incredible circumstances.

I and just about every Christian I know can testify of God's miraculous provision out of impossible circumstances. Yet if we allow such provision to sway us into thinking that we are on the right track without checking all the factors involved in obedience to God, those circumstances can cause us to be deceived into thinking we are in His favor when, in fact, we are in rebellion against Him.

The things of this sort that have happened to these men have happened to most Christians, including myself. But very few would use those things as evidence that they have a special prophetic anointing; nor is it conclusive evidence of God's favor. God will bless His enemies if it serves His purpose and will cement their delusion.

Preaching of Righteousness

Few would believe that someone who preaches righteousness and holy living is not of God. But if we examine most of the aberrant Christian cults that exist today, we'll see that they invariably stress just these things. Mormonism is noted for its family life and preaching of clean living. Sun Myung Moon's Unification Church has established a high moral code for its followers, and they boast of their success in rescuing people from drugs and prostitution. Those who think that the preaching of righteousness is evidence of God's hand on the preacher do not understand Satan's tactics. Most of the evil to which man succumbs in the flesh is the result of his own sin nature, not of Satan's control:

> But every man is tempted, when he is drawn away of his own lust, and enticed.
> Then when lust hath conceived, it bringeth forth sin: and sin, when it is finished, bringeth forth death. (James 1:14-15)

Satan's purpose is not primarily to keep us entangled in the lusts of our flesh, but to keep us from doing the will of God in our lives. If sins of the flesh will accomplish this, he will tempt us; but more likely, attitudes of self-righteousness, spiritual pride and the desire to dominate others interfere with doing God's will. It is easy to recognize the lusts of our flesh; it isn't so easy to recognize when we've gone beyond the point of *gratitude for* our salvation toward *pride in* our salvation. Thus, if Satan is going to deceive us, he will most often work in the areas of beliefs and attitudes. And what better way to do so than to preach righteousness:

> For such are false apostles, deceitful workers, transforming themselves into the apostles of Christ.

And no marvel; for Satan himself is transformed into an angel of light.

Therefore it is no great thing if his ministers also be transformed as the ministers of righteousness; whose end shall be according to their works. (II Corinthians 11:13-15)

It would be a serious error to say that righteousness should not be preached. We affirm its necessity. But the fact of such preaching does not in itself validate the preacher's ministry as sanctioned by God.

On the contrary, if we examine these men's preaching on righteousness, we find a great paradox: the "lay" person is to be judged by the prophets according to his godly or ungodly lifestyle; but the prophet is not to be judged by the people regardless of how ungodly his lifestyle is. This double standard is just the opposite of what God requires. He requires godliness on the part of all who call upon Him, leaders and sheep alike, but especially the leaders. For if the leaders of His people are ungodly, how can they lead the people into true godliness?

Humility of the Prophets

We are struck by the testimonies that many of the alleged apostles and prophets—from Branham to Cain—exhibit a genuine humility in their lives. But this, too, is insufficient evidence that they speak for God.

Many people who deny that Jesus is the only way to the Father have been spoken of as humble. Besides Buddha and Confucius, three contemporaries that come to mind are the late Mohandas Gandhi, Mother Teresa, and Pope John Paul II. All are considered humble people, yet all have stated that there are ways to God other than Jesus.

Humility is a wonderful virtue, but it is not the only mark of a true servant of God. True humility is not outward self-abasement, but total submission to the will of the Father. Such submission does not allow for error when speaking in His name.

Again, this does not mean that the servant of God will be sinless, but it does mean that everything done in the name of the Lord will be in accordance with the Lord's will. There is no room for error in prophecy when spoken in the name of the Lord. Those who prophesy error may appear humble before men, but they are not truly humble before God.

Caring for the Poor

As with all outward demonstrations of compassion, there is no quarrel with benevolence. Certainly charity is a vital ministry. But again, these outward demonstrations do not validate the ministry of one who claims to speak for God. Many benevolent works are conducted by the ungodly. The Freemasons have their charities, as do many established denominations. Probably no single religious organization has built more hospitals and has so many other charitable outreaches than the Roman Catholic Church. And there are many self-sacrificing priests and nuns whose hearts of compassion toward the poor are openly evident.

Yet like all outward righteousness, benevolence merits nothing before God unless done in obedience to His will. And even when it is done in obedience to God, that particular work stands on its own account; it does not validate another work such as prophecy which may be out of line with God's will.

If there is any failure on the part of Christians to discern good and evil it is the validating of one work by the evidence of another work. Yet each work must stand on its own ground of testing.

A prophet cannot be validated by works of righteousness alone, although these should accompany him. But he must ultimately be validated by his meeting the scriptural standard: 100% accuracy, 100% performance *when speaking in the name of the Lord* (or leaving that impression), and 100% conformity to Scripture.

Zeal for God's Kingdom

If there is one element of the alleged apostles and prophets that stands out, it is their zeal. There is much evidence of self-sacrifice and tireless work. And zeal is a good thing if accompanied by truth. But it appears as if zeal has blinded their eyes to the truth that we have no need of teachers to discern the will of God for our lives.

> *These things have I written unto you concerning them that seduce you.*
>
> *But the anointing which ye have received of him abideth in you, and ye need not that any man teach you: but as the same anointing teacheth you of all things, and is truth, and is no lie, and even as it hath taught you, ye shall abide in him.* (I John 2:26-27)

CONCLUSION

There are two primary sources one may observe to witness the growing emphasis of dominion teachings among charismatics. These are Strang Communications Company (publishers of *Charisma and Christian Life* and *Ministries Today* magazines, and others), and Trinity Broadcasting Network. These two sources, more than any other, impact charismatics on a regular basis with exposure for alleged apostles and prophets, and the general dominionist philosophy. *Charisma*, especially, is replete with ads beckoning readers to conferences and rallies designed to procure dominion. I believe the Lord is using these to send the strong delusion that will result not in the expected revival, but in the apostasy prophesied in God's Word.

Yet there is no denying that He is also using them to introduce people to Jesus. Many have come to the Lord after initial response to TBN's ministry. The same may be said about many other churches and organizations mentioned here. Let's not lose heart; some leaders who are currently in error are acting in good faith. They will be found faithful in the end. In the meantime, whenever they are the source for truth, we may agree with the Apostle Paul's approach in Philippians 1:15-18:

> *Some indeed preach Christ even of envy and strife; and some also of good will:*
> *The one preach Christ of contention, not sincerely, supposing to add affliction to my bonds:*
> *But the other of love, knowing that I am set for the defence of the gospel.*
> *What then? nothwithstanding, every way, whether in pretence, or in truth, Christ is preached; and I therein do rejoice, yea, and will rejoice.*

A HISTORY OF ESOTERICISM VS. GOD'S REVEALED TRUTH

The chart on the facing page is by no means a complete representation of the history of esotericism and its conflict with God's Truth. Nor is it possible to compile such a representation. The interaction of diverse cultures throughout the five thousand years of human history since Noah's flood has produced many religious philosophies, and their links to one another are lost to antiquity. Yet there are obvious similarities found in all of the world's religions, including much of what has passed for Christianity since the first century.

It should be noted that even the most learned esotericists cannot find definite links from one philosophy to another. But the exceptional similarities of philosophy should be adequate evidence that a central source of occult knowledge (satanic spirits) is behind them all. Our chart is at best a poor representation of an extremely complicated subject.

To avoid too much complication, we've eliminated some connecting lines, such as gnosticism's lead into the New Age Movement, and into charismatism. The Eastern Religions are especially difficult to trace and, for most purposes, are not as relevant to the subject as are the Western esoteric traditions out of which the Holy Roman Empire arose. So we've only shown their link to theosophy and to the New Age Movement.

The purpose of the chart, therefore, is merely to demonstrate generally how our specific subject, dominion theology, grew out of a blending of Christianity with esoteric tradition. It also shows that those caught up in dominion theology can be restored to biblical truth, and thus avoid the eventual melding into the one-world religio-political system of Mystery Babylon. So, too, can all who are part of the world's religious systems, including Protestants, charismatics, and Roman Catholics.

Even some of those who are not saved, and who are involved in pagan religions, will enter into the Millennial Kingdom. However, out of the Millennial Kingdom, at the end of the thousand years, many will be cast into the Lake of Fire because of their rebellion against the Lord Jesus Christ. Those who have proven faithful to the end will enter into the Eternal Kingdom of God.

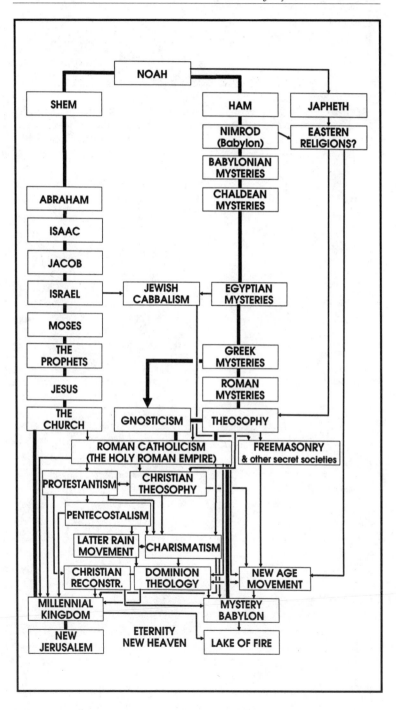

PART III - RECONSTRUCTION

1

An Overview

In contrast to the Charismatic Dominionists, Reconstructionists generally classify themselves as fundamentalists or at least evangelicals. Many avoid association with Charismatic Dominionists because they are embarrassed by the charismatic approach. Most Reconstructionists do not accept the idea of apostles and prophets for today, for example, nor are they particularly mystical in their religious expression. Rather, they tend toward orthodoxy, finding common ground with the "high churches." Because of the common denominator of a dominion mindset, however, many Charismatic Dominionists are beginning to fraternize with Reconstructionists and vice versa.

While Charismatic Dominionists stress impassioned prayer, exuberant praise, and prophetic exhortation combined with stomping on the devil, Reconstructionists are generally more restrained. Yet there is the common thread of reliance upon liturgy that promises to be one of the uniting factors for both groups.

Reconstructionists are also more biblically literate than their charismatic counterparts, but both find another common ground in allegorizing Scripture. Literalism takes a back seat to biblical imagery in both camps, and neither is ashamed to admit it.

In their approach to dominion, Reconstructionists are excellent expositors of the covenant model: God does everything in relation to covenants He establishes with His creation; He does nothing outside of those covenants. Because of this emphasis on covenant keeping, Reconstructionists hold a high view of God's Law as contained in both the Old and New Testaments. They affirm that God's Law is always applicable to all men, believers and non-believers, and that all penal sanctions against man, including the final, eternal sanction, will be established in accordance with how the Law was kept.

Rouses John (R.J.) Rushdoony, considered by many the father of modern Reconstruction, believes sin and its consequences (evil) to be an ethical rather than a metaphysical problem.[1] In essence, this view implies that the *solution* to sin and its consequent evils is ethical and not metaphysical. If that is the case, then salvation rests not on the efficacious sacrifice of Jesus, but on the ethical behavior of mankind.

Rushdoony is correct in saying that sin and its consequent evils are ethical; he errs in saying they are not metaphysical. Actually, they are both ethical and metaphysical. They are metaphysical because they are relevant to the soul, and stem from man's sin nature; sin is inherent to man by virtue of our being the offspring of Adam. In Adam, all die because of sin (I Corinthians 15:22). But sin and its consequent evils are also ethical because the sins we commit personally are the result of choices we make in life.

By emphasizing the ethical aspect of sin and its consequent evil while denying the metaphysical aspect, Rushdoony in effect places the keeping of the Law above the grace God has provided through the sacrifice of Jesus. This amounts to salvation by works.

Reconstructionists would deny that they believe or teach salvation by works. Yet their spiritual father, Rushdoony, believes a Christian has denied God if he does not actively work to transform society:

> A godly law order will work to disinherit, execute, and supplant the ungodly and to confirm the godly in their inheritance. For Christians to work for anything less is to deny God.[2]

I doubt that most Reconstructionists would see the implication of such a statement without it being pointed out to them; most are followers who haven't thought out the rationale of their leaders.

The Coming New Order

Because they perceive sin and its consequent evil as ethical, Reconstructionists believe that the Old Testament penal sanctions against certain sins are still in effect, and that it is the responsibility of government to implement those sanctions; because government has been usurped by atheists and humanists, it has perverted the role entrusted to it and is about to experience God's judgment. That judgment will come in the form of destruction upon all human institutions that do not comply with God's Law, and their replacement with Christian-oriented leadership. It is the Church's responsibility to place itself in the forefront of political and social action in order to take the reins of control out of the hands of the ungodly (e.g., the unethical), and implement rule under a theonomic structure (*theo*: God *nomos*: Law). This will establish Jesus Christ as Lord over His creation through the ministry of His body, the Church, while He remains in heaven.

It is Rushdoony's belief that there are only two factors at work to control men's thoughts and actions: Satan and God. All who do not surrender to God are under the influence of Satan. He's right. But there is a catch to this: Rushdoony believes that it is a mandate for all Christians to diligently work toward instituting God's Law throughout the creation and to bring into subjection to that Law everyone who is currently living outside of it. Thus, mankind will be redeemed from the influence of Satan and placed under the influence of God.

If this were not contrary to Scripture's clear prophecy that the establishment of human government under God in this present age will never occur, it would seem that the Reconstructionists should be followed. Because up to that point, just about everything they say is true. This is why it is so difficult to argue with them; they're so right.

But they are not entirely right. For no such mandate to redeem man's social institutions exists.

Social Evangelization

With their emphasis on political and social action, the Reconstructionists' concept of evangelization is not necessarily to save souls, but to preach their version of the Gospel of the Kingdom: all men are called to ethical living under the terms of the Old Covenant in order to be found worthy to dwell in the restored Paradise on earth.

Consequently, there is a willingness of some to overlook the unbelief of those with whom they join in political and social action, and to accept them as brothers in the ethics of Scripture. Moonies, Mormons, Roman Catholic hierarchy—all are seen as brethren, not necessarily in Christ, but in a common cause to eradicate social evil in society.

Two Major Camps

Reconstruction is basically divided into two camps, one led by R.J. Rushdoony, and the other by Rushdoony's son-in-law, Gary North. Both are brilliant spokesmen for their position, and both have garnered rather large followings among Christians of both fundamentalist and charismatic persuasions.

North looks at Rushdoony as the one to whom credit must be given for the existence of today's Reconstruction movement. Rushdoony looks at North as a heretic; he will have nothing to do with North until North repents of what Rushdoony calls blasphemous heresy: the teaching that the menstrual blood of a virgin bride is a type of Jesus' blood shed on the cross. At the time of this writing they are not on speaking terms. (So much for "unity.")

Rushdoony has been heavily influenced by reformed theologian Cornelius Van Til's assertion that there are no options in living one's life but two: 1) self-government (autonomy); 2) government by God (theonomy). Van Til's application of this rule was primarily toward individuals. Rushdoony has expanded this philosophy to humanity as a whole, including all of man's social institutions.

Rushdoony's outreach is principally through personal appearances and the writing of books. His organization is Chalcedon, named after the Council of Chalcedon, held in A.D. 451.

North, an economist, is prolific in his writing of books and has established two publishing houses: 1) Institute for Christian Economics (ICE), a non-profit educational organization that publishes works on Christian ethics authored primarily by North; 2) Dominion Press, a publishing company that produces books by North and other authors on aspects of dominion theology, specifically the Reconstruction viewpoint.

Differing Views Of Charismatism

North recognizes the strong force that charismatics offer to the Reconstruction cause, and has even appeared on the same platform with Charismatic Dominionists. Rushdoony, however, denounces charismatism in strong terms, stating that the mysticism of charismatism is detrimental to the establishment of a society based on God's Law:

> If man wants a spiritual or mystical religion, then the law is his enemy. If he wants a material religion, one fully relevant to the world and man, then Biblical law is inescapably necessary for him.[3]

Rushdoony accuses charismatics and Pentecostals of stressing a mindless religion, with an emphasis on mindless experience as power:

> The charismatic who learns to babble insanely in what is no tongue at all has no answer therein to moral and intellectual problems, but he "witnesses" eloquently to others of the feeling of "power in the spirit," power which is in essence a cultivation of what is mindless and subterranean. . . .
>
> Power from below is a faith which insures the triumph of mindlessness and violence. No calls for law and order can stem this intense faith of the new pagans. The so-called religious revivals of recent years have only been a part of the same ugly faith. Instead of "turning on" with narcotics, the call is for "turning on" with Jesus. Instead of the great narcotic "trip," the

"trip" with Jesus (and the "great trip," the Rapture) are offered, so that religion is made a part of the same tradition as the pagan creed, and mindlessness is not challenged.[4]

Rushdoony has neglected the common ground by which Charismatic Dominionists are found in agreement with him, particularly regarding the "great trip." But he no doubt will find favor with fundamentalists who consider charismatism a heresy.

When there are two so diverse factions within a common belief, we can be reasonably sure that the truth lies somewhere between the two. While Rushdoony categorically denounces mysticism, there is no denying that, biblically, there is a mystical quality to our Faith. One cannot even pray to an unseen God without being somewhat mystical. Nor can one expect that God will answer prayer without being mystical. While Rushdoony doesn't want anything to do with mysticism, who wants a God who refuses to hear and respond to the pleas of His children? That is a mystical God by human perception, albeit in the biblical sense as opposed to the occult sense.

On the other hand, the excesses of charismatism have brought justifiable reproach from those who rightly believe that the Faith is also rational; God did not call us to mindless conformity to mystical "feel-good" religion. The Faith is foolishness to those who perish, but it is only logical to those who, with the mind of Christ, perceive it as the only possible solution to the problem of sin.

Proliferation Of Works

For sheer bulk of information on the extent to which evil has permeated society, particularly in the United States, both Rushdoony and North offer some of the finest material available. Their solution, of course, is the implementation of God's Law over all aspects of human life: government, art, science, education, occupation, home, church, etc. They are, after all, correct in their assessment that only the application of God's Law can cure society's ills and restore righteousness in the earth. Where they go wrong is in their belief that God's Law not only can, but one day will, be implemented worldwide in secular society before Jesus returns.

Never In A Million Years

Reconstructionists tend to believe that, over a period of centuries—even millennia—mankind will come to the realization that his attempts at self-government have failed miserably. In this, they are correct; to a large extent, man has already come to that conclusion. But, Reconstructionists would say, with that realization will come a concurrent realization that only God's Law offers any rational approach to government; having become fed up with his own mess, mankind will seek out those who know God's Law to take the leadership of the world system. After this is accomplished, the Lord will (or may, or may not, or any number of options depending on the particular Reconstruction model one follows) return to bring judgment on all evildoers. The earth will immediately be burned up along with all the elements, and God will establish a new heaven and a new earth wherein dwelleth righteousness.

Accordingly, there is not going to be a rapture or catching away of the saints to be with the Lord while He pours out His wrath upon the earth; there will be no Millennium because, depending again upon which Reconstruction model one follows, 1) we are already in the Millennium; 2) there is no Millennium; it is merely an allegory for a long (or short) period of time during which God's righteousness will increase in the earth through the preaching of the Gospel; 3) there will be a Millennium, but the Lord will be reigning from heaven, and His saints will be governing and judging the earth in His absence; 4)any or all interpretations are acceptable as long as Jesus isn't here to run (or ruin) the show.

2
The Dominion Mandate

The Reconstructionists' concept of dominion is virtually the same as that of the Charismatic Dominionists. If there is any difference it is in the way dominion will be achieved. Whereas the Charismatic Dominionists are convinced that supernatural manifestations of power will be instrumental in bringing about the visible Kingdom of God on earth, Reconstructionists tend toward a more subtle, but no less effective, approach by the Holy Spirit: the conversion of souls through the preaching of the Gospel coupled with a dissatisfaction with the conditions that will become increasingly worse under the present world order.

Reconstruction is decidedly postmillennial in its eschatology, and looks upon premillennialism as an escapist dream. Postmillennialism is defined as

> the idea, simply put, that the Christian faith will progressively gain dominion over the earth, geographically in the nations, but first in people's minds, hearts, and lives, and then in all areas of life, until Christ returns. At that time, the kingdom will be complete.[1]

The author of this statement, R.E. McMaster, Jr., asserts that one proof, or at least indication, that postmillenialism is the truth is the fact that the New Age is counterfeiting postmillennial optimism for the earth:

> What's the essence of evolution? That things are getting better and better over time. Which Christian perspective is evolution most closely attempting to counterfeit? Post-mil, the concept that Christians will make the world better and better over time until Christ returns. *Satan's counterfeit, evolution, is*

attempting to substitute itself for the post-mil reality. The New Agers are close to being on track, but they have bought the truth with a deathly Satanic warp.[2] (McMaster's emphasis)

McMaster's rationale might just as easily be applied to the idea that the New Age is attempting to counterfeit the premillenial position. The New Age proclaims that there is coming a Christ who will institute and oversee a new era of peace and brotherhood among all men. All the nations of the earth will recognize him as their leader, and all dissenting voices will be done away. This could easily be a counterfeit claim to the Millennial reign of Jesus Christ on earth.

The fact is that the New Age Movement is far more complex than McMaster has portrayed. There are many nuances to it that can be rationalized to fit any particular point of view. Besides, what New Agers believe should not be used to validate what we believe. Rather than try to see a parallel where none clearly exists, it is better to stick to Scripture. If we do not allow ourselves to become enamored by the flights of fancy found in dominion theology, we will see the plain biblical truth that when Jesus returns the nations will be allied against Him, not waiting to welcome Him with open arms (Matthew 24; Mark 13; Revelation 6-7).

In spite of the lack of clear biblical support for their position, the Reconstructionists are just as adamant as the Charismatic Dominionists that it is the *duty* of Christians to take over the world system. In fact, those who do not become involved in social and political action are looked upon as lesser Christians; they are accused of having denied the Faith. As we look at some of the statements of leading Reconstructionists we find lacking the singular quality of mercy toward those who do not see things their way.

R.J. Rushdoony

The goal of occultism, atheism, and unbelief is the inheritance and possession of the earth and power without God and in defiance of Him. The goal of covenant man is the inheritance and possession of the earth and power and dominion over the earth under God and according to His law.

When God struck down the firstborn of Egypt in the tenth plague, He thereby destroyed the heirship of apostate man. By declaring Israel to be His firstborn, to be delivered from Egypt, He affirmed the heirship of covenant man to the earth. A godly law order will work to disinherit, execute, and supplant the ungodly and to confirm the godly in their inheritance. For Christians to work for anything less is to deny God.[3]

To say that those who do not follow the Reconstructionist agenda are denying God is a serious charge. It makes obedience to the Faith dependent upon obedience to a perceived mandate based on an inference gleaned from Scriptural passages that do not state such a conclusion. This violates Rushdoony's correct assessment that commands based on inference are wrong:

> Unhappily, too many people over the centuries have insisted on seeing commandments where there are none. They base their rules, and their determination to bind the conscience of the faithful, on inferences, sometimes wrongful ones. Not even a valid inference is a commandment. . . .
>
> Operation Rescue builds its case on inferences; so too do those who oppose birth control, smoking tobacco, and interest, and so on and on. In his personal life perhaps a man can seek ways which his conscience feels are important, but can he bind the conscience of other men? God's law is very plain, so that all may understand. Inferences take us into the realm of human conclusions. Anything important enough to be a law and bind our conscience is plainly stated by God: it is not left for men to discover.
>
> Inferences can be very, very dangerous, not only to the life of faith but to our standing before God. People who major in inferences wind up trying to be holier than God, a particularly evil state.[4]

In view of his own criticism of creating laws predicated on inference, it seems somewhat paradoxical that Rushdoony would base his entire life's work on such an inference and hold the Body of Christ responsible to it. Considering Rushdoony's condemnation of inference as a means to bind men's consciences to man-made agendas, I would ask where God's Word speaks clearly of the dominionist mandate to work for political and social change in the world system. Yet because of the inability of dominionists—both charismatic and Reconstructionist—to present plainly stated commands of God ordering us to salvage the dying world system and implement the rule of godly men to enforce God's Law, obviously all their arguments rest upon inference.

There is yet to be stated any unequivocal command that all Christians are to embroil themselves in the world system other than to proclaim the Gospel of salvation in Jesus Christ. That includes the Gospel of the Kingdom which, upon surrender of one's personal life to Christ, one enters as a citizen. But to follow the Reconstructionists' agenda is to attempt to meld the Kingdom of God with the kingdoms of this world before Jesus comes to personally oversee it.

Gary North

North is a leading Reconstructionist author and publisher who is outspoken in his beliefs that America is a Christian nation, and that American Christians must lead the way in establishing the Kingdom of God on earth. He suggests that the wicked will get their comeuppance at the hands of the Reconstructionist troops:

> The eschatology of dominion has once again revived, as it has not since the period of the American Revolution. . . . This is not the end of the world. The Church is not about to be raptured. The humanists, occultists, and New Agers are about to see their world ruptured. This process could be delayed by God's external judgment on the West, but it cannot be delayed until Christ's return in final judgment. It will happen long before Christ returns in glory.[5]

North is among the most visible Reconstructionists and is, in his own words, "one of the two primary publishers of dominion theology."[6] It is North's belief that David Chilton's *Paradise Restored* is the most definitive, virtually irrefutable book on what North calls "dominion eschatology":

> Dominion theology is the wave of the future. David Chilton has written the two primary eschatological manifestos of dominion theology. Whoever comes after him will inevitably be labeled a "me, too" postmillennialist. Chilton has established the terms of the debate over eschatology for the next hundred years, at the very least.[7]

This is quite a claim. Obviously North is convinced that no one will be able to challenge Chilton's dominion eschatology in our lifetime. But the question is, if it can be challenged at all—one hundred years, or one thousand years from now—why must we accept it today? God's Word is open to us for understanding as much today as it will ever be. If the Church has been slow to grasp understanding it's because it has tried to spiritualize the Word rather than take it for what it says, and/or it has leaned to tradition and its own understanding rather than rely on humble yielding to instruction from the Holy Spirit. In any case, one hundred years or today means little. Had North said that Chilton has established the terms of the debate once and for all, I'd be impressed. Better for his position had he not qualified it.

As much as some don't like to admit it, there is a debate going on. The Reconstructionists comprise the intellectual arm of dominion theology and, except for their eschatology, they're just a little better grounded in the study of theology than their charismatic counterparts. As such, the Reconstructionists' arguments are somewhat viable. And since one of the major publishers of dominion theology has established that David Chilton is *the* voice for dominion eschatology, we couldn't do justice to the subject without addressing Chilton's arguments.

David Chilton

Referring to Matthew 5:13-16, Chilton says:

> This is nothing less than a mandate for the complete social transformation of the entire world. And what Jesus condemns is *ineffectiveness*, failing to change the society around us. We are commanded to live in such a way that someday all men will glorify God—that they will become converted to the Christian faith. The point is that if the Church is obedient, the people and nations of the world will be discipled to Christianity. We all know that everyone *should* be a Christian, that the laws and institutions of all nations *should* follow the Bible's blueprints. But the Bible tells us more than that. The Bible tells us that these commands are the shape of the future. We *must* change the world; and what is more we *shall* change the world.[8] (Chilton's emphasis)

Matthew 5:13-16 is hardly a "mandate for the complete social transformation of the entire world." It is a mandate, yes. But it is a mandate that requires *personal* holiness that will manifest itself as salt and light. Of course, as a result of our godly living and witness for Christ many will be saved and brought into the Kingdom of God. But social transformation of one nation, let alone the whole world, doesn't even enter the picture.

Scripture tells us that when Jesus returns the nations will be allied against Him; they will not be waiting to welcome Him (Revelation 16:14; 19:19). Whether anti-Christ is a man or—as stated by many dominionists—a system, the fact remains that, when Jesus returns, at least a vastly major portion of the world will be under the rule of anti-Christ, not under the rule of the Church.

What Chilton has done in spiritualizing Matthew 5:13-16 is not academically honest. In waxing eloquent for his eschatological bias he often accuses those with whom he disagrees of making Scripture say what they want it to say. Has he not done the same?

Chilton goes against another of his own rules by referring to Matthew 28:19-20, and then assuming that all the nations, not just individual souls from out of all the nations are to be discipled:

The Great Commission to the Church does not end with simply witnessing to the nations. Christ's command is that we disciple the nations—all the nations. The kingdoms of this world are to become the kingdoms of Christ. They are to be discipled, made obedient to the faith. This means that every aspect of life throughout the world is to be brought under the lordship of Jesus Christ: families, individuals, business, science, agriculture, the arts, law, education, economics, psychology, philosophy, and every other sphere of human activity. Nothing may be left out. Christ "must reign, until He has put all enemies under His feet" (1 Cor. 15:25). We have been given the responsibility of converting the entire world.[9]

This is the major premise upon which the early papacy established the Holy Roman Empire. In view of current overtures for unity with the papacy heard among many dominionists, it is not surprising that the mindset toward temporal rule of the earth would be so much a part of their agenda.

One point Chilton makes over and over again is that literalism must be considered secondary to consistent biblical imagery. Who made that hard, fast rule, we don't know; but in this instance he has gone against his own rule. To "disciple all the nations," or, more accurately, "make disciples of [out of] all the nations," does not mean that every nation as a whole is one day going to sit at the feet of the dominionist gurus and learn the ways of Truth. The Great Commission requires us to go into all the nations and preach the Gospel, and then to disciple "whosoever will" be saved. Using Chilton's exegetical rule, if this "mandate" encompasses all the nations as saved entities, it must encompass all believers as missionaries to foreign lands. After all, is the Lord not speaking to each of us as individuals?

And if Chilton's "biblical imagery" rule is good for Matthew 28:19-20, it must be good for Matthew 24:9: ". . . ye shall be hated of all nations for my name's sake." Therefore, everyone in every nation will hate all Christians. Ergo, no one will ever be converted.

As usual, the use of biblical imagery is used to establish a commandment where none is stated. This violates Rushdoony's rule that commandments should not be based upon inference whether real or imagined. It is out of an imagined command that the Reconstructionists perceive their means to take over the world:

Our goal is world dominion under Christ's lordship, a "world takeover" if you will; but our strategy begins with the reformation and reconstruction of the Church. From that will flow social and political reconstruction, indeed a flowering of Christian civilization (Hag. 1:1-15; 2:6-10, 18-23).[10]

In his book, Chilton correctly points out that postmillennialism has been a dominant theme in Church history. But it is not Scripture he uses to support that contention. Rather, he uses the writings of the early "Church Fathers" (Augustine, Athanasius, etc.), and some recent sources such as C.H. Spurgeon. But what Chilton fails to recognize is that the only legitimate early Church fathers were the apostles. Those early Church Fathers he quotes were products of a religious system already sliding into apostasy.

They were the fathers of Roman Catholicism. And it was the Roman Catholic Church that first attempted to take dominion over the governments of the earth. It succeeded to some degree, in that most of Western Civilization came under its control. But in order to establish and maintain control, the Roman Church had to acquiesce to pagan cultures and enforce its mandate at the point of the sword. The result was that, although the biblical ethic (as much as was allowed under Romanism) did bring a measure of enlightenment, the Church itself suffered corruption and became paganized. This affected not only its liturgy but its doctrinal position in some crucial areas.

Yet even to achieve the modicum of success it enjoyed in establishing its compromising rule, the Roman Church had to resort to bloodshed not only through the fomenting of wars, but through pogroms against dissenters such as took place in the Inquisition.

Failing to learn from history the disastrous and ungodly results of attempting to establish a theonomic social order, Chilton (an alleged historian) has also failed to understand that there are varying points of view even among premillennialists. As a staunch postmillennialist, he lumps all premillennialists under the mantel of "dispensationalism," and accuses of being a defeatist anyone who doesn't hold to his concept of dominion:

> The eschatological issue centers on one fundamental point: Will the gospel succeed in its mission, or not? Regardless of their numerous individual differences, the various defeatist schools of thought are solidly lined up together on one major point: The gospel of Jesus Christ will fail. Christianity will not be successful in its worldwide task. Christ's Great Commission to disciple the nations will not be carried out.[11]

> A good deal of modern Rapturism should be recognized for what it really is: a dangerous error that is teaching God's people to expect defeat instead of victory.[12]

There are many who would take umbrage at Chilton's accusations. It is patently ridiculous to accuse any Christian of believing that "the gospel of Jesus Christ will fail." Every premillennialist I know expects victory, including Hal Lindsey (whom Chilton takes special delight in denigrating). There are several points on which I disagree with Lindsey, but no one can legitimately accuse him—or many other non-dominionists—of having a defeatist attitude. Were that true, they would not be writing books with evangelistic themes.

The trouble with dominionists is that they don't do their homework. Otherwise they wouldn't lump all premillennialists into one grab bag of escapism.

Has The Gospel Failed?

Another problem is that they see as defeat anything less than domination of the world system (which is condemned to destruction) before Jesus returns. This is not spiritual-mindedness, but carnal-mindedness, even when based on the assumption that the transformation of society will result from the changing of men's hearts through the Gospel.

We are not called to "win the world for Christ." We are called to be witnesses for Him. It is the Holy Spirit that draws men to God as we share the Word about Christ (Romans 10:17). To think that the Gospel of Jesus Christ will have failed because the whole world isn't converted would be the same as to think it has failed because every person who hears the Gospel doesn't fall on his or her face in repentance.

What's the difference if not everyone at a given moment is converted, or anyone throughout history is not converted? Somewhere, according to the reasoning of dominion theology, not only the Church has failed, but so has the Holy Spirit.

"But," some would say, "we don't expect every person to be converted; we just want to make sure their lives are conformed to Christian principles; God delights in righteous living whether or not the person is a believer in Jesus Christ."

Well, if not every person is converted, we will have less than total dominion, even if we can control their actions. If even one person remains unconverted, the Holy Spirit will have "failed" just as He has "failed" throughout history by not converting everyone who ever lived.

To think that God delights in man's righteousness without faith is contrary to His Word which calls unregenerate man's righteousness "filthy rags" (Isaiah 64:6). God hates for men to appear righteous while their hearts are far from Him (Isaiah 29:13).

Even if the Church were to rule the world, as long as there are unconverted souls, the privilege to run society will be challenged. Ultimately there will be confrontation and the need to apply force to maintain control. Bloodshed and corruption (yes, even among "Christians") will be an ongoing result of religious domination.

Human nature being what it is, even were we to succeed in converting every soul and ruling society under God's spiritual direction, within two generations at the most, the rebellious nature of those to be born will manifest itself.

Without the visible, tangible presence of Jesus and His *resurrected* saints administering the Kingdom of God on earth, the world would be at the mercy of arrogant, religious autocrats whose own peculiar understanding of "God's will" will keep men in bondage.

PURGING THE EARTH

One teaching that joins Reconstructionists with Charismatic Dominionists is their belief—even their heart-felt desire—that the earth will be purged of evildoers by the established New Order.

David Chilton

In reference to Revelation 8:3-5, Chilton instructs on his understanding of God's method of executing judgment:

> God rains down His judgments upon the earth in specific response to the liturgical worship of His people. As part of the formal, official worship service in heaven, the angel of the altar offers up the prayers of the corporate people of God; and God responds to the petitions, acting into history on behalf of the saints. The intimate connection between liturgy and history is an inescapable fact, one which we cannot afford to ignore. This is not to suggest that the world is in danger of lapsing into "non-being" when the Church's worship is defective.
>
> In fact, God will use historical forces (even the heathen) to chastise the Church when she fails to live up to her high calling as the Kingdom of priests. The point here is that the official worship of the covenantal community is cosmically significant. Church history is the key to world history: When the worshiping assembly calls upon the Lord of the Covenant, the world experiences His judgments. History is managed and directed from the altar of incense, which has received the prayers of the Church.[13]

The fact is that God has more often executed judgment by His own volition than in response to the prayers of His people for vengeance upon their enemies. And the chronology of Revelation 8 shows that the events to follow the Church appearing in heaven take place after the Great Tribulation (ch. 7).

There is no scriptural precedent for liturgical services conducted with the expressed intentions of calling God's wrath down upon the enemies of the Church. Yet in all the dominionist movements there are teachings about the necessity for the Church to rise up and take vengeance upon those who do not reform. It is not necessary that all people become Christians, even nominally. What is important to the dominionist agenda is that everyone live a moral life or suffer God's judgment either supernaturally or at the hands of God's servants: Christian administrators of God's government on earth.

Reconstruction philosophy is very methodical, insisting that penalties incorporated under the Old Testament civil law for Israel be implemented in civil government today.

Ray Sutton

(Reconstructionist author and pastor of Westminster Presbyterian Church in Tyler, Texas):

> First, Paul's Romans 1:18-32 language indicates that New Testament penal sanctions are *similar to the Old Testament*. The vast majority of Old Testament penalties should still be instituted. As earlier sections of this book indicate, the proper hermeneutic for determining what carries over into the New Testament is the principle: continue what is not changed in the New Testament. This would apply to the penal sanctions of the Old Testament. The death penalty offenses that should be extended into the New Testament are witchcraft (Deut. 18:10-11), idolatry (Deut. 13:10), murder (Gen. 9:6), blasphemy (Lev. 24:11-23), homosexuality (Lev. 18:22-29), bestiality (Lev. 18:23), rape (Deut. 22:25-27), adultery (Lev. 20:10), incest (Lev. 20:14), incorrigibility of teenagers (Deut. 21:18-20), kidnapping (Exod. 21:16), and some instances of perjury (Deut. 19:19-20).
>
> ... not every convicted homosexual would have to be put to death according to I Corinthians 6. In the New Covenant Age, only the "unreformable" element would be put to death.[14] (Sutton's emphasis)

I address this statement in more depth in a future chapter. For now, suffice to say that, in view of the Reconstructionists' agenda, I'm afraid we'd end up with a bloodbath that would virtually wipe out the next generation of humanity were these penalties instituted today.

3
The Theonomic Structure

Reconstructionists, as do many other dominionists, consistently maintain that they are not trying to force anything on anyone. They deny that they are attempting to institute a "theocracy," preferring instead to use the term "theonomy." They take great pains to avoid using the word "theocratic" when describing their New Order. An example is Ray Sutton's disclaimer:

> The final question to be answered is, "How do we establish a society based on the concepts presented in this book?" I raise it because I do not want there to be any confusion about how a Christian society is created. I do not want the reader to leave this book thinking a covenantal culture comes from the top down, meaning by some "theocratic elite" forcing everyone to be a Christian, or believe a certain way. Nothing could be farther [sic] from the truth.
>
> God told the Israelites that their Biblical culture would come "little by little." It did not come *suddenly*, or overnight. It came gradually.[1] (Sutton's emphasis)

Sutton's conclusions demonstrate the illogical nature of such a claim. How can they have a Christian civil government guided by God's Law and not use any governmental influence (force, sanctions, etc.) to insure that the people obey God's Law? The Reconstructionists say they do not plan to force everyone to be a Christian or to believe a certain way. But regardless of how people are allowed to *believe* contrary to the truth, they will not be allowed to *live* contrary to the Reconstructionists' interpretation of God's Law. The Reconstructionists are not so concerned with saving souls as they are with establishing an ethical society.

This drive for an ethical society reveals what is wrong with the dominionist approach to evangelism. While evangelism is a critical responsibility entrusted by Jesus to the Church, it should be engaged in with proper motives: to save lost souls. The dominionist approach is predicated upon a desire for world conquest and the establishment of an ethical society. Any souls saved are icing on the cake, so to speak.

Although Paul was unconcerned with motives as long as the Gospel was preached (Philippians 1:15-18), we must remember that it was the *true* Gospel that was preached even out of contention, not the dominionists' gospel. Their gospel can only lead to a replay of the Roman Church's attempt at world conquest through compromise.

Sutton's conclusion is also erroneous in his thinking that Israel's biblical culture came "little by little." Israel's biblical culture was established by God through Moses. Whether they ever entered the Promised Land did not determine their biblical culture. It merely established their residency in the land promised by God *for their faithfulness* to their biblical culture. They had to remain faithful to remain in the land. Their biblical culture was established while they were in the wilderness for forty years, and even when they went into captivity they took elements of their biblical culture with them. From this erroneous premise, however, Sutton tells us how we are to take dominion "little by little":

> The expansion of the Gospel from Jerusalem to Rome serves as an example. Jesus says at the beginning of Acts, "You shall receive My power when the Holy Spirit has come upon you; and you shall be My witnesses both in Jerusalem, and in all Judea and Samaria, and even to the remotest part of the earth" (Acts 1:8). This verse summarizes the spread of the Gospel from one part of the world to the rest. It began in Jerusalem, and ended up in Rome. The method was *little by little evangelism*, just like the land of Canaan.
>
> Yes, Acts parallels the Book of Joshua. Joshua is the account of the conquest of the land; Acts is the story of the conquest of the world.[2] (Sutton's emphasis)

Before I comment on Sutton's reasoning, I would point out that Jesus said His disciples would "receive power," not "My power." This is not a mere technicality to those who understand the dominionist mindset. It reflects an attitude of autonomy on the part of the believer in exercising power: we have "His power," therefore we can do all that we determine to do.

But we do not have autonomy. One who has power of attorney to administer the affairs of another's estate cannot exercise that power in accordance with his own will, but must execute his duties according to the will of the person he represents. So, too, we are to exercise authority in accordance with God's will, not our own. Jesus did not give us "His" personal power. He sent the Holy Spirit who works through us according to the Father's will. The Holy Spirit exercises His power through us. We are not the ones who exercise power by using the Holy Spirit; any such attempt is witchcraft. It's a matter of who's will is being implemented.

We received power when the Holy Spirit came upon us. But Jesus said that power would be used to make us His witnesses. He said nothing about using the His power to further our own religious agendas or to take dominion over the cursed world system.

Witnessing Defined

This brings us to what is meant by "witnessing." Remember that Sutton's statements relate to establishing not only the Gospel in men's hearts throughout the world, but to establishing civil rule throughout the world. It follows, then, that to be witnesses does not mean merely to proclaim the Gospel, but to take dominion over civil governments. This is how dominionists define witnessing.

Okay. For the sake of argument, let's accept their interpretation. In that case, in order to be faithful to Jesus' command, the first place to work for a Christian society is in Jerusalem, not in the United States where this aberration is under full sail. Therefore, according to the dominionist interpretation, Jesus' words have not been fulfilled because Jerusalem has never been "Christianized"— unless we want to believe that the ungodly Roman Catholic Crusaders established Christian civilization there. But even the Crusaders' rule lasted only for a short period of time. It was not permanent. So the rest of the world cannot be Christianized until Jerusalem is Christianized—permanently.

From Jerusalem the dominionists will have to go throughout all Judea. Once that province has been Christianized they can go to Samaria. Where they wish to go from there would be up to them.

The dominionists cannot have their cake and eat it too. Either this passage is speaking of witnessing only ("you *will be my witnesses*"), or it is speaking also of taking dominion over all civil governments ("you *will take dominion*"). Since Jesus set the terms and prophesied how it would be accomplished, if it doesn't begin in Jerusalem, He was wrong.

If the dominionists want to prove Jesus correct and be true to their understanding of this Scripture, they must leave America, go to Jerusalem, and do what the apostles failed to do: establish Jerusalem's civil law under Christians.

THEONOMY: CIVIL OR INDIVIDUAL?

When dominionists define theonomy, they are not confining their definition to the individual's obedience to God's Law. Yet some attempt to convince us that, regardless of what we *say*, we all really *think* as they do. They label as "theonomists" all who are obedient to God's Law—even those who do not profess their mandate for world dominion. Reconstructionist Gary Crampton quotes Cornelius Van Til (whom Reconstructionists have adopted as one of their own, but whom many consider a Reformed theologian rather than a Reconstructionist) to make the argument that all Christians are theonomists whether or not we realize it:

> Cornelius Van Til has stated that "There is no alternative but that of theonomy (i.e., God's law) and autonomy (i.e., self or man's law)." He is correct. All Christians, by their confession of the Lordship of Christ in their lives, are theonomists. There could be no such thing as a Christian who would opt for self-law over God's law. God's law is the only rule of faith and life (2 Tim. 3:16-17). This is covenant theology.[3]

I don't dispute Van Til's statement, but I do dispute Crampton's application of it. In the context of the principle tenets of dominionism in general and Reconstruction in particular, the word "theonomy" carries the specific connotation of applying God's Law to civil government. In this regard, Reconstructionists build upon Van Til's definition, extending it to unintended dimensions.

To answer this question we must see what proponents of theonomy for civil government offer to substantiate their belief that civil rule is mandated by Scripture.

In his stretching of the application of theonomy, Crampton also quotes the Westminster Confession of Faith to demonstrate that theonomy does apply to civil governments. Well, the WCF does not demonstrate that theonomy applies to civil government. It demonstrates the opinion of the Presbyterian Churches in America who drafted the Westminster Confession of Faith in the seventeenth century, and later revised it toward the end of the eighteenth century.

Because the WCF (or Calvin, or Spurgeon, or any myriad of Christian leaders of Church history or early American history) applied theonomy to civil government, does not validate the philosophy. Only Scripture can do that. And, it doesn't.

The critical question is, does *God's Word* apply theonomy to civil government today, or is His covenant binding only upon those individuals who enter into His covenant by choice?

According to Greg Bahnsen, a noted Reconstructionist, the concept of theonomy is stated in two parts. In contradiction to other Reconstructionists, however, he treats theonomy strictly as a matter pertaining to civil government:

> The first is that Old testament [sic] laws are taken to be binding unless the New Testament particularly/specifically abrogates a given law. This is in opposition to Dispensationalism which contends that only those laws affirmed by the New Testament are binding today. Deuteronomy 4:2 and Matthew 5:17-19 serve as a Scriptural basis for the theonomic position. The second part of the concept is that the law of God applies to the social and political arenas as well as to the spiritual or religious aspects of life.[4]

That the Old Testament laws were not done away with entirely, I would agree. Just because the New Testament does not reiterate all the laws of God as stated specifically in the Old Testament does not mean they have been abrogated. But that is not the key issue. The key issue is whether or not the Church is to take dominion over the nations before Jesus returns.

I state this because the Reconstructionists have a clever way of convoluting the question: they create a straw man by giving a truth (God's laws are still in effect), then stating their own conclusion (the law of God applies to the social and political arenas), then implying that those who do not accept their conclusion do not believe the truth. This is why they label all who do not believe in postmillennialism (or who at least do not possess some form of dominionist mindset) as Dispensationalists.

They make Dispensationalism the either/or straw man as if there were no other positions. Because of their narrow focus, they have essentially made the argument one between Dispensationalism and dominionism. By so doing, they are ignoring a large segment of the Christian populace. There are many who find problems with both positions. But it does make the dominionists' arguments seem reasonable to themselves if not to anyone who understands God's Word.

And for Bahnsen to use Deuteronomy 4:2 to validate a theonomic structure for today's civil governments is not proper and violates Rushdoony's rule against making commandments out of inferences. In fact, there isn't even an inference that this Scripture establishes a dominion mandate. It refers specifically to Israel's duty to obey the commandments given to them as God's chosen people. These commands may apply to the Church government to some degree, but they do not apply to civil government.

> *Now therefore hearken, O Israel, unto the statutes and unto the judgments, which I teach you, for to do them, that ye may live, and go in and possess the land which the LORD God of your fathers giveth you.*
> *Ye shall not add unto the word which I command you, neither shall ye diminish ought from it, that ye may keep the commandments of the LORD your God which I command you.* (Deuteronomy 4:1-2)

If these verses apply today, then all three Law categories apply, because all three were included in this pronouncement. There is no distinction made between them. If the dominionists wish to claim that the ceremonial laws were specifically abrogated in the New Testament, whereas the moral and civil laws (and let's not forget the dietary laws) were not, they must still abide by the rules of covenant: that a covenant must be predicated upon the consent of all parties. The New Covenant is predicated upon the consent of God and those who profess faith in Jesus Christ. This did not include consent of civil governments.

Also to the point, this was a word to Israel as they were about to enter the Promised Land under Joshua's command. There is nothing in this verse to suggest that Old Testament laws "are taken to be binding unless the New Testament particularly/specifically abrogates a given law."

Bahnsen has created yet another straw-man: this Scripture verse does not prove anything either way. It can be used neither as an argument to support the dominionist position, nor can it be used to dispute the dominionist position.

Now let us see what Matthew 5:17-19 has to say about this same claim by Bahnsen:

> *Think not that I am come to destroy the law, or the prophets: I am not come to destroy, but to fulfil. For verily I say unto you, Till heaven and earth pass, one jot or one tittle shall in no wise pass from the law, till all be fulfilled.*

Does this prove either the theonomist or the Dispensationalist viewpoint? No. It merely states that the law is still valid for believers. It neither abrogates specific laws (the theonomist position), nor affirms specific laws (the Dispensationalist position). But within the context of the Sermon on the Mount, during which it was stated, it does affirm the whole moral law. There is not even a hint of an allusion to the civil law.

Jesus' own words that His Kingdom is not of this world (John 18:36) indicate that He did not affirm Israel's civil law as binding upon His disciples or for the nations during the present age. Nor can one Scripture be produced to show that He ever confirmed the civil laws of Israel over the civil laws of pagan Roman society. He tells us we must obey all governments regardless of their ungodly character. Thus, the second part of the concept of theonomy relating to civil government is likewise unsupported by Scripture.

Of all the dominionist materials I've read I have yet to see a single, *accurately exegeted Scripture reference* that substantiates the dominionist mandate for subduing the nations and/or ruling the world prior to Jesus' return. They either spiritualize, allegorize, or erroneously apply the Scriptures in their attempts to justify an otherwise untenable position.

Another of Bahnsen's statements bears looking at in view of the importance that dominionists attach to the theonomic worldview:

> Yes, theonomy is not the be-all or end-all of life; it is simply a part of the whole picture of the Christian life. It has its place and is important, but it is not the only issue. I compare it to God's sovereignty or to the virgin birth; both are important and foundational, but they are not the whole of Scripture.[5]

What is *this*? In attempting to give the impression that he is downplaying theonomy, he compares it to the sovereignty of God and the Virgin Birth! These are cardinal doctrines of the Faith!

How can he compare theonomy with these? He isn't downplaying theonomy by saying it is "not the be-all or end-all of life." In fact, he is putting his philosophy on a par with essential truths, and implying that those essential truths are not the be-all or end-all of life either.

What an incredible analogy! Yet it accurately reflects the dominionist mindset that considers activism in the political and social arenas of life the *essential duty* of every Christian.

THEONOMY VS. THEOCRACY

Dominionists tend to shun the word, "theocracy." This is because "theocracy" carries a stigma. It conjures in people's minds the religious zealotry of intolerable religious systems capable of wielding the power of the political sword. Dominionists opt instead for the word "theonomy" which is less ominous in its connotation, mainly because most people are unfamiliar with that term. But for all practical purposes theonomy and theocracy are synonymous. You cannot have a civil government operating under God's Law (theonomy) without the power and inclination to enforce that Law (theocracy).

Whether or not a religious state is ruled by the true God is a moot point. False religious philosophy makes such a government structure no less a theocracy. Iran is a theocracy, yet it has nothing to do with Jesus Christ. A theocracy can be implemented in the name of any god, true or false.

But, the dominionist would say, under theonomy the people live by God's Law not because of any outside force, but by the conviction of the Holy Spirit.

Such naivete reminds me of Karl Marx's promise that, under communism, the state would one day just "wither away." States never wither away—they just change hands, few of which rule righteously. By the same token, nobody lives by conviction of the Holy Spirit except those born of the Spirit.

History has proven that every attempt to institute a theonomic state has resulted in persecution of those who do not see eye-to-eye with the established order. Even the former "Christian" Geneva under Calvin, which the Reconstructionists like to point to as an example of theonomy at work, made second-class citizens of all who did not adopt Calvin's dogma—even other Christians. Many were persecuted under the theonomic structure of Calvin. The same is true of the theonomic Anglican system in England.

And we've already mentioned the horrible example of the Holy Roman Empire under the papacy.

THE NEUTRALITY BUGABOO

Another flaw in dominionist thinking is reflected in Ray Sutton's implication that those who reject the dominion mandate are neutral toward God's Law. He begins by pointing out that those Christians who think abortion should be legal are resting "on the belief that killing a baby and not killing a baby are morally equivalent acts; God is neutral regarding the killing of babies. That such Christians should also adopt a theory of judicial and political neutrality is understandable."[6] But then he introduces another dominionist straw man:

> But what is not easily understandable is that Christians who recognize the absurdity of the myth of neutrality in education and abortion cling to just this doctrine in the area of civil law and politics. This is a form of what Rushdoony calls "intellectual schizophrenia."[7]

Sutton is reaffirming the Reconstructionists' belief that those who do not accept the dominionist mandate are politically neutral. They don't want to get involved. This is untrue. Many Christians who reject the dominionist mandate are active in civil and political affairs, working to change the system as best they can. And in terms of neutrality, why do the dominionists not storm abortion clinics and kill the doctors performing abortions? Are they making a distinction between an unborn child and a child in the crib?

The dominionists to a man would say, and I would agree, that there is no difference between a child in the womb and a child in the crib. They are equally precious lives before God. But if the dominionists wish to be truly non-neutral in their approach toward abortion, they would have to take the same steps to protect from attack the child in the womb as they would the child in the crib.

A Neutrality Scenario

Consider the following dialogue which, to various degrees, I've had with anti-abortionists who insist that everyone should take up their cause with the same fervor as they:

Question: Is there any difference between a child in the womb and a child in the crib?
Answer: No.
Q: If you saw a man standing over a child in a crib, ready to plunge a knife into the baby, what would you do?
A: I'd stop him.
Q: How would you stop him?
A: By any means I could.
Q: Would you kill him if necessary?
A: Yes.
Q: Why would you not kill an abortionist about to kill a baby in its mother's womb?
A: Well, that's different.
Q: Why is it different? You've already stated that there is no difference between a child in the womb and a child in the crib.
A: Well, there are laws that would prevent me from killing the abortionist.
Q: Would you stand by and watch a man kill a child because you fear the law? Which is more precious to you, the law or the child?
A: The child.
Q: Then which is more important to you, the law or the child in the womb?
A:

Do not take this scenario as evidence that I favor abortion; I am vehemently opposed to it. My point is that while claiming non-neutrality toward politics, by their own actions (or lack thereof) dominionists prove that they do indeed take a neutral position once the price becomes higher than they wish to pay. Using Sutton's logic, I would paraphrase his own statement:

> But what is not easily understandable is that dominionists who recognize the absurdity of the myth of neutrality toward

the child in the crib cling to just this doctrine in the area of the child in the womb.

Until the Reconstructionists and all other dominionists are ready to take to the limits their own convictions, they have no business placing the onus of those convictions upon others.

THE PATIENCE OF SAINTS

The Church Age is not the time to "possess the land," as the dominionists like to tell us. It is a time to bring "whosoever will" to faith in Jesus. We will possess the land when Jesus returns.

There is a proper time for everything according to God's plan. Had the Israelites attempted to enter the Promised Land before the time prescribed by God they would have been routed and destroyed for disobedience. In fact, that's just what happened to those who tried to enter after the Lord told them they must wait because of their initial disobedience. Dominionists insist that they are not really trying to force anything on anybody—that they really believe in a constitutional republic. But a constitutional republic under a theonomic system is an oxymoron unless the population as a whole endorses it. It would take a constitutional convention to implement the thing. And if anyone thinks a majority of any society will ever embrace God's Law to the extent that they will tolerate a theonomic government, they don't know human nature.

While the dominionists decry the concept of a pluralistic society based on freedom of religion (and well we all should for the evils it begets, let alone tolerates), there's a better chance that, in frustration and prideful willingness to admit they cannot implement their theonomic society, many will join with Roman Catholicism. That religion boasts a membership of one billion souls—a formidable ally for those who wish to wield political power over a significant portion of mankind.

In either scenario, the evil generated by a religious state would far outweigh the evil of any pluralistic society unless the Lord Himself were here to administrate that state.

Claiming to reject pluralism, the dominionists would have us believe they can form a true, lasting constitutional republic based on God's Law. But there are some serious flaws in their thinking.

In the first place, if such a government could be established it would not last past two generations—four at the most. The human condition simply does not allow for the tolerance of righteous rule. Every society that became "Christianized" slid back into its former ungodly lifestyle within a few generations. Sanctity is not something that can be passed on through the genes. Everything in nature inevitably degenerates; everything is dying and will continue to do so until the new heaven and new earth. History demonstrates a basic flaw in man: his sinful nature. That is why it will be necessary even for Jesus to implement His righteous rule with a rod of iron when He does establish His millennial reign on the earth.

In the second place, God's Law in the Old Testament was predicated not on a constitutional republic, but upon a theocracy guided by prophets and kings. The prophets were stoned, and all but a few kings became corrupted with idolatry. And this at a time when God's displeasure was palpable and brought swift, dire consequences. Yet Gary North points to Israel as an example of theonomy in action and poses the following questions:

> But then someone may ask: Wouldn't biblical law lead to tyranny? I answer: Why should it? God designed it. God mandated it. Was Israel a tyranny? Or was Egypt the real tyranny, and Babylon? Tyranny was what God visited upon His people when they turned their backs on biblical law. His invitation unto the land of Israel was unto shalom or peace and blessing![8]

Wait a minute, Gary. Religious tyranny is just as evil as political tyranny—even more so. Israel was tyrannical at many stages in its history, and not just when it forgot God's Law. The best example of Israel's tyranny was the religious establishment which, though not being the state per se, ruled the nation unrighteously by enforcing God's Law even beyond the parameters that God required.

The religious leaders were champions of God's Law, but their hearts were evil and they used His Law to enslave the people. The implementation of God's Law does not guarantee peace or insure that those enforcing the Law will do so under the spirit of the Law. The spiritual condition of those in power determines how God's Law will be implemented. And there are enough loopholes in the rules of administration to test the heart of any religious leader.

The point is, do we want to trust men to implement God's Law according to their own understanding? Or would we rather look for Jesus Christ to return and implement it personally?

THE DEATH PENALTY

The dominionists assert that theonomy is necessary in order to   establish Jesus' lordship over the earth. It will therefore be necessary to invoke the death penalty and other harsh disciplines in their efforts to keep society godly.

I am not saying that the death penalty has no place in keeping law and order. But the death penalty is not an invention of God's theonomic structure alone. It has been in force by civil government since the beginning of civilization. So have less severe penalties for certain crimes. These penalties are not the exclusive property of the dominionists, although they'd like us to believe that if they were in power, somehow corruption in high places would be non-existent (or at least dealt with swiftly), and all penalties would be meted out according to a just, biblical standard.

Nor is the mercy of God extended to man through Christ really a part of the dominionist agenda as they might like us to believe. Had theonomy been the rule during the time of their own ignorance or rebelliousness, many of dominionists would be bankrupt today from having to restore four or more times what they stole from others through unreputable business practices. They may even have been put to death for adultery, breaking the Sabbath, or just plain rebellion as teenagers.

God's mercy is okay for them, but not for future sinners who, if the dominionists have their way, will never know the salvation of God. What they are promoting is a modern Phariseeism, using the name of Christ to validate their own righteousness.

They broaden their phylacteries through the writing of many books, professing wisdom that displays an utter foolishness devoid of mercy, while presenting themselves as examples of righteousness. And every day they break God's Law because they don't really understand His Law beyond the rudiments.

Those who would rule so ruthlessly can thank God that the extent of Church discipline allowed by the Scriptures went no further than excommunication during their own time of rebellion.

We know from Scripture that certain Old Covenant laws carried the death penalty. These penalties applied to all inhabitants of the land, both Israelites and foreigners living in their midst. The dominionists want to reimplement those Old Covenant laws and penalties in today's society. In fact, if they do have such a mandate from God, they *must* implement those laws and penalties. Sutton states their case as well as anyone:

> First, Paul's Romans 1:18-32 language indicates that New Testament penal sanctions are *similar to the Old Testament*. The vast majority of Old Testament penalties should still be instituted. As earlier sections of this book indicate, the proper hermeneutic for determining what carries over into the New Testament is the principle: continue what is not changed in the New Testament. This would apply to the penal sanctions of the Old Testament. The death penalty offenses that should be extended into the New Testament are witchcraft (Deut. 18:10-11), idolatry (Deut. 13:10), murder (Gen. 9:6), blasphemy (Lev. 24:11-23), homosexuality (Lev. 18:22-29), bestiality (Lev. 18:23), rape (Deut. 22:25-27), adultery (Lev. 20:10), incest (Lev. 20:14), incorrigibility of teenagers (Deut. 21:18-20), kidnaping (Exod. 21:16), and some instances of perjury (Deut. 19:19-20).

> ... not every convicted homosexual would have to be put
> to death according to I Corinthians 6. In the New Covenant Age,
> only the "unreformable" element would be put to death.[9]
> (Sutton's emphasis)

Sutton says that Paul's Romans 1:18-32 language *indicates* that New Testament penal sanctions are *similar* to the Old Testament. But this indication of similarity for penal sanctions is Sutton's view. And even if valid, it does not mean that the Church is to see that civil governments implement them; it merely states that those who do the things he describes are worthy of death. But Paul also tells them that he is persuaded that God's judgment would be upon those who commit such things (Romans 2:2). His language and the context give no hint that God's judgment would come through the Church ruling or even advising civil governments. God will deal directly with all the ungodly in His own time. Paul also told the Corinthians that such were some of them before God's grace was shed upon them (I Corinthians 6:11), demonstrating that God is far more patient than men in showing grace toward those who are lost.

Conviction because of the laws of a church hierarchy does not bring genuine salvation; only the power of the Holy Spirit can do that. Under church laws many are convicted of sins that aren't even sins except as defined by the hierarchy of the church.

How Would The Law Be Implemented?

Debates over which specific crimes would incur the death penalty rage even within the Church. How many of today's most "godly" dominionists were rebellious teenagers themselves? Was God's mercy okay for them, but not for future generations?

If the Old Testament laws are to be implemented at all, they must be implemented fully. The issue of which laws to implement carries a very sticky proposal. Consider the laws against idolatry. There are many practices that can be construed as idolatrous within the Roman Catholic Church. To implement those laws would be to take on a religious institution whose adherents—nominal and devout—number some one billion souls. This is nearly one-fifth of the earth's present population.

Are the dominionists ready to take on the political state of the Vatican? On the contrary, there is every indication that the quest for unity will eventually bring about an integration of Protestantism with Roman Catholicism. Even Sutton is willing to overlook this problem:

> Of course, during this discussion, it should be kept in mind
> that Biblical religion is the only one that truly allows for
> religious freedom. The reader may think that the position on

pluralism that has been taken in this book would not allow for religious diversity. Actually, Biblical Law allows for "private worship," in this sense a "limited" freedom of religion. The basis is the Old Testament "stranger in the land" concept. As long as he obeys the commandments of God that are legitimately enforceable by civil government, he enjoys the benefits of a Biblical society.

During the Reformation, this concept was used to solve the problem of how Protestant countries should deal with Catholicism. In the Netherlands, for example, post-Reformation Catholics were allowed to continue to hold worship but not to conduct processions down the street. But the Netherlands is one simple example to show how religious diversity could be tolerated. Perhaps in a multi-denominational society, the Apostles' Creed could be used as a minimum standard of orthodoxy.[10]

In the first place, the "stranger in the land" could no more practice idolatry than the Israelites. If the dominionists want to be absolutely true to their concept of a biblical mandate to rule the nations, they would zealously execute all who do not surrender to their Christ. Even if non-believers worshipped other gods in private, were they found out they would be executed. Need I once again remind the reader that this is exactly the position the Holy Roman Empire took in its conquest of the nations until it realized that the best it could do was compromise? Today, in many Roman Catholic countries, that compromise is evident in pagan ceremonies conducted in Catholic churches under the watchful eyes of their priests.

In the second place, as far as the Apostles' Creed goes, it was a fine minimum standard to define the Faith for its day (though there is far more to the Faith than the Apostles' Creed addresses). Cults operating in the name of Jesus Christ have adopted the language of the Church and have perverted it to suit their own demonic doctrines. So any test of orthodoxy today would require a much more definitive article than the Apostles' Creed.

Also, what would happen to those who do not subscribe to the Apostles' Creed? Sutton's language implies that they will not be allowed to remain in society; at best they would be non-citizens, shunned and persecuted because they don't meet the dominionists' standard.

What we really see in Sutton's comments is that Christian civil government would punish idolatry outside the Church, but tolerate it if it is practiced in the name of Christ behind closed doors. God's Law is to be enforced, but not if it causes consternation to the Roman Catholic Church.

Some Sticky Problems

What decision would be rendered by a Christian civil government were an idolatrous religious system allowed to apply for a building permit? Besides the architectural restrictions (no statues, no esoteric pagan symbolism of any kind), the weightier matter would be to regulate what goes on inside should permission be granted. How can a godly civil government grant permission to build an edifice to house idolatrous worship?

No matter how they cut it, the dominionists are biting off a lot more than they will ever be able to chew.

Assuming that this compromise rule applies to the idolatrous religious systems, would it not also have to apply to all other laws that would normally incur the death penalty? (*Remember, idolatry was one sin not abrogated by New Testament law, and is reaffirmed by Sutton as being worthy of the death penalty.*)

Would it not be unjust to fail to apply the same standards to homosexuality (private homes and clubs for homosexual activity; just keep it out of the public eye)? Wouldn't the same apply for bestiality, adultery, and other sins? Logically, it would have to apply to any personal sin (one that does not directly affect another person, such as murder or theft) not committed in public. Otherwise, to abrogate this rule in order to implement Christian civil law in these areas, civil government would have to abrogate it in regard to religious worship that is not in strict conformity to Christianity, simply because all other forms of worship are, by definition, idolatrous.

The challenge before the dominionists, therefore, is this: when you take control, enforce the law without respect to any individual or any ostensibly "Christian" institutions. Do away with Easter, Christmas, Mother's Day, Hallowe'en, Valentine's Day, birthday celebrations, and any other current cultural festivity that involves idolatrous practices and symbols, whether they are part of "Christendom" or heathenism.

And be prepared to take on the Roman Catholic Church, Islam, Hinduism, Buddhism, Mormonism, and every other religion currently outstripping evangelical Christianity in its growth.

4
Covenantalism

There is an aspect of dominion theology that requires close attention due to its infringement upon the individual believer's relationship to the Father. It is the belief that the dominion mandate is part of God's covenantal requirements for Christians. In essence, this means that to fail to work for political and social reform to establish dominion over the world system is to break covenant with God. This is a serious charge when we consider the ultimate condition of the soul that is out of God's covenant.

Covenantalism is gaining impetus and will continue to do so in the coming years as teachings on "covenant bonding" proliferate among local churches. Much of what is taught under covenantalism is true and has been neglected by the Church for many centuries. But if there are some truths of covenant living conveyed by the dominionists, there are also serious errors.

The implications of this teaching go far beyond the mundane personal decisions of the believer. For to break covenant with God is to incur His judgment. By implication of the dominion mandate, then, it logically follows that to break the covenantal bond with God by remaining politically neutral would result in loss of one's salvation, or at least some form of judgment from God. In some churches, those who oppose covenant bonding under the dominion mandate risk being shunned.

Covenant theology is not new. John Calvin is perhaps the earliest Reformer to formulate the idea that God does everything in relation to His covenants with man. Later, the Puritans claimed to be a covenant people, and attempted to colonize the New World as a means to advance the Kingdom of God in the Western hemisphere. That attempt was short-lived once the humanists that fomented the American Revolution and founded the federal government gained ascendency.

That all Christians are under covenant with God we must agree. Exactly what the terms of the covenant are and how far they reach in our ministry to the world is the question in dispute. In relation to the dominionists' agenda, the critical question is whether someone who is not politically active in working to establish Christ's lordship over the whole earth is guilty of breaking God's covenant. Most dominionists would say yes, he is breaking God's covenant. This would be stated in terms similar to this: "We deny that a Christian can fully discharge his duty to God apart from social, cultural, and political action aimed at influencing society for God and for human good."[1]

In order to properly address this question we must understand why dominionists say this, and we must test what they say by God's Word. There is no other criterion by which we can judge. We must be careful not to reject what one says because it bothers our sense of personal freedom. To toss off the dominionists' challenge because we do not want to be called to accountability under the terms of the covenant is not to challenge the dominionists, but to challenge God. If we cannot establish a biblical basis for rejecting or accepting anything, then we are trusting in our own wisdom.

Regarding the covenant model, there is one writing that Gary North claims is the apex of covenant theology. This is Ray Sutton's *That You May Prosper: Dominion by Covenant* (Tyler, TX: Institute for Christian Economics, 1987).

North thinks Sutton's exposition of the covenant is the single most important writing for the Reconstruction movement:

> Because this is the book that verifies theologically the brilliant monographs by Rushdoony and Chilton, I regard this as the key book in the Christian Reconstruction movement. On this book's thesis I am "betting the store."[2]

North's accolades for Sutton's book go beyond mere superlatives. What he is saying is that, if Sutton is wrong, the Reconstruction movement is wrong. More than this, he tells us that without this book we cannot really understand Scripture:

> . . . the author has found the key above all other keys to interpreting the Bible. . . . We have waited over three millennia for someone to say plainly: "This is what the Bible is really all about."[3]

> No doctrine of the Bible can be properly understood without the outline or covenant model found in this book.[4]

The fact is that North is probably right in much of what he says (though, heaven forbid, not in all he says). Sutton's book is a brilliant exegesis of the covenant model. And though Sutton's covenant concept is not new, he has built upon the works of earlier writers in presenting formidable arguments for the dominionist view of God's covenants. Further, he has broadened the covenant model to include a "five-point structure" for what the dominionists believe are "all three of God's covenants": church, family and civil government,.[5]

Briefly, these five points are that the covenant model contains 1) a transcendent view of God: that he is distinct from His creation; 2) a concept of authority, or hierarchy, based on representation; 3) a society based on ethics, particularly the laws of the Bible; 4) a system of sanctions based on an oath; 5) a system of continuity based on something other than blood relations.[6]

Not all Reconstructionists have bought into Sutton's covenant model. Reconstructionists are divided into two camps on this as well as on other issues.

Using Deuteronomy (which Sutton believes is the "Book of the Covenant" referred to in II Kings 22:8) as the model for his five-point structure, Sutton presents a plausible argument that establishes a sound rationale for the dominionist mandate. But because it's a sound rationale doesn't mean that it's biblical.

Granting that most of what Sutton says is true in regard to the covenant model and that Christians are indeed under covenant with God, our concern is not with the true statements found in his book, but with the errors upon which arguments for the dominionist mandate rest.

It is on these areas, therefore, which I will concentrate. In so doing, I hope to convince the reader that the dominionist mandate has no sound basis in God's true covenant and, therefore, is not scriptural.

GOD'S TRUE COVENANTS

As Christians we are aware of God's covenants that He established in both the Old and New Testaments. Before we examine the dominionists' covenant mandate, we should briefly review the major covenants expressly implemented by God, and consider the extent to which they may or may not apply to us today. This will be important when we later examine covenant principles within the context of the dominionists' agenda, and how covenants are used to bind Christians to political action and areas of responsibility not required by God's Word.

The covenants of God with man are many, but all of His covenants fall under the three major covenants that have continued throughout history and affect God's people today: the Adamic Covenant, the Old Covenant, and the New Covenant. For puposes of brevity the Adamic Covenant here includes what some call the "Edenic Covenant," which relates to God's covenant with Adam before his sin.

The Adamic Covenant (Genesis 1:14-2:17):

This was made by God with Adam before the fall (the Edenic Covenant), promising endless seasons and fruitfulness, and giving him dominion over the earth and all the animals. The condition for blessing was that he not eat of the tree of knowledge of good and evil. The penalty for disobedience was physical and spiritual death.

All mankind is included under the terms of the Adamic Covenant. When Adam sinned he brought a curse upon the whole human race, because we were all "in him." This covenant is still in effect and all men are born under its curse for Adam's breaking it. Until the resurrection which will occur when Jesus returns, physical death will continue to inhabit our bodies even though we have been spiritually regenerated, and are now "in Christ."

Many dominionists actually believe contrary to this. They assert that they will restore Paradise—that obedience to biblical law (ethics) can restore man to the pre-fall Adamic state. This is known as "progressive sanctification." As man is sanctified through obedience to biblical law he will become immortal, the earth will be transformed: food will be plentiful, wild animals will become tame, diseases will no longer take their toll, and all nature will be in harmony.

The Old Covenant (Genesis 15:18):

This was made by God with Abraham, giving him all the land from the Nile to the Euphrates. This covenant has not yet been fully implemented; God promised that the land into which He led the Israelites under Joshua would be an eternal inheritance.

The Old Covenant was inherited by the nation of Israel, having been ratified through Moses. It showed the way to God, and established laws and conditions for obedience to demonstrate the faith necessary for redemption. Although Israel as a nation was God's chosen people, not all Israelites were believers. Yet the Old Covenant laws applied to all Israelites because they were born into the covenant family. It also applied to Gentiles who dwelt with them in Israel, with some specified exceptions. To break the laws of the covenant incurred the penalties prescribed by those laws. The Old Testament laws were of three categories: civil, religious (or ceremonial), and moral.

The Civil Laws pertained to Israel as a nation, guided by the prophets, kings, and priests. They protected the rights of the individual, provided justice for the poor, and pronounced judgments upon those who were rebellious. These laws established Israel as a theocracy: a nation ruled directly by God through His prophets, and guided by a theonomic structure (God's Law), mediated through the teachers of the law, the priests and rabbis.

The Religious or Ceremonial Laws provided the means by which the people could have their sins atoned. They also provided for worship, praise, fellowship, and restitution prescribed by God's Word. The prescribed method of atonement involved blood sacrifices which were done away after Jesus' perfect sacrifice.

The Moral Laws as encapsulated in the Decalogue (the Ten Commandments), and refined by Jesus in the "two greatest commandments" (Matthew 22:34-40), were binding upon all individuals as a means to demonstrate the faith they professed. If they truly loved God and their fellow man they would live by these laws as a demonstration of that love.

Salvation By Grace

None of God's Laws could save from sin. To remain in covenant it was incumbent upon each person to live by the Law through faith in God. They were not given as a means to attain salvation. "Therefore, by the deeds of the law shall no flesh be justified in his sight" (Romans 3:20). Nor could the blood of bulls and goats remove completely the sins of the faithful (Hebrews 10:4). Salvation, even under the Law was still dependent upon God's grace.

The promises of this covenant are specific to the natural descendants of Abraham through Isaac and Jacob (Israel), and will be fulfilled by the remnant of that nation during the Millennium. It cannot apply to Christians of all nations, because all nations will dwell throughout the earth. Therefore, it must apply to a believing remnant of Israel. Since the promises have not been fully realized (Israel has never possessed in perpetuity the entire portion described in the covenant) its fulfillment is future.

It must be remembered that this covenant was not predicated upon Israel's obedience, but upon Abraham's. Even though Israel has rejected their Messiah for the most part, the promise of God will be fulfilled in Abraham's natural, believing descendants out of God's honor for Abraham's faithfulness. These will not be distinct spiritually from other believers (Galatians 3:28), but are distinct in the physical realm just as there remain differences between male and female, and even between the bond and free, in the physical realm.

The New Covenant (Matt. 26:28; Mark 14:24; Luke 22:20):

This is God's Covenant made available to all who by faith enter into salvation through Jesus' blood shed for the remission of sins. This covenant was reiterated and expanded upon in Romans 11:27, I Corinthians 11:25, II Corinthians 3:6 (not of the letter but of the Spirit), Galatians 4:21-31 (contrasts the New Covenant with the Old), Hebrews chapters 7 through 10 (establishes the New Covenant as better than the Old, with laws written on our hearts and put into our minds through the Holy Spirit).

The Old Covenant laws had a purpose in showing man his utter incapability to live righteously in the world. But with Jesus Christ's death was provided the final and complete sacrifice for sin that need never be offered again (Hebrews 10:12). As the sinless Lamb of God, the Word of God incarnate, Jesus Christ's blood is sufficient for the redemption of the entire human race from Adam to the last soul yet to be born.

To procure the free gift of redemption provided by God it is necessary to enter into the New Covenant established through the blood sacrifice of His only begotten Son. This involves repentance from sin and coming to Jesus Christ in faith believing that His death and Resurrection provide the only means to eternal life and fellowship with the Father. To repent from sin involves obeying the terms of the New Covenant; it is not a one-time decision, but a lifetime commitment. Anything that adds to or subtracts from this Gospel as clearly defined in the New Testament is a false teaching, and those who bring those additions or subtractions are accursed (Galatians 1:8).

There is a sacredness to our covenant relationship with God; the Church really is a covenant people. In fact, a major problem for the Church has been that it has forgotten what it means to be in covenant with God. The responsibilities go far beyond "accepting Christ." Once we have entered into the New Covenant established through Christ we must keep His commandments by faith, for faith without works is dead (James 2:20). Jesus said, "If ye love me, keep my commandments" (John 14:15).

There is no disputing the fact that when we come to Christ for salvation we are not merely the recipients of the blessings of His covenant. We also assume the responsibilities of that covenant. The covenant is a legal contract. To keep the terms of the covenant is to reap its benefits. To violate it (to sin) is to incur its penalties.

God, in His love and mercy, has provided the means by which the covenant can be renewed should it be violated by our sin. Under the legal terms of the covenant, "if any man sin, we have an advocate with the Father, Jesus Christ the righteous" (I John 2:1). Jesus sits at the right hand of the Father to make intercession for us when we violate the covenant. "If we confess our sins, he is faithful and just to forgive us our sins, and to cleanse us from all unrighteousness" (I John 1:9).

All who profess faith in Jesus Christ enter into relationship with the Father under the terms of the covenant. We are all, therefore, bound by those terms. The willful breaking of the covenant results in apostasy and brings into effect the penalties prescribed in Hebrews 6:1-12 and 10:26-31.

That there are consequences to breaking the covenant no right- thinking Christian will dispute. Those who think they can "accept Christ" while continuing in sin and in love of the world do not understand the ramifications of their easy-believism.

This misunderstanding is the Church's fault more often than it is those who come to Christ on the basis of the Church's careless treatment of the Gospel. The Church's responsibility is to first state the terms of the covenant to those it evangelizes, and then make them accountable to those terms after they agree to them.

While the Church should not infringe on the believer's personal relationship with the Father, neither should it allow him to think he can call himself an heir of God without fulfilling the requirements of the covenant that makes him an heir.

This is not legalism. Legalism is the belief that salvation comes through works of the Law. God's Word is clear that salvation through works is not possible (Galatians 2:16). But neither is it possible to claim faith in Christ while rejecting the responsibility to live by His commandments. For one to believe he can do so is to deny the faith that he claims to have. As Jesus said, "If ye keep my commandments, ye shall abide in my love; even as I have kept my Father's commandments, and abide in his love" (John 15:10). Conversely, if we do not keep His commandments can we say we abide in His love? Such a "faith" is dead.

Additional Covenants

Besides the three major covenants, of course, there are numerous promises to individuals and, within the New Covenant, to believers in Jesus Christ. All of God's promises are conditional upon obedience to His Word. They are not conditional upon obedience to religious leaders and their personal "revelations" or their particular understanding of Scripture (I John 2:27).

Are The Laws Still In Effect?

The dominionists equate Jesus' commandments with all the Old Testament laws. To them, rejection of the dominion mandate constitutes rejection of Jesus' commandments and, therefore, the whole of God's Law. For this reason it is necessary to differentiate between the ceremonial laws, the moral laws, and the civil laws of the Old Testament. This is especially important because dominionists promote what they often refer to merely as "theonomy" (rule by God's Law). While in their writings they make the distinctions between the three categories of law, for the most part they use the phrase "God's Law" ambiguously.

We know from the Scriptures relating to Christ's sacrifice that the Old Testament sacrifices and laws pertaining to atonement have been done away. At the instant of Jesus' death, God Himself tore asunder the veil of the temple, thus exposing the Holy of Holies as a sign that entrance into the presence of God was now available to all who would come through Jesus (Matthew 27:51).

After some forty years, the temple was destroyed, removing all opportunity for Israel to come to God by any sacrifice other than Jesus'. The ceremonial laws were not only rendered null and void by Christ's death, it became impossible to implement them. Therefore, like all of mankind, those Israelites who reject Christ remain outside the covenant of their fathers, as well as outside the New Covenant in Jesus' blood.

As far as the moral laws are concerned, Scripture indicates that they are still binding upon the believer. Keeping them cannot save us, but willful disobedience incurs God's judgment (Hebrews 6:1-12; 10:26-31). These are the laws of which Jesus spoke when He said, "Think not that I am come to destroy the law, or the prophets: I am not come to destroy, but to fulfil. For verily I say unto you, Till heaven and earth pass, one jot or one tittle shall in no wise pass from the law, till all be fulfilled" (Matthew 5:17-18).

That Jesus was referring specifically to the moral laws is evident because He makes mention of them in verses 19 through 48. Also, in verse 20 He tells His followers that, unless their righteousness exceeds the righteousness of the scribes and the Pharisees, they could not enter into the Kingdom of Heaven. This righteousness pertains to the keeping of the law not only outwardly, but inwardly as a matter of faith.

These words were part of the Sermon on the Mount, following the beatitudes which reflect the perfect life of one who lives by faith. The beatitudes are not commandments, but illustrations of what it means to follow Christ. One cannot choose to be a peacemaker while refusing to be meek and humble, and still demonstrate the righteousness of Christ in his life.

The Civil Law Mandate

So up to this point we see that the ceremonial laws were done away with, and the moral laws were reinforced by Jesus. But what of the civil laws? For that is the crux of the dominionist mandate:

that God's civil laws must be imposed upon all governments so that the whole earth will come under the lordship of Christ.

Sutton attempts to establish the dominion mandate for civil government by stating that Christians are to take dominion by means of the covenant:

> Some Christians do not understand their Commission from the Lord. It is a renewal of the cultural mandate; it has the covenantal structure; it means Christians are to take dominion by means of the covenant.[7]

By what authority does Sutton make the statement that the Lord's Commission is a renewal of the "cultural mandate"? If it is made on the basis that the Great Commission has the covenantal structure, Sutton is assuming more than the Scriptures allow.

But there is a reason to this madness. For this claim is in keeping with the dominionists' belief that the Old Covenant, as a means of implementing a theonomic or theocratic world rule, was not done away with entirely. Rather, the New Covenant merely established the Church as the new means by which God would implement His dominion over the earth.

It is believed by some that Israel failed under the Old Covenant to establish God's rule over the nations. But such reasoning implies that God's initial plan failed, necessitating Jesus' coming in order to establish the New Covenant. A further implication of this belief is that the Cross was an afterthought. Unable to see this discrep-ancy, Sutton attempts to bring what he calls "the power State nations" (earthly governments) under the covenant by claiming that the cross of Christ has conquered them:

> Consider Christ. The movement of history reaches the apex of conflict at the cross. The power-State nations of the world crucify their Savior. The weapon of destruction (the cross), however, becomes that which brings them to ruin. Power States were brought under the covenant.[8]

Sometimes people strive too hard to prove their point. The so-called "power-State nations" did not crucify Christ. The Father ordained His crucifixion. If any human agencies were to blame it would have to be the Jewish leaders. Outside of Pontius Pilate and the local Roman garrison, the "power State nation" of Rome was not even aware of what was going on in Jerusalem. And even that state's ruling magistrate, Pilate, wanted to release Jesus.

True, there was a spiritual battle being waged; but it wasn't just waged at the Cross. It was waged during Jesus' entire tenure on earth, and will culminate with the new earth. To make the Cross a conflict over earthly governments is to read into the Gospel what is not there. While the Cross provided the means for the redemption of man, which redemption includes the eventual conquest of the nations, Scripture is clear that the conquest of the nations will not take place until Jesus returns. When Jesus defined the terms of the New Covenant He made no mention of bringing the "power State nations" under its terms. The New Covenant is specifically stated by Jesus and by the writer of Hebrews as dealing with the remission of sins once and for all for those who believe (Matthew 26:28; Mark 14:24; Luke 22:20; Hebrews 10:9-18). Jesus made this covenant with His disciples, not with the power State nations.

Like the individual who refuses to believe in Christ, the governments of the world are also under the curse of the Adamic Covenant; they are not under the New Covenant. All rebellion was judged from before the foundation of the world. God's judgment upon sinful man affects man's institutions including his governments. The final implementation of His judgment will not take place until the establishment of the new heaven and new earth. For Christians to take it upon themselves to execute judgment upon those outside the Body of Christ is itself sin because it seeks to implement something contrary to God's Word, which cannot fail.

Consent Required

Even though they are instituted by a transcendent, personal God, His covenants always rest upon *acceptance and promise of obedience* through faith by those with whom He makes them. This is faithfulness on His part to the legal requirements of the covenant principle: the consent of all parties.

Although Sutton stresses the legal implications of a covenant, he neglects that very important legal technicality: by definition, a covenant involves the *consent of all parties*. Thus, he addresses the roles of both God and those who enter into His covenant, but he fails to adequately address a third category: those outside the covenant. If someone is not party to a covenant or agreement he cannot be held to its terms.

I can draw up all the agreements and legal contracts I want between myself and another party. But until a contract is ratified by that other party it has no legal basis for implementation. Throughout his writing Sutton violates his own principles of covenant, specifically the third: "the covenant implemented a system of sanctions based on an oath."[9]

Consider this very carefully: where no oath exists, no covenant exists. This is a very important point—even, I might say, critical—to understanding the distinction between the believer's role under the New Covenant, and the non-believer's total estrangement from it. It also demonstrates why we cannot impose the terms of the New Covenant upon non-believers. Yet Sutton continually seeks to impose consequences upon those who have not taken any oaths to obey the covenant.

Rushdoony makes this very point by applying the status of citizenship exclusively to those under the covenant:

> In Biblical law, neither equalitarianism nor an oligarchy have any standing. God as the source of law established the covenant as the principle of citizenship. Only those within the covenant are citizens. The covenant is restrictive in God's law.[10]

Now, the dominionist would say that the laws apply to everyone who lives in the land, not only to citizens; but only citizens have a right to govern or involve themselves in the legislative and juridical processes. And this is true. However, the presupposition of dominion theology—that since the nations belong to God, only His people are citizens of the nations—does not hold water in view of Scripture's recognition of the validity of other nations' existence apart from His covenants. In other words, the nations are not under covenant with God, and we are not citizens of the nations, we are citizens of heaven.

We recognize, however, that although not all men are under the New Covenant, all are under the Adamic Covenant. The terms of the covenant that condemn mankind were stated thusly: "In the day that thou eatest thereof thou shalt surely die." Through Adam, all have partaken of the tree of the knowledge of good and evil. All are born under the terms of the Adamic Covenant whether or not we like it. The evidence is that all have sinned and fallen short of God's glory (Romans 3:23). Therefore, all are cursed.

This curse is the result of being born under the Adamic Covenant which is distinct from both the Old Covenant given to Israel, and the New Covenant given through Christ to the Church. Although physically we bear the marks of the Adamic Covenant until we are resurrected, when we enter into the New Covenant through faith in Jesus Christ we are given new spiritual life, born again by the Spirit of God through faith.

Those who do not enter into the New Covenant cannot be held accountable to it; they are already held accountable under the terms of the Adamic Covenant that condemns them both physically and spiritually. The power State nations have not accepted or agreed to abide by the terms of the New Covenant, so they remain cursed under the terms of the Adamic Covenant. This condition will persist at least until Jesus returns; it will not be alleviated beforehand. That is why Jesus said, "My kingdom is not of this world" (John 18:36).

Therefore, anything the Church wishes to impose upon civil governments it must do illegally. We are outside our jurisdiction if we attempt to judge those outside the Body of Christ. That's why Paul made a distinction between the unbelieving sinner and one who calls himself a brother, yet continues in sin. He told the Church to continue in company (in association, not in spiritual fellowship) with the former but to shun the latter:

> For what have I to do to judge them also that are without? do not ye judge them that are within? But them that are without God judgeth. Therefore put away from among yourselves that wicked person [the professed believer who continues in sin] (I Corinthians 5:13).

It might be argued that this refers to individuals, not to civil governments. But the entire premise of the dominionist mandate involves Christian civil government judging individuals for their failure to live in obedience to God's Law. The principle, therefore, still applies, whether to individuals or to any human agency outside the Body of Christ.

Righteous Judgment

The dominionists reject the idea that we are not to judge those outside the Body of Christ. Sutton cites I Corinthians 6:2-3 to argue that Christians are to exercise judgment not just upon each other but upon the world: "Christians are the judges of the world (I Cor. 6:2-3)."[11]

But this is a serious misquote that changes the meaning of what Paul was saying. These verses do not say that we *are* judges of the world. They say that we *shall* judge the world:

> Do ye not know that the saints shall judge the world? and if the world shall be judged by you, are ye unworthy to judge the smallest matters?
> Know ye not that we shall judge angels? how much more things that pertain to this life?

Paul makes a distinction between judging things pertaining to "this life," and the future judging of the world and of angels by God's saints. I should make it clear, however, that although we are not to judge those outside the Body of Christ, *we are to make judgments* based on God's Word as to what the world does. And we are to make our judgment known even when we know it will not lead to repentance. This is how the Church is to maintain its separation from the world.

An Irrational Conclusion

Sutton neglects to see this vital truth, that unbelievers are not bound by the Old or New Covenant. Further, he uses the faulty rationale that those who don't believe that all civil governments are under the New Covenant have no basis for evangelization:

> Someone who wants to argue that the "unbeliever" is not bound by God's covenantal standard ultimately has no basis for presenting the Gospel to the unbeliever. If he is not accountable in the area of civil rule, then he has found a loophole in the gospel, an area of neutrality, a "King's X" from God. He therefore does not need the Christ of the Bible.
>
> The New Testament clearly teaches that civil authorities are supposed to rule by the Bible. Their purpose is ethical. If their purpose is not ethical, then it becomes manipulative.[12]

First of all, Sutton equates God's covenantal standard with obedience to civil law; but, as stated before, this standard only applies to those under the covenant. It is *after* the unbeliever recognizes his need for the Christ of the Bible that he enters into the covenant and *then* becomes accountable to all righteous laws, including civil law. Before that, in the eternal picture, it doesn't matter whether he obeys or disobeys every law in every law book, including the Bible, because he is lost anyway; he still needs to be evangelized.

This doesn't mean, however, that governments should not enforce the laws necessary to keep an orderly society. But if every government existed in total anarchy, God's people would still need to fulfill their purpose through evangelization.

Granted, the *ideal* is for civil authorities to rule by God's Law. But what should be is not what is. Nor is it what shall be until Christ returns. This condition exists because God's mercy is being extended to all through the preaching of the Gospel by His people. If civil law enforced the Old Testament standards many would not find salvation. They would be put to death after their first rejection of those standards.

The dominionists do not hold their extreme position arbitrarily. They hold it because it is the Old Testament's position. But they fail to understand that it was applicable only within the Israelite community. Even then Israel was never commissioned to extend theocratic rule to the nations. It is through Jesus Christ, after He has come to rule in person, that the nations will be so blessed.

By their desire to implement the Old Testament civil laws in all the nations, the dominionists effectively deny the concept of the "Age of Grace." This is primarily because they reject every aspect of the Dispensationalist point of view. Granted, many Dispensationalists have an erroneous view of the "Age of Grace" because they equate the Old Testament era with an "Age of Law," as if salvation rested on keeping the law during that time. At least as far as they have stated their case, they seem to not understand that God's grace has been operative since the Fall (really since Creation). The Law itself was an extension of God's grace.

On the other hand, neither do the dominionists have a biblical concept of grace as it applies to this age. In a sense, Jesus did inaugurate an "Age of Grace" in that, during this "time of the Gentiles," God's wrath is largely held back until the people of all nations have the opportunity to respond to the Gospel. Another purpose is to test the hearts of those who profess Christ. This test will continue until He returns.

During the visible Millennial reign of Christ on earth His Law will be enforced with a rod of iron because all men will know the truth and will experience the presence of its author. Unrighteousness will be dealt with quickly; justice will be swift and sure.

In the meantime, God's people must walk in humility, ministering grace toward all men. We cannot know all men's hearts. Yet where an individual Christian has the authority to influence legislation he should do so, trusting that God will guide him. But the sinful condition of our unregenerate flesh precludes even Christians from having absolute—or near absolute—control.

THE CIVIL COVENANT

In spite of the unscriptural premise for the dominion mandate, Sutton states that the formula for victory is simple: keep the Covenant (his concept of the Covenant) and dominion will be the proper effect. But here we are not speaking of the Old or New Covenant. Remember that Sutton has posited three distinct covenants contained within both the Old and New Covenants: church, civil government, and family. Yet even while he makes these distinctions he concludes that it is the Church's corporate obedience that establishes the covenant for civil government.

But just because the Church is faithful to the New Covenant does not necessarily mean we will have dominion over our nation. The nation itself must keep God's covenant in order to be blessed by God. If, as Sutton says, the governmental covenant is separate from the Church covenant (even though both are encompassed under the New Covenant), then the nation itself must covenant with God in order to be under covenant.

Theoretically, a nation could covenant with God, in which case it would enjoy His blessings as long as it didn't break that covenant and allow its unrepentance to continue past the time allotted by God's mercy. But a faithful Church cannot offset the sins of the nation. The nation as a whole, or at least its leaders as a whole, must repent and obey God's Word through faith in Jesus Christ. Outside of Israel, this has never happened. And even then, for most of its history Israel was rebellious.

Those who quote II Chronicles 7:14 erroneously equate "my people" with all the people of the nation. Yet not all citizens are counted among God's people. In fact, few are. This Scripture addressed the only nation God ever called "My people." Today His people are a new nation, the Church (I Peter 2:9), which has come out of all the nations. The nations themselves, however, are not His people. This is why He said, "My kingdom is not of this world." Not only do the dominionists ignore these vital words of Jesus, they ignore His words that follow immediately upon them:

> *If my kingdom were of this world, then would my servants fight, that I should not be delivered to the Jews: but now is my kingdom not from hence.* (John 18:36)

No doubt were the dominionists on the scene at the time, they would have taken up arms to prevent the Lord's death, thus in their ignorance condemning the world to its sin. God's purposes are higher than we can imagine in spite of how things appear. How vital it is that we not go beyond what is written (I Corinthians 4:6).

It is important to remember that, according to Scripture, the nations of the world will not repent before Jesus returns (Matthew 24; Mark 13; Revelation 6, 7 and 18). Therefore, the condition of the world does not necessarily reflect the obedience or disobedience of the Church; the condition of the Church reflects the obedience or disobedience of the Church.

The Church Laws

I would agree with Sutton that, under a theonomic system, civil law enforces the penalty for breaking the moral law. But the only government that is ordained by God to operate under a theonomic or theocratic order is the Church. And the Church may dispense penalties for breaking the moral law in order to keep itself pure from contamination, but its jurisdiction ends with its members. The most it can do is excommunicate, and how can it excommunicate those who are not communicants in the first place?

Considering the present spiritual condition of the churches, it is nothing less than amazing that so many leaders, even among the dominionists, want to dispense judgment in the civil arena, but are so lax in dispensing judgment in the Church or even in their own personal lives.

Is America A Christian Nation?

Regarding America (since this is the starting place for the dominionist mandate of world conquest), history disputes the idea that this is a nation under covenant with God. Were it so, the Founding Fathers would all have been Christians in the true sense. And they would have established belief in and obedience to Jesus Christ as the primary criterion for holding elective or appointed office. Government officials would then comprise the hierarchical structure of Sutton's covenant model for government. We cannot dispute that *some* of the early settlers in this country were Christians, at least nominally. And the Mayflower Compact did form a body politic, one of the purposes of which was to advance the Christian faith. But its framers also purposed to honor the king of England. Just because they had as one purpose to advance the Christian faith does not mean they meant to do so by establishing an independent Christian government. On the contrary, the Mayflower Compact specifically reaffirmed their loyalty to the king of England.

Nor were these all religious refugees. True, some of those aboard the Mayflower were Protestant Separatists who had fled England to Holland to escape persecution from the reformed Anglican Church prelates (an example of theonomy at work), but the principals were men commissioned to further the business of the Virginia Company.

The Mayflower Compact was an afterthought designed to keep the colony intact after they were blown off course from their intended landing at the mouth of the Hudson River, having landed instead at what later became Massachusetts. When they set sail, it was not a part of their original intent to draft the Mayflower Compact and form a Christian colony under its terms.

Although the document that the Mayflower passengers drew up did have some *influence* on the charters of a few colonies prior to the Revolutionary War, it had no *official* bearing on the federal government or on any of the colonies or states created either prior to or after the American Revolution. If we are going to call America a Christian nation we must see if its founding body, the Continental Congress, purposed to establish it as such. Did that body, in fact, covenant with God to form this nation?

No Mention Of Jesus Christ

When the Continental Congress drafted the Declaration of Independence and, later, the Congress formed under the Articles of Confederation drafted the Constitution of the United States of America, no mention was made of Jesus Christ. Rather, the only references to deity in the Declaration were to "God"; none are in the Constitution. In fact, many of the framers of these documents were anti-Christian, being comprised of Masons, and deists of many persuasions. (See the Media Spotlight special report, "A Masonic History of America.") Since, under the terms of the New Covenant, God does not enter into other covenants that do not invoke the name of His Son, there exists no covenant between the Father and the federal government of the United States, or with any state government. Had the constitutions of all these governments, including the federal government, named faith in Jesus Christ as the principle criterion for holding any elective or appointed office, there would truly be a covenant with God as a nation. But this would have had to be done in the name of Jesus Christ with full understanding of the true biblical character of His role as Savior and Lord. This the founders of this nation of sovereign states failed to do.

It is apparent that the Western European influences that shaped America were part of what had become known as "Christendom." But a culture based on the idea of "Christendom" does not of itself constitute a culture based on Scripture or an inviolable covenant with God. The history of Christendom is an ugly history fraught with tyranny and the enslavement of those who are less "enlightened." If God gave the knowledge and means to subdue the earth and take dominion in the name of Jesus Christ, then that privilege has been terribly abused. If, on the other hand, Satan gave that knowledge and means, his purposes have certainly been accomplished. The fruit of Western Civilization, in spite of its enlightened accomplishments, demonstrates that no attempt to institute the Kingdom of God on earth before Jesus returns can succeed. So the idea of a covenant between any nation and God is a fantasy.

If, then, there is no valid covenant between this nation and God, the Church cannot mandate civil dominion by obedience to the covenant. And if we are to treat any alleged civil government covenant as distinct from the family and church covenants, we cannot impose upon the former the requirements for the latter.

Although the Reconstructionists have managed to grasp some truths of covenant living, they have confused the issue by attempting to apply God's covenant with His people to the uncovenanted nation. It is precisely because of their confusion in this area that they have misunderstood why the nations will maintain the upper hand in the world system until Jesus returns.

THE CAUSE AND EFFECT PRINCIPLE

One premise upon which Sutton bases the dominion mandate is his belief that everything that happens in the physical universe is the result of a cause-and-effect principle contained within the covenant structure. He correctly affirms that "the mechanical view of cause and effect led to a collectivist concept of government, as do all utopian theories."[13] But he challenges the mechanical view with a poorly thought-out cause-and-effect theory based on covenant keeping:

> God is personal. He created the world. He also created mathematics. A formula may explain what happens in a physical sense, but not *why*. The water cycle can be studied, for example, but this does not explain why famines occur. God sends famines as a curse. *Everything that happens is the result of covenant-keeping or covenant-breaking.* Life is not mechanical. (Sutton's emphasis).[14]

To some degree, this is true. But Sutton's concept is somewhat simplistic and downplays another truth stated in Scripture: God "maketh his sun to rise on the evil and on the good, and sendeth rain on the just and on the unjust" (Matthew 5:45). This truth is stated by Jesus in context with His command that we love our enemies. It points out that, while all disobedience will eventually result in judgment, that judgment is God's, not ours. It will come in His time according to His will. During this age God's people are to concern themselves with loving their enemies and working toward bringing them into relationship with Him.

While everything that happens to God's people may be seen as the result of covenant-keeping or covenant-breaking, it must be remembered that this rule applies only to those under covenant, not to those outside the covenant. If calamities of nature are God's judgment upon the world, they are judgments under the Adamic Covenant, not the New Covenant. This, again, is the reason that the rain falls on the just and the unjust alike.

The assumption is that the covenant cause-and-effect theory is unimpeachable. But is it? If the principles of covenant are inviolate (and they are), then they must apply to the individual as well as to the Church, the civil government, and the family. And if everything that happens to God's people is the result of cause-and-effect, then all sickness, accidents, and other ills that befall Christians are the result of sin. This is contrary to Scripture. Some of God's most faithful servants (including Jesus' apostles) have suffered sickness and other personal calamities. They suffered persecution and even death at the hands of religious zealots and at the hands of the ungodly. We see, then, that part of God's New Covenant proposal includes persecution and tribulation in this world (John 16:33).

Persecution = Defeat

Contrary to Scripture, the dominionists see persecution of God's people as defeat. But the Scriptures say, "Precious in the sight of the Lord is the death of his saints" (Psalm 116:15). At the time of the Great White Throne Judgment all things will be reconciled under covenant cause-and-effect. But the tares will continue to exist with the wheat until God's angels separate us at the time of the end. In the meantime we must count it a privilege to suffer for the Gospel just as the apostles did (Acts 5:41).

Because dominionists see a persecuted Church as a defeated Church, eventually their "optimistic eschatology" will boomerang on them. They will be in terror and confusion when it finally becomes apparent that their eschatology has failed them and persecution against the Church has come like a flood to refine and purify God's people before Jesus returns.

When that persecution comes—when it is apparent beyond any doubt that Jesus spoke the truth when He said that, before He returns, sin will abound as in the days of Noah (Luke 17:26)—those dominionists whose hearts are right will look toward heaven and, in unity with all true believers, will cry, "Maranatha!"

THE COVENANTAL LAWSUIT

Let's assume that the dominionists do convert the world and take over civil government. What will be their legal grounds for enforcing the covenant (assuming, of course, that consent is not necessary to bring someone under that covenant)? One means that Sutton proposes is what he calls, a "covenant lawsuit" to be brought by individual Christians against those who harm them:

> Because the Biblical covenant commands Christians to be lawful, they are not allowed to use violence, except in the event of self-defense and a legally declared war by proper civil magistrates. Are they, therefore, left only with what some Christian activists call "a smile and a 'God loves you'"?
>
> No. The Bible specifies a special kind of *lawsuit* that can be filed with God against the wicked called a *covenantal lawsuit*. This Biblical concept is consistently used by prophets, many of their books being structured according to the Deuteronomic covenant. With a covenantal lawsuit, however, the five points of covenantalism are all turned toward accusations against lawless covenant-breakers and enemies of the Church, calling down God's sanctions on them. Yes, a covenant lawsuit asked God to *kill* the wicked. God destroys the wicked one of two ways: by conversion or destruction. So, a covenantal lawsuit is not "unloving." But is the *Biblical method for taking dominion when opposition is met!*[15] (Sutton's emphasis)

The fourth part of the lawsuit asks God to pour out His sanctions on the wicked. Deuteronomy tells how God "blesses" and "curses." Both should be asked for, but in the case of the lawsuit, the specific curses should be requested and mentioned. Also, it should be kept in mind that Revelation speaks of "plagues" that are not referred to in Deuteronomy. These would also be appropriate sanctions to ask for.[16]

According to Sutton's rule, the "covenant lawsuit" is not necessarily reserved for the time after the Church has taken dominion over the earth. It may be implemented now in order to take dominion over any individual or aspect of the world system.

If I remember correctly, didn't Jesus tell us to turn the other cheek? Didn't He also tell us to love our enemies? In fact, He commanded us not only to love them, but to do good to them. (Matthew 5:44).

Converting them is doing good; I'd agree with that. But killing them by calling down God's wrath upon them? Didn't Jesus rebuke His disciples for wanting to call fire down from heaven to consume His enemies? His rebuke should end the argument:

> *Ye know not what manner of spirit ye are of.*
> *For the Son of man is not come to destroy men's lives, but to*
> *save them.* (Luke 9:55-56)

The disciples had even appealed to the precedent set by Elijah. They had an Old Testament model to fall back on. Jesus had to remind them that He had not come to destroy His enemies, but to save them. The dominionists want to do all the works that Jesus did; but this one escapes them.

Would not their thinking be considered returning evil for evil?

Yet I think I understand better the reasoning behind Lester Sumrall's testimony of how he called down God's curse upon a bank that refused to negotiate with his son David over an excessive interest rate for a church building project in the Philippines.

Although Sumrall is a charismatic, and not a Reconstructionist, I include his words here because they demonstrate Sutton's "covenant lawsuit" principle, and they illustrate how little difference there is in the mindset of both:

> When the bank would not listen to him, I told David, "They cannot take our building. Have the congregation curse that bank in the name of God the Father, God the Son and God the Holy Ghost." Although the bank did not believe in God or what we were doing, they are out of business today.[17]

According to Sumrall, the payments were being raised based on a higher interest rate. Such a rate could not be implemented unless the terms of the mortgage contract allowed for it. This would have to have been agreed to by the church when it entered into the contract. Can Christians make agreements and then, when they find that they've hurt themselves, blame the other party? Sumrall mentions also that they had not only cursed the bank but the leaders of the bank. Some questions arise:

Did the leaders of the bank die or suffer other calamities? If not, how does he reconcile that the curse worked on the bank and not the bankers? If the curse was invoked under the authority to bind and loose, as Sumrall claims elsewhere in his account, then it must work with consistency. Does not the curse upon the bankers violate God's law for the Church that we not return evil for evil? Some in the Church are taking on more than the Lord intended.

We know that, as joint heirs with Christ, we will share in the Kingdom of God. But to attempt to grasp too much too soon is disobedience, which incurs the penalties under the covenant into which we have entered. Dominionists must repent of their desire to possess the land before God's time or they will remain outside the covenantal blessings. This may or may not mean loss of salvation, but at the least it will mean loss of rewards under the covenantal possession when it does occur.

CHURCH COVENANTS

Christians can generally recognize the overt evils of the world that tempt us to sin. Likewise, we recognize those obvious philosophies that denigrate Christ and lead men into spiritual error. What is not easily discerned is a religious philosophy that contains sufficient truth to gain our confidence while leading us into bondage to the dictates of men and into spiritual error.

This is because religious philosophies cater to an innate desire to prove ourselves worthy to God. By their nature they nullify God's grace and place works of righteousness in its stead. So subtle is this evil that even the most staunch defenders of the biblical doctrine of salvation by grace are seduced into implementing prescribed works not only for their own lives, but for the lives of those under their authority in the Church.

This spirit of religion is the greatest obstacle that we face in perceiving and living in obedience to the will of God. Only in the conquest of that spirit can we exercise true freedom in Christ which guarantees our salvation and allows us to serve Him according to His will, unhampered by the dictates of others.

One expression of the religious spirit is an inflexible liturgy: If we do certain things in certain ways we will grow spiritually,

God will answer our prayers, we will be blessed. The liturgical religious spirit also tells us we must know how to pray by some formula (usually patterned after an amplified version of the Lord's Prayer) in order to be heard by God.

Another expression of the religious spirit afflicts church leaders especially. It tells them they must get their flocks into line in order to please God. It strives for commitments from congregants that they will fully support the pastor's programs and vision virtually at all costs to personal freedom.

It isn't that these leaders are evil. Many are trying to do the best they can to disciple those under their care. But their perception of religious duty exceeds that of Scripture. They require conformity to their programs and uniformity of expression rather than unity of the Spirit and exercising of one's freedom in Christ. They perceive it their duty to line the sheep up and drill them on their responsibilities to the leadership.

Total Commitment

The Christian's commitment to Christ is to be total. But one's definition of total commitment to Christ might vary from person to person. Many leaders perceive total commitment to Christ as total commitment to their church or parachurch ministry. It is seen as a willingness to forego all for the benefit of the leader's vision, even by those whose labors are voluntary. Just as many corporations require those who would move up the corporate ladder to subordinate their personal and family responsibilities to those of the corporation, many pastors require their congregants to subordinate everything to the church.

Those who cannot or will not fall into line, forsaking even their own family's needs for the pastor's vision, are considered uncooperative and often treated as second-class church citizens. They are made to feel guilty or fearful of God's judgment for their failure to perform to the standards set by their pastor.

Pastors often don't understand why their congregants aren't as committed as *they* are to the church. They wonder why others can't make all of the meetings or get involved in all the things pastors like to see their leaders involved in. What those who make such demands seem not to realize is that it's easy to make the church one's life when the church is the provider of one's livelihood. It's another thing to have to work in the world every day, meet the needs of personal and family obligations, and still give a substantial amount of one's income and time to the church.

Most pastors don't have another job to consume their time. The meetings *are* their job. By and large the programs are *their* programs. The churches revolve around *their* schedules. This isn't the way it should be, but for the most part this is the way it is. Consequently, the less "cooperation" leaders get, the more they feel they must implement programs to ensure cooperation. The religious spirit glories in such a setting.

The Old Face

The Shepherding-Discipleship movement, which attained its greatest impetus during the 1960s and 1970s, exemplifies the manifestation of the religious spirit. In its implementation of discipleship toward a goal of developing holiness in the lives of its adherents, this movement destroyed marriages, split churches, induced poverty, and ruined the faith of many.

No one could make a move without the approval of their shepherd. Everyday decisions involving shopping for personal needs, what to wear, and with whom to associate came under the scrutiny of the shepherd. What had started as an attempt to build maturity in individual Christians' lives became the means to stifle spiritual growth and subordinate people to the whims of self-appointed prophets. The leaders of the movement failed to realize (or chose not to consider) that those they led were not *their* disciples, but *Jesus'* disciples.

The broken lives and resulting scandals that rocked the movement eventually caused those who initiated it to back off for awhile. But although the movement died in name, the spirit behind it lives on, and many of those who initiated the Shepherding-Discipleship movement are today working to implement their ideas among established churches.

The New Face

In the past the religious spirit of Shepherding-Discipleship was confined primarily to small cell groups which operated under extreme authoritarianism working autonomously from the established churches. Today it has gained ascendancy within the denominations and among many independent churches, both charismatic and fundamentalist. Within this new context Shepherding-Discipleship is called covenantalism. Its focus is, as before, on small home groups, but this time under the sponsorship of churches. Thus it has gained a respectability and acquired the confidence of pastors that it lacked in its previous life. In fact, covenantalism is increasing at a rapid pace among thousands of churches in the United States, and abroad.

Underlying the philosophy of covenantalism is a dominionist mindset which perceives the Church's mission as one of conquest over the nations. It is believed by those at the forefront of the covenant movement that the Great Commission is a mandate for the Church to take dominion over the governments of the world. This cannot be done unless a sufficient number of Christians submit to apostolic authority.

It is significant that Charles Simpson, one of the leaders of the old Shepherding-Discipleship movement, is the founder and Chairman of the Fellowship of Covenant Ministers and Churches (FCMC), headquartered in Orlando, Florida. One of FCMC's purposes is to promote covenantalism with the goal of establishing pastors as the disciplers of a dominionist agenda.

Ern Baxter, Simpson's old associate in the Shepherding-Discipleship movement, and a former associate of William Branham, is an Advisor to FCMC. In its first two years of operation, that organization has granted membership to some 120 churches as well as many independent ministries, and is growing steadily.

Although covenantalism originated in Shepherding-Discipleship, it has been adopted by non-charismatic dominion-oriented churches, particularly those that recognize its compatibility with the Reconstructionist cause.

A Special Appeal

According to the thinking of those at the forefront of covenantalism, dominion cannot be achieved without worldwide evangelism which, in turn, is dependent upon a sufficient number of Christians being groomed to "take their communities and nations by force." This does not mean preaching the Gospel, although that is a part of the program. Rather, it means taking control of the spiritual and temporal forces that govern the world system. By its very nature it is ecumenical and concerned more with establishing a society based on biblical ethics than on true righteousness in the hearts of individuals.

What seems to appeal the most to pastors is the idea that covenantalism implemented through home cell groups can result in growth for their ministry. Recognizing that the pulpit ministry is insufficient to build membership and to meet the needs of the people, they have come to realize that close-knit home fellowships can be used to their benefit.

The idea of home fellowships which form the nucleous of a congregation is in itself not wrong. In fact, it's a step in the right direction. Where those who promote covenantalism err is in requiring that those involved in the home fellowships meet certain standards that are not delineated in Scripture, but are outgrowths of the religious spirit of the Shepherding-Discipleship philosophy.

Those who would take the role of shepherd in these home cell groups must first demonstrate their loyalty to the pastor's vision, and a willingness to move those he disciples in the direction the pastor deems appropriate. In essence, the home fellowships are for the benefit of the congregation only to the degree that they benefit the pastor's programs. If any spiritual benefit is realized by an individual it is certainly acceptable and even touted as a reason for others to join. But if the leadership is not also benefitted the home fellowships are often dismantled or imbued with an even stricter authoritarian structure.

Proper application of God's grace nurtures an individual's freedom in Christ. The demands of leadership should be confined to those prescribed by Scripture, and should concern themselves with confronting sin and exhortation to service toward one another. No one should infringe upon the freedom in Christ to which all believers are entitled. At the same time, however, Church authority should be ready to implement discipline where discipline is needed, not for the sake of their own egos or to implement their programs, but with a humble caring for the spiritual benefit of those under their care. There should be no demands for performance according to the standards of men, regardless of how good they seem.

Written Covenants

The new method of implementing Shepherding-Discipleship in the churches is to require members to sign covenants with the pastor wherein they agree to perform certain duties in order to be considered in good standing. Among other duties, these include:

- commitment to a small group headed by one who has previously covenanted with the pastor to follow his "vision";
- commitment to hold one another accountable for their personal lives;
- commitment to tithe to the church;
- commitment to a minimum standard and time of prayer;
- commitment to consistent and faithful attendance at services and meetings.

No one would disagree that these are noble goals. But covenantalism by its very nature induces compulsion upon those who fall victim to it. Once a covenant is signed it is difficult to break without terrible feelings of guilt and fear at having failed not God, but the men to whom the allegiance was given.

It is not difficult to see that at the heart of these covenants is a shepherding mindset that gives leaders a psychological edge in herding the sheep into line with their "visions."

The Coalition on Revival (COR), headquartered in Mountain View, California, is an organization actively working to implement covenantalism in the churches. This is evidenced in the COR Covenant as well as many of its documents. (We examine COR in our next chapter.) In its sphere document, "The Christian World View of Pastoral Renewal," COR addresses the pastors vision:

> We affirm that every pastor, to accomplish his task and stay encouraged, needs to surround himself with a few trustworthy and loyal men from among his church's leaders who are in the process of catching his vision for their church and are eager to play their part in it and to be discipled by him in how to be Christ-centered, Bible-obeying men of God.[18]

> Local pastors and seminary administrators must be made aware of the pastor's need to create around himself a loyal, faithful band of elders and staff who are committed to his vision for their church and to helping that vision be accomplished, and who are being discipled by that pastor.[19]

There is no scriptural precedent for a pastor to "surround himself with a few trustworthy and loyal men" to catch his "vision." This is priestcraft. "Visions" for pastors invariably mean programs for growth in attendance. The more people one can get to sit in his pews and listen to him the more success he feels he has attained. And if church covenants can be used to garner loyalty to his programs so much the better. This evil has taken root because pastors have not examined their own motives in implementing their particular "vision."

The head of the Church is Jesus, not the pastor. Yet the approach of COR, and that of covenantalism in general, is based on the assumption that every pastor's vision is from God, and that most if not all pastors are de facto qualified to disciple others.

One of the paramount visions promoted among pastors by COR and other leaders of covenantalism is the taking of dominion over their communities and nations. This involves social action based upon the philosophical underpinnings of the religious right, and may include anything from protesting abortion and pornography to support of the free enterprise system and a strong military. One who holds a liberal viewpoint on economics, the military, or other non-scripturally mandated agendas, would not be considered in submission to Christ.

The answer to spiritual growth does not lie in tying Christians to their pastor's vision. It lies in an example of humility demonstrated by church leadership (the same example Jesus gave us). If all our churches were led by God-ordained elders in mutual submission to one another, and to whom the pastors were in submission, there would be fewer splits. There would be less idolization of proud men who speak great, swelling words that sway congregations to support their "visions." And there would be many who would seek to emulate Christ as they see their leaders emulate Him.

Compulsion

The requirement to submit to a pastor's vision induces compulsion and robs people of the experience of learning to submit to Christ in a spirit of humility. As one grows in his faith he comes to understand by the prompting of the Holy Spirit that his service in the Body of Christ should be generous—even sacrificial. Except in those situations clearly delineated by Scripture, if a person is disobedient to the Spirit's prompting in a given situation it is up to God, not the Church, to chasten him. And it is up to God, not the Church, to place upon his heart how much he should give in time, money and effort in his service to the Church.

Requiring congregants to sign a covenant that they will tithe or perform other stints of duty puts them under compulsion, particularly if they feel their tithe isn't being used properly or the ministry of the fellowship is lacking.

While it may legitimately be said that how one handles his money and his time reflects the depth of his commitment to Christ, it is up to no man to judge someone on the basis of how much he gives or how much he serves. In fact, pastors should encourage congregants to give secretly so no one can judge them in the matter but the Father who sees in secret (Matthew 6:2-4).

As much as possible, this same principle should apply to all our service. Signing covenants does not allow for privacy of one's benevolence, but makes an open show of it. The act in itself promotes a sense of pride in those who sign it, and leadership's disillusionment with those who do not sign it. The danger of ostracism and divisiveness among the brethren is increased when they are separated into the classes of those who do and those who do not sign a covenant. Should one not sign the covenant he is often looked upon as unsuited for ministry or for receiving the full benefits of the church's services. Those who do not agree to attend a minimum number of services or other church functions are discouraged from being involved at all, and are looked upon as second-class church members.

This approach disdains the personal freedom and the individual needs of the members. It says that their commitment to Christ isn't sufficient to allow them good standing in the congregation; they must make a special commitment to the pastor's vision.

The Taking Of Oaths

Once a person takes an oath (and that is what a covenant is) he is bound before God to fulfill that oath. The guilt and fear that comes from failure to perform can haunt people for the rest of their lives. Pastors who require the brethren to sign covenants in order to be considered in good standing are not acting in their best interests. They are acting contrary to Christ's admonition against the taking of oaths, which He stated in Matthew 5:33-37:

> *Again, ye have heard that it hath been said by them of old time, Thou shalt not forswear thyself, but shalt perform unto the Lord thine oaths:*
>
> *But I say unto you, Swear not at all; neither by heaven; for it is God's throne:*
>
> *Nor by the earth; for it is his footstool: neither by Jerusalem; for it is the city of the great King.*
>
> *Neither shalt thou swear by thy head, because thou canst not make one hair white or black.*
>
> *But let your communication be, Yea, yea; Nay, nay: for whatsoever is more than these cometh of evil.*

The Lord knows our weaknesses. Yet in spite of His prohibition against oaths, He requires us to be true to our word. Failure brings God's judgment upon the swearer.

It is argued that these covenants are merely reaffirmations of what the people already promised God when they came to Christ. But this is not true. A reaffirmation of faith does not require oaths to tithe or become involved in social action. To belong to the Body of Christ does not require oaths or signed covenants with men. We reaffirm our faith daily by personal commitment to God's will for our lives, not by commitment to men's religious ideas. Why should Christians be required to sign covenants in order to receive the full benefits of the ministry or to be considered worthy of leadership?

Can a minister really have at heart the interests of those he serves if he does not warn them of the danger of entering into covenants, let alone requiring them to do so? Is he really interested in their spiritual growth if he hides from them the danger of commitment to men, all of whom are at best untrustworthy?

Additionally, those who are new in the Faith may be threatened by the extreme authoritarianism characteristic of covenantalism. How difficult it would be to win souls if, in addition to the scriptural requirements to which they may be expected to adhere upon giving their lives to Christ, we saddled them with the obligation to tithe and support the vision of a pastor they don't even know.

A Matter Of Trust?

Those who require their followers to sign covenants often ask them to trust that they have their best interests at heart. Yet trust is a two-way street. If someone has confessed Jesus and kept his testimony pure, the leadership should trust him without requiring him to sign a covenant. He is accountable to the New Covenant.

As for pastors, we should trust them as long as they do not betray that trust. But we should not be so foolish as to risk our birthright at their hands. Short-term commitments to some enterprises may be acceptable, but long-term commitments apart from those ordained by God's Word, such as marriage, are foolish.

Commitment to a pastor cannot be equated with commitment to Jesus. If we are truly committed to Christ we will be committed to all our brethren including our pastors; but we must be ever aware that men may fail us no matter how godly they seem. And it may not be their fault that they fail us; if we put unreasonable demands on them we can be sure that they *will* fail us.

Many pastors are doing their best to minister in love; not all are self-serving. In many cases pastors appear self-serving because they learned their job from seminaries or Bible colleges that promulgate the philosophies of religious establishments.

If we choose to fellowship under a particular leadership we must support that leadership in its efforts to serve the brethren. Let us offer help to them rather than tear them down because we disagree with some methodology that is not addressed in Scripture, as long as it is not abusive of one's personal freedom in Christ. We can learn to work within any structure not in conflict with Scripture. And the leadership should be supported to the fullest extent. But each person must be the judge of that extent. Covenants not expressly sanctioned in Scripture are not of God, but are born of a religious spirit that seeks to rob people of their liberty in Christ.

CONCLUSION

Although we are expected to judge the teachings and the actions of all within the Church, including those who lead us, we must be careful to grant to them their own freedom in Christ to serve Him the best they know how. Our attitude must be one of humility and kindness predicated upon love for those under whose authority we have placed ourselves. Yet the fact remains that there are evil men in positions of leadership in the Church. Upon such, God has already pronounced His judgment:

> *Thus saith the Lord God unto the shepherds; Woe be to the shepherds of Israel that do feed themselves! should not the shepherds feed the flocks?*

> *Ye eat the fat, and ye clothe you with the wool, ye kill them that are fed: but ye feed not the flock. . . .*
>
> *Therefore, ye shepherds, hear the word of the Lord;*
>
> *As I live, saith the Lord God, surely because my flock became a prey, and my flock became meat to every beast of the field, because there was no shepherd, neither did my shepherds search for my flock, but the shepherds fed themselves, and fed not my flock;*
>
> *Therefore, O ye shepherds, hear the word of the Lord;*
>
> *Thus saith the Lord God; Behold, I am against the shepherds; and I will require my flock at their hand, and cause them to cease from feeding the flock; neither shall the shepherds feed themselves any more; for I will deliver my flock from their mouth, that they may not be meat for them.* (Ezekiel 34:2-10)

How aptly this Scripture applies to those who require covenants in order to bring the sheep into line with their "vision."

In their desire to keep the sheep from straying they herd them into pens rather than allow them to enjoy the wide pastures of God's grace and freedom in Christ. If they would tend the sheep within the boundaries of the pasture, rather than herd them into pens to feed on the grist of theological biases of what constitutes "Christian duty," they would prove themselves pastors worthy of the Lord's favor.

5
Coalition On Revival
Putting Feet on the Dominion Agenda

Among the dominion-oriented organizations having a profound impact on many churches is Coalition on Revival (COR). COR was founded in 1984 by Dr. Jay Grimstead, a former Executive Director of the International Council on Biblical Inerrancy. It isn't that we want to pick on COR particularly, but COR has not only articulated the dominionist agenda so well, it is militantly putting feet on that agenda. In the process, it is acting as a melting pot for Charismatic Dominionists and Reconstructionists.

It was Dr. Grimstead's concern over liberal attitudes toward essential doctrines of Christianity—biblical inerrancy, the Virgin Birth, the deity of Christ, etc.—that led him to institute COR.

COR is a coalition of some 500 Christian leaders from a wide spectrum of denominations, whose original purpose was to create a consensus statement on how the Christian worldview applies to seventeen spheres of life and ministry: Law, Government, Economics, Business, Education, The Arts and Communications, Medicine, Psychology and Counseling, Science and Technology, Church Unity, Evangelism, Discipleship, Helping the Hurting, Social/Political Action, Revitalizing Christian Colleges and Seminaries, The Family, and Pastoral Renewal. Seventeen editorial committees worked for three years to create these documents.

Since its inception COR has taken a new direction that has created considerable alarm among many Christians who would otherwise be pliant supporters of COR's agenda.

Rather than maintaining the role of merely defining the Christian worldview as a consensus of varied thought within the Christian community, COR has determined that it is mandatory for all Christians to implement that worldview in society, particularly as it applies to the dominionist interpretation of the Great Commission. According to Article 38 of "The Essentials of a Christian Worldview of the Coalition on Revival,"

> We affirm that it is always the obligation of believers to participate in promoting good government. We deny that a Christian can fully discharge his duty to God apart from social, cultural, and political action aimed at influencing society for God and for human good.

Without qualifiers to the terms, "always the obligation of believers," or "a Christian can[not] discharge his duty" unless he involves himself in social, cultural, and political action, such a statement disqualifies not only the Apostles, but Jesus. There is no scriptural or historical evidence that Jesus, His disciples, or the first-century Church ever engaged in cultural or political action.

This isn't to say that, insofar as God permits, Christians may not become involved in social, cultural or political action, but it is a serious infringement upon one's freedom in Christ when leaders place the onus of their own political convictions upon him.

In the face of unfavorable reaction COR would have us believe that it has qualified the dominionist mandate:

> Pre-, a- and post-millennialists are cooperating with each other, sharing the exciting task of getting God's will to be done on earth as it is in heaven insofar as that is possible between now and whenever Christ comes back to Earth.[1]

Even the qualifier, "insofar as that is possible," is consistent with dominionist thinking. Many dominionists believe that total control will not occur until Jesus returns. But they do believe that sufficient control will be gained to keep the ungodly in check and to be able to turn the earth over to Jesus. So even this qualifier does not sufficiently offset the dominionists' influence. And influence in COR the dominionists do have.

DOMINION INFLUENCES IN COR

While COR states that its philosophy developed as a result of input by some 500 Christian leaders of varying backgrounds, those 500 played minor parts during the primary stages of the documents' development; most are not actually members of COR.

The initial input for COR's sphere documents was in the hands of its Steering Committee, at one time comprised of 112 men and women of varied theological backgrounds. Approximately 25% of the Steering Committee members openly subscribe to the dominionist mandate.

But the real influence as far as the documents' final form is concerned has been the Editorial Committee comprised of Jay Grimstead, Dennis Peacocke, Bob Mumford, Cal Beisner, Gleason Archer, Gary DeMar, Larry Walker, Bob Simonds, Duane Gish, and Henry Krabbendam. Grimstead, Peacocke, Mumford, DeMar, and Walker are admitted Reconstructions; Mumford and Peacocke are strong Shepherding-Discipleship advocates and seem to cross the line between Charismatic Dominionism and Reconstruction. Bob Simonds agreed with the original intent of COR, but wrote to Grimstead in June 1986, warning him about dominion theology and encouraging him to keep COR pure from its influence.

With 25% of the Steering Committee and 50% of the Editorial Committee comprised of dominionists, it was inevitable that the dominionist mandate would find its way into the COR documents. Although Grimstead did make attempts to pass the documents by those who would normally oppose the dominionist position for their input, the response was minimal compared to that of the dominionists. So the dominionists may have been outnumbered, but they were more conscientious in seeing that their viewpoint was heard. And the fact is that most theologians and religious leaders are not schooled in the language of dominion theology and thus would be unable to spot it unless it was pointed out to them.

Grimstead claims that only nine of the original 112 members of COR's Steering Committee are postmillennialists. But this is begging the question. Postmillennialism is not the issue; the dominionist mandate is the issue, and this transcends postmillennialism. There are many dominionists (including Jay Grimstead himself) who are premillennialists—what Gary North likes to call "operational postmillennialists."

In view of the dominionists' militancy, COR is tailor-made for establishing a dominionist worldview under the aegis of a coalition of varied opinions. I am not suggesting a conspiracy; the dominionists have been very open about their intentions. But those who comprise half of COR's Editorial Committee have obviously influenced the outcome of the final documents, as we shall see.

COR'S SPHERE DOCUMENTS

COR's sphere documents offer strong evidence that COR has taken a turn from its original intent and become an activist organization heavily influenced if not controlled by dominionists. The language of the COR documents is replete with dominion clichés, and is particularly Reconstructionist in its tone.

The COR documents we are about to examine reveal only some of the dominionist influences in that organization. There are far too many to cite here.

The Christian World View of Social, Political and Moral Issues

Ray Allen, Chairman; Marshall Foster, Co-Chairman

Article 5a:

> We affirm that man is depraved as a result of original sin
> (Romans 5); that man's fallen nature, essentially exploitative
> and self-centered, requires restraining by God's Law (Romans
> 7); and that that Law must be either written internally and
> enforced by the Holy Spirit (Romans 2:14,15), or written exter-
> nally and enforced by legitimate authority (Romans 13:1-7).

Using Romans 7 to assert that man's fallen nature requires
restraining by God's Law is an inaccurate assessment of that chapter. Paul was merely speaking of how the Law reveals our ungodliness and how, after we come to Christ, we are free from the curse
of the Law. His words weren't meant to be construed that the Law
is to be implemented in secular society as a means to keep men
under restraint.

Although it's true that the best civil law is based on God's
moral law, the context of Romans 7 has to do with restraint by the
Holy Spirit upon God's people. It has nothing to do with civil law
or the implementation of God's Law (theonomy) in society.

Article 20:

> We deny that God and His truth should ever be separated
> from the State; that absolute separation of Church and State is
> either right or possible; and that Christians should ever be silent
> in the face of evil.

If the Church were in the hands of men possessing absolute
spiritual integrity, all Christians could agree with this statement.
But that is not possible before the resurrection. In any case, this
should put to rest the Reconstructionists' claim that the Church will
not control the government in a theonomic society. Both Ray Allen
and Marshall Foster, co-chairmen of this sphere document, are
Reconstructionists. Their statement reflects the doublespeak mentality of Reconstructionism: the Church will not control the state;
the state will be in the hands of individual Christians who are in
submission to God's Law under Church authorities; the Church
will advise the state.

But if those who control the government are under the control
of the Church, who, in fact, is in control of the government? And
how can God's Law (theonomy) be "enforced" unless the government implements that force. Despite the Reconstructionists' claims
to the contrary, that would be theocracy.

Article 22:

We affirm that Christians must be involved in all processes and offices of civil government in obedience to the Lord Jesus Christ, so that the government may rest upon His shoulders (Isaiah 9:6,7), and that such involvement is part of the Church's prophetic role in society.

Where in Scripture is this "prophetic role" of the Church? It doesn't exist. Where, too, are we commanded to involve ourselves in the political process in order to be "in obedience"? Citing Isaiah 9:6,7 in this context erroneously assumes that the "government" is secular government in this age. No such idea is even implied.

Article 23a:

We affirm that Christians have a duty to pray for those in authority (1 Timothy 2:1-4), to register to vote, to be informed about candidates' stands on issues, to cast their votes faithfully as bond-slaves to Christ, and to be willing to be sent by God into civil government, the political process, or social and moral action.

If COR can affirm the first portion with properly understood Scripture, why is any scriptural reference lacking for the latter portion of this statement? Because none exists. Certainly we must be willing to be sent anywhere by God. But the implication in total is that unless a Christian gets involved in the political process he is being disobedient to God by not fulfilling his "duty." But our freedom in Christ makes this a matter of personal conviction.

Article 23b:

We deny that inactivity, prayer alone, or prayerless activism alone can constitute the faithful exercise of a believer's full Biblical responsibilities.

The rest of this statement aside, it has been God's call upon some to be active prayer warriors alone, with no hint of activism. Prayer alone *can* "constitute the faithful exercise of a believer's full Biblical responsibilities," simply because God may wish an individual to concentrate on prayer to the exclusion of all other works not mandated by Scripture. Note, I said, "not mandated by Scripture," because we do have other responsibilities. But political activism is not mandated by Scripture. And what about those who are physically unable to become politically or socially active?

The Christian World View of Local and World Evangelism

Al Whittinghill, Chairman

Article 21a:

We affirm that the ultimate goal of missions, while generally beginning with evangelism and church planting, goes far beyond this to making disciples of all nations, and that the message of the missionary must be the totality of the gospel and the necessity of Christ's lordship in all of its fullness for all the life of individuals, families, churches, states, and other aspects of society.

If the drafters of this document had omitted the word "states" there would be no quarrel. But nowhere in Scripture are missionaries mandated to even exert influence on states let alone bring them under the lordship of Christ. All states are already under the lordship of Christ whether they realize it or not, or whether or not they are in obedience to Christ.

If, in the course of our work in the world, we can lawfully change government, fine. But we can't invent causes that mandate Christian activism to take over the governments of the world by ignoring Scripture or taking it out of context.

The Christian World View of Helping the Hurting

Gladys Dickelman, Chairman; Robert Martin, Co-Chairman

Preface:

In addition to organizing united efforts to help the hurting, the Church must conform social, economic, legal, educational, medical, and governmental structures to Biblical order. [page 5]

Had COR said "influence" rather than "conform," there would be no quarrel. One word can make a vast difference. Subtle, yet so precise, is this dominionist language.

The Christian World View of Business And Occupations

John Beckett, Chairman; Ted DeMoss, Co-Chairman

Preface:

Because man is under God, as God's image-bearer, he possessed limited sovereignty over nature. Therefore man is responsible, as God's faithful servant, to co-labor with Christ to bring all nature under God's rulership, that His will might "be done, on earth as it is in heaven" (Matthew 6:10). This mandate to subdue the earth (Genesis 1:26-28) was part of God's provision for man in the creation, and was fully affirmed in Jesus Christ's victorious Death and Resurrection, by which His eternal, triumphant reign is established. [page 3]

Again, nature is already under God's rulership. And the earth has always been under the subjection and dominion of man. What they're really saying is that nature must come under *their* dominion. This is not even implied by the Scripture verses they quote.

Summary:

The extension of God's rule is required in all occupations. We are admonished to exercise dominion by taking every part of the world away from the power of Satan and laying it at the feet of our Lord. He then places these areas under our stewardship, rewarding faithful service with trust and increased responsibility: ". . . to whom they entrusted much, of him they will ask all the more" (Luke 12:48).

Again violence is done to Scripture. Luke 12:45-48 deals only with the Lord's return and how He will deal with His servants. For COR to here cite Luke 12:48 gives the erroneous impression that Scripture sanctions the dominion mandate.

The Christian World View of Art And Communication

Theodore Baehr, Chairman; Dave Clark, Co-Chairman

Preface:

God has given all authority in heaven and on earth to His Son, Jesus Christ. Since Jesus Christ is entitled to have lordship over all areas of life, Christians must bring all art and communication under His authority. [page 3]

All art and communication must be brought into captivity to the mind of Christ. [page 4]

Had these statements said Christians must bring *their* art and communication under Jesus' authority there would be no quarrel. But we're not required to bring *all* art and communication under His authority. If we look at what passes for art even in the Christian community we'd have to admit that here, too, the Church needs to get its own house in order before trying to clean up the world.

Article 27a:

We affirm that restoration of art and communication to Christianity is a Biblical mandate. [1 Corinthians 10:31]

Here is another misapplication of Scripture. I Corinthians 10:31 has nothing to do with restoring anything, let alone art and communication, to Christianity:

> *Whether therefore ye eat, or drink, or whatsoever ye do, do all to the glory of God.*

All this Scripture tells us is that whatever we do as Christians we are to do to the glory of God (i.e., not without faith or not with sinful motives). Art and communication cannot be "restored" to Christianity, because it was never the exclusive property of Christianity. In fact, true Christianity has never had a large role in the world system. The question is not one of "restoration," but of taking dominion.

The Christian World View Of Pastoral Renewal

Jay Grimstead, Chairman; Ron Sadlow, Co-Chairman

Article 3b:

We further deny that the majority of pastors can arm themselves properly, get their hearts into proper perspective, or accomplish adequate intercession for their flocks without spending at least one hour per day in prayer.

At the risk of seeming flippant, how can COR take it upon itself to determine what the majority of pastors need in the way of time spent in prayer? And why is this applicable only to the majority? Why is it not applicable to all pastors? For that matter, who has established that one hour is the time required by God, as if they had His mind? Perhaps He requires a minimum of four hours per day. Maybe He just requires thirty-eight minutes and twelve seconds.

COR could have better stated this article in a less stringent fashion: ". . . without spending considerable time (preferably at least one hour) per day in prayer."

This would allow pastors their freedom in Christ to address their needs for personal prayer time according to the leading of the Holy Spirit, while still stressing the importance of a consistent, diligent prayer life.

Article 15a:

We affirm that every pastor, to accomplish his task and stay encouraged, needs to surround himself with a few trustworthy and loyal men from among his church's leaders who are in the process of catching his vision for their church and are eager to play their part in it and to be discipled by him in how to be Christ-centered, Bible-obeying men of God.

Specific Actions, Article 6:

Local pastors and seminary administrators must be made aware of the pastor's need to create around himself a loyal, faithful band of elders and staff who are committed to his vision for their church and to helping that vision be accomplished, and who are being discipled by that pastor.

As stated before, there is no scriptural precedent for a pastor to "surround himself with a few trustworthy and loyal men" to catch *his* vision. This is priestcraft. While we may allow for latitude in the form of authority which has established senior pastors, the fact remains that the head of the Church is Jesus, not the pastor. Many pastors are not even themselves "Christ-centered, Bible-obeying men of God."

If COR wants to get back to biblical basics, it would do well to challenge the present ecclesiastical structure by including in its documents a call for repentance from the ungodly system the churches have operated on for centuries. It would require that all pastors submit themselves to the elders in their churches with a humble spirit ready to receive correction if needed.

Many pastors are being swayed by dominionists to think of themselves as "God's anointed" on the basis that they happen to have been placed in the position of "priest" to some church. They are told that, as "God's anointed," no one is to touch them or challenge their "vision." Those who do—even the elders—are to be dealt with in a manner that will strike fear in the hearts of others.

Media Spotlight receives letters from all over the world testifying of abuse by pastors who have been puffed up at some "pastors' conference" conducted by dominion-oriented teachers. Their congregations live in confusion, and much division has resulted due to the forcing out of the congregation those who perceive error.

COR would do better to phrase Article 15a in this manner:

We affirm that every pastor must be in submission to a body of elders in the congregation of which he is a member.

Apart from administrative duties, he is an elder on a par with the other elders. All elders should share the teaching responsibilities and in cooperative effort seek God's direction for the church body.

Such a statement could help prevent the abuses against God's people that are prevalent in many churches today. A proud pastor who wishes to hold on to his "vision" at the expense of the people's welfare should be left to his own devices. Perhaps he would find it of greater benefit to himself and to the congregation to leave the ministry and go to work in some productive material capacity.

I don't say this to demean pastors. But difficult conditions require difficult words. I have a love for pastors whose hearts are for the people, and who are trying to minister effectively against all the odds devised by an ungodly system. Their health suffers. Their family relations suffer. They take the brunt of attacks from insensitive people who think the pastor is there to wipe their noses day and night.If the pastoral duties were shared by elders of equal standing there would not be these abuses by or against pastors.

It would take a humble man to relinquish his place of pre-eminence for the benefit of the body, but that is the kind of person that would command the loyalty of God's true servants.

Article 16:

> We affirm that, though tithing one's income and material gain may not be commanded in the New Testament, it is a Biblical and wise way to support the church's expenses and outreach.
> We deny that those churches that encourage or require their members to tithe their income to Christ's work on earth are therefore legalistic or unbiblical.

We have a problem here. Article 16 is correct in stating that tithing is not commanded in the New Testament. Yet it also states that it's not legalistic or unbiblical for churches to "require" their members to tithe. What other laws and regulations might a church "require" its members to obey even though Scripture does not require it? All giving should be done without compulsion, cheerfully as God has placed it upon the individual's heart:

> But this I say, He which soweth sparingly shall reap also sparingly; and he which soweth bountifully shall reap also bountifully.
> Every man according as he purposeth in his heart, so let him give, not grudgingly, or of necessity: for God loveth a cheerful giver.
> (II Corinthians 9:6-7)

God may require us to give 1% or 100%, and varying amounts at different times. At times it may be one should give nothing. We have the Holy Spirit to guide us in our service to God. He isn't interested in percentages; He's interested in our heart attitude. If a man gives sparingly he will reap sparingly, whether money or time; but that is between him and his Lord, and no man may compel him to do anything more than the Scriptures require of him in order to be obedient to biblical authority.

In view of the prevalent unscriptural demands placed upon believers today, I would add two more articles to the sixteen in this sphere document. Article 17 would read:

> We affirm that church leadership should encourage members to be generous in their giving, and that all giving should be done in secret according to the Lord's command (Matthew 6:1-4). Thus, the giving of cash or by other means that preserve the privacy of the giver should be encouraged.

Article 18 would read:

> In keeping with I Timothy 5:3-10 and James 1:27, we affirm that every local body has a responsibility to *adequately* support faithful widows, orphans, and others in the fellowship who, for reasons beyond their control, are unable to support themselves.

Specific Actions, Article 7:

> Those pastors and churches that mistakenly think that neither pastors nor churches have any business trying to change society and stand for social righteousness by constitutional means must become exposed to the COR Manifesto and the COR sphere document "The Christian World View of Educating Christians [on] Social, Political, and Moral Issues" in order to disabuse their minds of that false dichotomy.

This is the dominionist commission for the churches, not Christ's.

The Christian World View of the Making of Disciples

Mike Kiley, Chairman; Peter Doane, Co-Chairman

Article 1:

> We affirm that the making of Bible-obeying disciples of all nations and the bringing of all things under the lordship of Christ is the primary purpose and defined objective of the Great Commission (Matthew 28:19,20; 2 Corinthians 10:5).

Do these Scriptures confirm this statement, or are we once again falling under the influence of dominionist doublespeak?

> *Go ye therefore, and teach all nations, baptizing them in the name of the Father, and of the Son, and of the Holy Ghost:*
> *Teaching them to observe all things whatsoever I have commanded you: and, lo, I am with you alway, even unto the end of the world. Amen.* (Matthew 28:19-20)

Dominionists love to quote this Scripture to "prove" that they have a mandate to "disciple" or "discipline" all nations, not just those souls who come to Christ from out of all nations. But if we assume that "teaching" or "discipling" the nations means the governments and institutions of the nations, then so too must these be "baptized." The nations should be "baptized" (i.e., "dunked") in water. Does the latter (baptize) apply only to individuals? Then so too does the former (teach) apply to individuals.

Let's quote II Corinthians 10:5 in context with verses 3 & 4:

> *For though we walk in the flesh, we do not war after the flesh:*
> *(For the weapons of our warfare are not carnal, but mighty through God to the pulling down of strong holds;)*
> *Casting down imaginations, and every high thing that exalteth itself against the knowledge of God, and bringing into captivity every thought to the obedience of Christ.* (II Corinthians 10:3-5)

The full context of these Scriptures covers three chapters (10:1-13:10). These demonstrate that Paul was dealing with sin in the Church and, specifically, those who had challenged his authority as an apostle. He is telling us that Christians are to bring their thoughts into captivity to Christ, and are not to be rebellious against God's authority. Other Scriptures extend this requirement to obedience to secular government regardless of whether or not it is under the dominion of the Church.

Specific Actions, Article 3:

We must launch a program to re-educate the Church about the nature of Christian discipleship that includes the following points: ... Biblical discipleship involves participation in intimate relationships, commitment, confrontation, and accountability. It must reach down into the daily details of life: decision making, finances, relationships, habits, values, etc. Much of what travels under the name of "discipleship training" is merely the transfer of academic Biblical principles from one notebook to another without the essential ingredient of accountability and changes in thought and behavior.

"Intimate relationships?" "Decision making?" "Finances?" "Habits?" "Values?" "Etc.?" What do these entail? Inasmuch as the two co-chairmen for this sphere document are pastors of dominion-oriented churches we can guess what these statements portend: robbery of the Christian's freedom in Christ.

Discipleship must concern itself with correction for sin, and exhortation to good works and sound doctrine. In some cases it may require public repentance, chastizement, and even excommunication. But when men want to control "intimate relationships," they not only can affect, but historically have affected, relationships of husbands, wives, and entire families beyond what is scripturally allowed. It is not unusual for wives to be made subject to their pastors even above their husbands.

Even if the framers of this document adhered to sound scriptural discipling in their own churches, and their intentions were of the holiest nature, the language is far too broad and vague to be of any value to the Body of Christ. In fact, as stated, it opens the door to all sorts of abuses.

For a clear, concise statement outlining the areas of discipleship to which the Church can adhere, this statement should be amended to read:

> Biblical discipleship involves participation in teaching sound doctrine. It also involves nurturing the individual's personal relationship with Christ through discipline of sin as it is clearly defined in Scripture (what is not forbidden by Scripture is not to incur discipline from the Church), exhorting to good works, and developing a sense of freedom in Christ from unwarranted intrusion by Church authority.

It's bad enough that these disciplers infect the believers in their own churches, but COR has given them a platform to infect others with their aberrations:

> For those churches that wish to structure or restructure their congregations along these lines, the names and addresses of churches that are doing this successfully and of parachurch organizations that effectively help churches to accomplish [this] are available from the Coalition on Revival . . . and from various denominational headquarters and seminaries.

The dominionist agenda, including the aberrant philosophy of the Shepherding-Discipleship movement, is sprinkled throughout most of COR's sphere documents and other official publications.

ESCHATOLOGY: A NON-ISSUE?

In COR's "Commitment Sheets For Coalition On Revival Steering Committee Members, Pastors, Parachurch Staff, Key Laymen, and Regional, County, and Local Committee Members," Document #3 contains the following commitment:

> As long as I am a member of the Coalition on Revival (COR) I commit myself to its "Non-Quarreling-Policy" and will refrain from fighting or arguing over the following doctrinal points with other member[s] of the Coalition on Revival.
> 1. Ecclesiology
> 2. Eschatology
> 3. Baptism and Communion
> 4. Calvinism, Arminianism and Dispensationalism
> 5. Christian freedom differences regarding activities which are not forbidden in scripture
> 6. Tongues and other charismatic activity
> 7. Modes of worship and methods of evangelism and follow up
> My commitment to not quarrel over these doctrinal issues is not to say that I do not consider them important, or that my own stand at these points cannot be biblically defended. Rather, my commitment to the "Non-Quarreling-Policy" stems from an understanding that I am not doctrinally omniscient and that it is simply too much to expect other Christians to view all theology exactly as I view it. This liberates me to labor for Christ together with other Christians who know and love God even though our doctrinal views may differ.

While COR requires that eschatology not be made an issue, COR's dominionist perspective de facto makes eschatology an issue. The COR agenda is fraught with eschatological inferences via the dominionist influences. Because its documents reflect the dominionist agenda, in essence COR is endorsing a particular eschatological viewpoint: the dominionist allegation that Jesus cannot or will not return until the Church establishes dominion over the world system, if not wholly, at least in part.

Regardless of one's millennial position, the dominion mandate cannot be separated from eschatology. Even Gary North refers to the "eschatology of dominion,"[2] proving that, at least as far as some dominionists are concerned, dominionism is in itself an eschatological position. Thus, by adopting dominion theology to any degree, COR has indeed demonstrated a bias toward a particular eschatology. More than this, it has mandated the adoption of that eschatology in order to be in harmony with the "Christian World View."

In spite of COR's claim that eschatology is not to be a factor in the development of its worldview, eschatology did become an issue for several of COR's Steering Committee members. This resulted in several notable Christian leaders leaving COR. These included Dr. Norman Geisler (Professor of Systematic Theology at Dallas Theological Seminary), Jimmy Williams (Executive Director of Probe Ministries), Dr. Harold Lindsell (Editor Emeritus of *Christianity Today*), Dr. Joseph Aldrich (President of Multnomah School of the Bible), and others.

Jay Grimstead stated that Dr. Geisler was asked to leave COR because of his "quarreling" over eschatology. But those with whom he was "quarreling" were not asked to leave.

THE MANIFESTO-COVENANT

On July 4, 1986, COR's Continental Congress III was held in Washington, D.C. At the culmination of the Congress a formal ceremony was held on the steps of the Lincoln Memorial, at which fifty members of COR's Steering Committee signed "The Christian Manifesto for the Christian Church, Declaration and Covenant." The Manifesto stated COR's position on where the Church must stand and what action it must take into the next century.

The Manifesto-Covenant that was signed is actually a short version of the larger COR Manifesto, which contains a "boildown" of all seventeen worldview documents. Those who sign it are, in essence, agreeing to all the statements in those documents. But do all the signers realize the implications of the dominion mandate to which they lent their names? Within the Manifesto is "A Solemn Covenant" which binds the signers to live by its terms until death:

> Now, for the Glory of God, having repented of our sin and counted the cost of true discipleship, [remember, "discipleship" according to COR means political activism to take control of society for Christ] willing either to be martyred or to reign with Him, we hereby solemnly covenant with Almighty God and with one another, to live henceforth in full, serious obedience to all the Bible's commands that apply to us today, to the best of our ability and in dependence on the power of the Holy Spirit, from now until the day we die, so help us God.
>
> We hereby voluntarily invite others in the family of God to hold us accountable to live in full obedience to the Bible and to show us with demonstrated love whatever discrepancies they observe between our lives and what is written in the Bible. We submit in advance to Biblical church discipline as described in Matthew 18:15-20.
>
> We commit ourselves, in the presence of God Almighty and of our Christian brothers and sisters:

to live to glorify God and to enjoy Him forever—the chief reasons for our existence in time and eternity;

to offer ourselves as living sacrifices to be used as God wills to build up the Body of Christ on earth that it may become biblical, holy, strong, courageous, unified, and effective in fulfilling its commissioned task on earth;

to do all we can, in the lives of our fellow humans and in the societies in which we live, to see God's will done on Earth as it is in Heaven, insofar as that is possible between now and the physical return of our great God and Saviour Jesus Christ.

Jesus' command in Matthew 5:33-36 is not a suggestion. It is an admonition for His followers not to enter into any oaths either before God or man. It's because He knows our weaknesses that He gave this command for our protection. To fail in the performance of an oath brings God's judgment upon the swearer.

Dying For The Cause

There is another portion of the covenant that we must address: the words, "willing either to be martyred or to reign with Him." "Either"? "Or"? Will not all martyrs reign with Christ? But we see in this language the dominionist mindset, to wit, if we do not take control we must be willing to die. Or, more precisely, we must be willing to die in our attempt to take control. Remember that discipleship, according to COR, requires political activism. What COR is asking of those who sign its covenant is to be willing to die in the attempt to establish a theonomic political state. This statement makes the COR Manifesto-Covenant more than just a covenant; it is a blood covenant, sworn to on the life of the signers.

It has been argued that the Manifesto is nothing more than a reaffirmation of the signers' original commitment to Christ. This simplistic answer does not recognize the unscriptural elements to which the signers of the Manifesto bind themselves.

The Manifesto in its entirety incorporates the "Christian World View" contained in the seventeen sphere documents and the "42 Articles" that comprise the "Essentials of a Christian World-view." Thus, the signers of the Manifesto endorse these documents and, in effect, bind themselves to live by them. To speak against any of them would constitute a breach of their oath before God. The Covenant, therefore, is an instrument that can be used to silence dissent and burden with guilt those whose eyes become opened.

In spite of the dangers inherent to taking oaths, COR is determined to have as many pastors as possible sign the Manifesto-Covenant and, in turn, have their congregations sign it. The potential for damage to the Body of Christ is incalculable.

THE "NON-NEGOTIABLES"

The original purpose of COR was to develop a consensus of a Christian worldview to which all Christians could subscribe. The final documents were to reflect those things that are essential and non-negotiable to the Faith. This is why COR likens its *42 Articles of Affirmations and Denials* to Luther's "Ninety-five Theses" that sparked the Reformation. COR claims that it is nailing a new, more complete form of Luther's Theses to the door of the modern Church. The final result, however, is far more than a consensus; it is an intrusion into the individual Christian's relationship with the Father. If an individual does not adhere to the COR's essential and non-negotiable dominionist pronouncements he has denied the Faith. This may not be Grimstead's understanding, but that's what is meant by the terms "essential" and "non-negotiable" when it comes to the Faith.

In regard to these "essential" and "non-negotiable" elements, there are several matters which require our attention. Remember that the 42 Articles contained in this document are, in COR's words, "essential" and "non-negotiable" for Christians. "Essential" and "non-negotiable" means that one is not a Christian if he does not subscribe to them. Well, here are some "non-negotiables" with which many Christians would take issue:

Article 37:

> We deny that any citizen is obliged to obey any government when it transgresses its God given mandate or requires him to disobey God's Laws.

Of course, as stated earlier, if a government requires us to disobey God's laws we must disobey that government. But because a government transgresses its "God given mandate" does not arbitrarily mean we can disobey it.

The problem lies within the definition of "God given mandate." What exactly is God's mandate to government? According to COR it is to administer God's Law (theonomy or theocracy). In this case, no government on earth is fulfilling its "God given mandate." It logically follows, therefore, that all governments as they are presently constituted may be disobeyed if they do not find favor with the dominionist agenda. Romans 13:1-6 makes this Article negotiable at least.

Article 38:

> We affirm that it is always the obligation of believers to participate in promoting good government. We deny that a

Christian can fully discharge his duty to God apart from social, cultural, and political action aimed at influencing society for God and for human good.

I dealt with this Article earlier. This must be negotiable, or COR is imposing upon our brethren obligations that are not clearly stated or required by Scripture.

Although the sphere documents themselves are said by Jay Grimstead to be exempt from the "non-negotiable" and "essential" requirements, he maintains that they must be adhered to by those who sign the Manifesto and Covenant. So while they are not required of the Church at large, they are required of those who would associate themselves with COR.

But remember that COR wants every pastor and congregation to sign this document. If that goal is realized would it not bring the entire Body of Christ under COR's dominionist agenda? Since these documents are fraught with opinion, presenting as biblical truths points of view that have been challenged for years—even centuries—by other Christians, the sphere documents must be addressed under the "essential and non-negotiable" clause as a warning to any who would sign the COR Manifesto and Covenant, even though on the surface they are not part of the 42 *Articles of Affirmations and Denials*.

The Christian World View of Law

Virginia Armstrong, Chairman; Michael Farris, Co-Chairman

In the Preface to this document, reference is made to the "Judeo-Christian jurisprudence of earlier America." This is debatable. Many would say that American jurisprudence, gleaned from English jurisprudence, is more likely predicated upon Roman law than on Scripture. In fact, even America's earlier jurisprudence can be found both compatible and in conflict with Scripture in many areas. But this can be said of every government in the world. All Islamic cultures have a strong moralistic jurisprudence. In some respects their jurisprudence is more "scriptural" than that of earlier America.

This may be regarded as my opinion, but the fact remains that this is a negotiable point.

"The Christian World View of Law" document has many areas that reflect American jurisprudence but which, in other countries, might not be practical or even desirable. For example, as much as Americans would like it to be, "consent of the governed" is not a Scriptural principle. Neither are some of the specific "requirements" of governmental structure.

The Christian World View of Government

Gary DeMar, Chairman; Colonel Doner, Co-Chairman

Article 18b:

We deny that absolute pacifism, which would resist arming local policemen with guns or maintaining a national standing army equipped with the best weaponry available resources can provide, is Biblical.

This is negotiable to many Christians, especially those who abhor the thought of Christians being conscripted to serve in one government's army to kill Christians conscripted into another government's army. This doesn't negate governments having armies, but it is not the business of the Church to define what constitutes God's view of a nation's military posture.

Article 20:

We affirm that civil government has the God-ordained authority to collect personal taxes (not property taxes) to support its Biblically stated jurisdictional duties.

The issue of personal taxes as opposed to property taxes is likewise negotiable to many Christians. Jesus indicated that the children of the Kingdom should not be required to pay civil taxes, but "lest we offend them," He had Peter catch a fish with a coin in its mouth in order to pay the tribute *after* He was confronted for not paying tribute (Matthew 17:24-27).

It isn't that the state has the right to tax God's people, it's that God's people pay taxes in order to set an example of being law abiding. By this we win souls and live at peace. It is also proper to support those who administer the state (Romans 13:6). The type of taxes is not referred to.

In Article 37 of the essential and non-negotiable "42 Articles" of faith, COR said we are not obliged to obey any government when it transgresses its God-given authority. In this "Christian World View of Government," COR says in effect that property taxes are a transgression of God-given authority. Have any of COR's dominionist members surrendered their homes to the state rather than give in to the ungodly property tax? Are they willing to disobey the government and endure suffering in order topioneer righteousness? If not, they have violated the oath of which they were the authors. For if they will not pay with their material goods, how will they pay with their lives?

The Christian World View of Economics

E. Calvin Beisner, Chairman; Daryl Borgquist, Co-Chairman

Article 33:

> We affirm that the God-ordained functions of civil government—law enforcement, defense, the judiciary, and such functions as are necessary in discharging these duties—ought to be provided for by taxation at a uniform percentage rate of the income of its citizens and by uniform user fees for services.

Certainly this is negotiable. I suggest *no* income tax. Can I still be a member of Christ's Body?

Article 23:

> We affirm that the Biblical requirement of giving one tenth of one's net income (tithing) to the Church remains in force under the New Covenant; that the Christian committed to building God's Kingdom ought to go beyond tithing in His giving to the Church insofar as he is able; that he who sows sparingly will reap sparingly; that he who sows bountifully will reap bountifully; that Christian giving should be done voluntarily rather than under coercion; and that God will always provide everything His children need if they seek first His Kingdom and righteousness (2 Corinthians 9:6-11; Matthew 6:33).
>
> We deny that God ceased commanding a tithe from His people with the advent of the New Covenant, and that the voluntary nature of Christian giving excuses refusal to tithe.

This sphere document contradicts the sphere document on Pastoral Renewal. There we are told that tithing is not commanded under the New Testament. Obviously this subject is negotiable.

In fact, this whole Article is negotiable, being designed to propagate a hierarchical structure that is unscriptural. For the most part, churches today do not use the monies received for the purposes God intended. Besides, there were three tithes required under the Law. Perhaps these people should study this subject more before making their pronouncements.

Although they say the tithe is voluntary, they also say it's mandated by Scripture. But the COR philosophy is that whatever is mandated by Scripture is essential and non-negotiable. This requirement to tithe is itself a form of coercion. Also, under a theonomic system the tithe would have to be enforced. It would then become a tax to keep the churches solvent.

The Christian World View of Science And Technology

Duane Gish, Chairman; Arthur C. Cunningham, Co-Chairman

Article 15:

> We affirm that the genealogical histories recorded in the Bible, as well as many physical time clocks, indicate that the earth is young.
>
> We deny that Biblical history and empirically verifiable physical processes establish an age of either the earth or the universe on the order of billions of years (Luke 3:23-38).

Luke 3:23-38 merely records the genealogy of Jesus from the time of Adam. It does not tell us how old the earth is. There are many Christians who would find these statements negotiable based on the idea that the Earth was not created void and without form, but became (Hebrew, *hayah*) void and without form. From the time of the *re-creation*, or *refurbishing*, of the heavens and the earth, it would appear to be young. But there is scientific evidence to support the idea that the earth and the universe *are* billions of years old. At the least this is negotiable.

There are other "negotiable" points that are too numerous to mention here. And in spite of the narrow parameters established by COR, most Christians would not be so narrow in dealing with them. On most of these points that COR has deemed "non-negotiable," I would have no problem with anyone who did not agree with me. Why is it necessary to establish non-negotiable tenets that Scripture does not even address, then imply that those who do not agree with them have denied the Faith?

COR'S POSITION PAPER ON THE KINGDOM OF GOD

Due to concern among some of COR's non-dominionist members it was necessary for Jay Grimstead to call for a position paper to address the subject of the Kingdom of God. This presents a good lesson in futility due to the inflexible positions taken by both sides on certain dominion-oriented elements within the paper. Because of this, there is doubt that it can ever be finalized. Some points of contention, taken from the initial draft of the position paper follow:

> **We affirm** (a) that the New Testament phase of the Kingdom of God was inaugurated in fact and in history at Jesus' first coming to earth, and (b) that it now operates in reality and power among men in this present age.

We deny that the Church must await the second coming of Christ for the Kingdom of God to be inaugurated on earth in time-space reality and in power. [page 3]

We affirm (a) that the Bible reveals God's intentions for the growth of His Kingdom in all nations of the earth during this present age through the proclamation and obedient application of His stated will in Scripture, and (b) that His intention includes the increasing manifestation of His rule over individuals, voluntary associations, families, the church, the state, and all spheres of human activity, some of which are law, government, economics, business occupations, education, sports, medicine, science, technology, arts, and media.

We deny that God's rulership is limited to transforming only the private lives of individuals to His will. [page 4]

We affirm that Christ alone, as representative man and last Adam, by His life, death, resurrection, and ascension to the throne at the right hand of the Father, accomplished redemption, the defeat of Satan, and the beginning of the restoration of man's godly dominion over the earth as God's vice-regent.

We deny that the restoration of man's God-ordained dominion (a) lies outside the scope of Christ's redeeming work as mediator on the Cross, or (b) awaits the physical presence of the returned Christ for its inauguration and expansion.

We affirm (a) that Jesus, the Son of David and Son of God, was given all authority in heaven and on earth by God the Father; (b) that after His ascension He sat down on the throne at the right hand of God; (c) that from this position of absolute authority in the universe He is bringing all things into submission under His feet, exercising His authority ever more widely and fully on earth as the gospel spreads and people are converted to Him; and (d) that His exercise of that authority will become more fully manifest after His second coming.

We deny that Christ will ever be given more power or authority over the earth than He was given at His first coming. [page 5]

We affirm (a) that when people—individuals or societies, Christian or non-Christian—generally follow, consciously or unconsciously, the moral, economic, and practical commands of the Bible, they tend to reap earthly blessings as a result, and (b) that when people generally fail to follow the moral, economic, and practical commands of the Bible, they tend to reap earthly judgments as a result.

We deny (a) that God will forever allow people to sow the wind without reaping the whirlwind, and (b) that obedience guarantees the believer whatever he claims from God. [page 10]

As usual the dominionist influences in COR stress orthodoxy over Scripture. But orthodoxy to the dominionist applies to Roman Catholicism as well as to the first three centuries of Church history. So they can point to "orthodoxy" to prove that their dominion mandate is historical. As previously stated, that mandate is a revival of the papal mandate implemented through the Holy Roman Empire. But there are no definitive Scriptural references that can be cited to support their position.

Surprisingly, there are some non-dominionist voices still left working within COR to offset the dominionist influences. Were it not for them, COR's position paper would be pure Reconstructionist in its language. Other portions of the paper were altered somewhat to leave ambiguous wording that could be interpreted according to one's particular understanding. But whether future work on the paper will ever resolve these areas of dispute may depend upon one side or the other walking out.

KINGDOM COLLEGE

If there is any question that, in spite of the efforts of good men to the contrary, COR has adopted a dominionist agenda, its creation of Kingdom College should put them to rest. Kingdom College, an outreach of COR, has as its purpose to "help recreate a generation of Christians who will systematically and effectively rebuild their civilization on Biblical principles."[3]

Restrictive Requirements

At the time of this writing, the suggested requirements for enrollment into Kingdom College are stringent, and designed to keep all but the most militant dominionists out. The student must provide "his own statement of his testimony and his reasons for wanting to participate in a 'world-changer' training school and his estimate as to his own calling in the Body and his gifts." He must also sign the COR Manifesto, 42 Articles and the Biblical Inerrancy Statement of the International Council on Biblical Inerrancy.

To be absolutely sure that the students are predisposed toward a Reconstructionist mindset, they must have read Gary DeMar's *The Reduction of Christianity*, Francis Shaeffer's *Christian Manifesto*, Greg Bahnsen's *By This Standard*, and Jay Grimstead's own *Let's Have a Reformation*.[4]

Such restrictive requirements will assure that no one who can think for himself will have an opportunity to put the curriculum to the test; the students will already be predisposed toward a dominionist mindset. This also reduces the chance for the curriculum to come under the scrutiny of those who disagree with COR's dominionist agenda.

In addition, COR will institute its own Shepherding program through "personal Christian maturity growth groups," in order to prepare the students to "function productively and effectively as a clear-thinking activist 'world-changer' within any kingdom-oriented church or parachurch ministry."[5] They will network with leaders in some 60 major cities where COR has contacts.[6]

The apprenticeship fields being developed revolve around COR's seventeen spheres of life and ministry.

CONCLUSION

In view of COR's dominionist agenda, and the unscriptural requirements placed upon those who agree to it, I encourage anyone who is approached to sign the COR Manifesto-Covenant to reject it.

PART IV - ESCHATOLOGY

1
Whose Eschatology Is Optimistic?

Reconstructionists and Charismatic Dominionists both accuse those who look for Jesus' soon return of having a pessimistic eschatology, while they themselves lay claim to an optimistic eschatology. If they applied the term "eschatology" properly they would see that it is they who have the pessimistic eschatology.

Eschatology relates to events that are associated with the end of this present age. More specifically, to Christians it relates to the Second Coming of Christ. Now, what is the dominionists' position on the Second Coming of Christ? It is that He will not return until all the nations have come under the control of God's people so they can turn them over to Him. This, some say, could take hundreds of thousands of years.[1]

On the other hand, what is the eschatology of the non-dominionist Christian? It is that Jesus is coming soon to punish the nations and to institute His visible reign on earth. How soon, we don't know, but soon. In the meantime, until He comes we are to occupy and win those who will be saved. How many souls will be converted only He knows, although His Word says there are few who will find salvation (Matthew 7:13-14).

Which is the more optimistic eschatology? One that says we may have to wait hundreds of thousands of years for Jesus to return, or one that says He will return soon according to the signs of the times?

Granted, for the world system the dominionists' eschatology is more optimistic; but for God's people the dominionists' eschatology is pessimistic. What the dominionists propose, in reality, is not an optimistic eschatology, but an optimistic future for the world system. There is a difference. And we shouldn't let them get away with their error any longer. If they don't know the difference between eschatology and science fiction that promises a rosy future for the world system they have no business even attempting to define an eschatological position.

But more to the point, why try to justify any theological belief on optimism? Optimism or pessimism doesn't prove anything. Certainly there is sufficient pessimism in God's Word relative to human nature to tell us that just because one theological or eschatological position lays claim to optimism doesn't necessarily prove that it is true to God's Word. In fact, just the opposite is often true. However, had the dominionists not raised this issue it wouldn't have had to be addressed.

Let's remember Jesus' words that many would take the path of destruction, and few the path of salvation (Matthew 7:13-14). Those who are tempted to think otherwise and fall for the dominionists' misplaced optimism might well consider that the dominionists themselves are an important element in God's prophetic description of the mindset that would prevail just prior to Jesus' return:

> . . . *there shall come in the last days scoffers, walking after their own lusts,*
> *And saying, Where is the promise of his coming? for since the fathers fell asleep, all things continue as they were from the beginning of the creation.* (II Peter 3:3-4)

Jesus also told us that at such an hour that we think not, He will come (Matthew 24:44).

And contrary to the dominionists' statements that the Church has historically been postmillennial, only some have held that view. Many in the Church—particularly the first-century Church revealed in Scripture—looked for Christ's imminent return. John the Revelator, in closing the final book of the Bible, revealed his expectation of the Lord's return:

> *He which testifieth these things saith, Surely I come quickly. Amen. Even so, come, Lord Jesus.*

Would John, inspired by the Holy Spirit of God, call upon Jesus to return quickly were there no expectation of His imminent return?

Yet today the Church is being led away from that expectation. Does this not, in itself, cast some doubt on the validity of any teaching that scoffs at the Lord's soon return?

2
The Kingdom Of God

Much of the confusion engendered by dominion theology has resulted from a lack of proper understanding of just what constitutes the Kingdom of God. This is on the part of both dominionists and those who have opposed them.

Some see the Kingdom of God as something yet to come, which will not be implemented until Jesus returns to the earth. Others see it as a very present reality which was inaugurated at any time from the Lord's birth to Pentecost, depending upon one's particular understanding of the Kingdom. Still others assert that the Kingdom of God is eternal, and that the earth has, from its creation, been under the jurisdiction and influence of the Kingdom.

Few would dispute this last view. Charismatic Dominionists, Reconstructionists, Dispensationalists, and Biblical Realists would not argue that the Kingdom of God is eternal. Why then the confusion? Because it is not the Kingdom of God that must be defined as much as it is how the Kingdom operates from eternity to eternity, including during this present dispensation (sorry, Gary, R.J., et al; dispensation is a valid concept).

It is unfortunate that Reconstructionists and other dominionists do not recognize the validity of the Dispensationalist concept: that God has manifested His will for man through different dispensations. It is also unfortunate that many Dispensationalists have not understood the validity of the covenant concept: that God deals with His people through covenants, and that it is the covenant responsibilities to which we must be answerable regardless of which dispensational period we happen to live in.

The fact is that God's dispensations have operated under different covenants. So again the truth lies between two extremes. But what is most unfortunate is that both Dispensationalists and

Covenantalists perceive both viewpoints relative to the earth rather than to God's Kingdom. It isn't so much that God's dispensations work for the benefit of the earth as it is that they work for the benefit of the Kingdom. The same can be said about His covenants. All things work in accordance with God's plan for His entire Kingdom; the events which transpire upon the earth at His initiation are Kingdom-centered, not earth-centered.

So because the Church at large has viewed the Kingdom of God in terms of its benefit to the earth rather than in terms of the earth's benefit to the Kingdom, those who hold intractable positions on both sides of the eschatological question have proven themselves in error to some degree.

Now, if all things work for the benefit of the Kingdom, if all the nations are already the Lord's, and if it is the Lord who establishes the basest of men over the nations (Daniel 4:17), then what more can be deduced than that human history is going according to God's plan after all? In that case, without a clearly stated mandate for the Church to establish dominion in this age over the kingdoms of the world, the best the dominionists have to offer is inference, allegory, and personal conviction. And as Rushdoony has said, "not even a valid inference is a commandment."

All we know about the Kingdom of God is what Scripture reveals. To add to or to subtract from what the Scriptures clearly state (and there is much that is revealed therein), is mere conjecture to which the Body of Christ must not be held accountable.

There are various designations of God's Kingdom in Scripture: the Kingdom of God, the Kingdom of Heaven, and the Kingdom of Christ. Some say these are all the same, while others make distinctions.

The Eternal Kingdom

Although there are those who contend that the Kingdom of God had a beginning (during Christ's sojourn on earth), by its very name the Kingdom of God implies an eternal Kingdom—without beginning or end—as ancient as the Ancient of Days. As long as God has existed the Kingdom of God must have existed, even if within that Kingdom there were no subjects yet created. This is simply because God, being eternal, dwells in a timeless reality. He sees the beginning from the end without respect to what we would consider "the present." Yet I would not contend for this beyond what I've stated here. More importantly, we must see that the Kingdom of God was a reality before Jesus came on the scene.

The Kingdom of God did not begin with the birth of Jesus, or at Pentecost, or any time in between. Rather, we find it revealed in the Old Testament Scriptures, only two of which we will cite here:

> *The Lord hath prepared his throne in the heavens; and his*
> *kingdom ruleth over all.* (Psalm 103:19)

> *How great are his signs! and how mighty are his wonders! his*
> *kingdom is an everlasting kingdom, and his dominion is from genera-*
> *tion to generation.* (Daniel 4:3)

There are many such Old Testament Scriptures that reveal clearly that the Kingdom of God was a reality at the time they were written. Indeed, who would be so foolish to say that God did not have a Kingdom before Jesus came into the world? Yet there are those who, when they speak of the Kingdom of God, narrow their perception to a future time, specifically the millennial reign of Christ on earth. By the same token, others, particularly among the dominionists who have coined the term, "Kingdom Now," have no less a narrow view of the Kingdom of God. They speak almost exclusively of the Kingdom as relevant to the establishment of God's rulership over the nations during this present age.

With equal resolve we must admit that the Kingdom of Heaven is really just another name for the Kingdom of God. This is proven in Scriptures that refer to the Kingdom in both these terms. John the Baptist called for repentance and baptism because the Kingdom of Heaven was at hand, that is, it was about to be revealed to the people through Jesus Christ:

> *In those days came John the Baptist, preaching in the wilderness*
> *of Judea,*
> *And saying, Repent ye: for the kingdom of heaven is at hand.*
> (Matthew 3:1-2)

Likewise Jesus Himself, at the beginning of His public ministry, warned the people that the Kingdom of Heaven was about to be revealed to them:

> *From that time Jesus began to preach, and to say, Repent: for the*
> *kingdom of heaven is at hand.* (Matthew 4:17)

However, in Mark's account, Jesus' reference is to the Kingdom of God:

> *Now after that John was put in prison, Jesus came into Galilee,*
> *preaching the gospel of the kingdom of God,*
> *And saying, The time is fulfilled, and the kingdom of God is at*
> *hand: repent ye, and believe the gospel.* (Mark 1:14-15)

So we see that the Kingdom of God is synonymous with the Kingdom of Heaven, and that it has been in existence at least as long as the creation.

In God's dealing with Nebuchadnezzar, king of Babylon, we see that the Kingdom of God is a present reality on earth and has, from the creation of man, exercised authority over human endeavor including all governments and social institutions:

> *This matter is by the decree of the watchers, and the demand by the word of the holy ones: to the intent that the living may know that the most High ruleth in the kingdom of men, and giveth it to whomsoever he will, and setteth up over it the basest of men.* (Daniel 4:17).

It is clear that the Kingdom of God is presently in effect. The problem for dominionists, therefore, is not that the Kingdom of God is not in effect, but that it operates in a manner they resent: God establishes the basest of men over the governments of the world.

Another problem—and one with which we find ourselves in agreement with the dominionists—is that the rulers of the kingdoms of this world lack understanding of their de facto subservience to the God of the universe. But we part company with the dominionists who seek to make the kingdoms of the earth become the kingdoms of our Lord and of His Christ (Revelation 11:15) before Jesus returns. In effect, they wish to make the kingdoms of the earth the kingdoms of the dominionists.

The dominionists' "Gospel of the Kingdom" is best suited to Western Civilization which, incidentally, is the projected seat of power for the anti-Christ's kingdom. The democratic societies—whether under the reign of an anti-Christ or under the reign of the dominionists—must inevitably become themselves totalitarian governments.

Lest we become alarmed at this prospect, we must remember that God is the one who decides who will hold the seat of power in the nations' governments. So although outwardly the dominionists do not perceive God's hand in human governments today, the fact remains that they are operating at His behest. They are already His kingdoms by default. At Christ's return to establish His millennial reign, Revelation 11:15 will be a manifested reality to the peoples of the earth.

The Future Kingdom

That Jesus saw the Kingdom not only as an eternal reality, but as a future reality, is revealed in His statement to His disciples at the Last Supper:

> *But I say unto you, I will not drink henceforth of this fruit of the vine, until that day when I drink it new with you in my Father's kingdom.* (Matthew 26:29).

This is also recorded in Mark 14:25 and Luke 22:18, where the authors rendered it "the Kingdom of God."

So, although the Kingdom of God is present, and it was revealed to man through the appearance of Jesus 2,000 years ago, there is also going to be a future revelation of the Kingdom in which we will be with the Lord, eating and drinking. It is misunderstanding of that future revelation of the Kingdom of God that is causing all the confusion. And herein lies understanding of what has brought confusion into the issue of God's Kingdom. There are times when Scripture speaks of the Kingdom of God or the Kingdom of Heaven as a present reality operative in a manner which mortals cannot comprehend without understanding granted by the Holy Spirit through the Scriptures: a righteous God overseeing and moving the decisions of unrighteous rulers on earth.

But there are other instances when the Scriptures speak of the Kingdom of God as the future, earthly millennial kingdom over which Jesus will preside when He returns to the earth after having put down all rebellion. Although outwardly the nations of the earth will confront Him at Armageddon at the prompting of the anti-Christ, the spiritual reality is that God will put hooks in their jaws to draw them to battle with Christ.

Those who seek to establish the operative Kingdom of God on earth before Christ returns are fooling themselves. The Kingdom of God is already established on earth, but the operative Kingdom which will control the nations will not exist until Jesus returns. Thus, in their attempts to bring about the visible manifestation of God's rulership over the nations, the dominionists will be found fighting God. He has chosen not to give rulership of the earth to His children until after Jesus returns. So once again we must remind ourselves of Jesus' words to Pontius Pilate:

> *My kingdom is not of this world: if my kingdom were of this world, then would my servants fight, that I should not be delivered to the Jews: but now is my kingdom not from hence.* (John 18:36)

Until Jesus returns to establish His Kingdom on the earth, the rulership of the earth is in the hands of the "basest of men" by God's decree. Those who are truly His servants will not be found fighting to establish Him as King over the present world system, which is doomed to destruction.

3
A Short Course In
Biblical Eschatology

The Revelation is the most definitive Biblical record of the events connected with the Lord's return. Since all other prophetic Scriptures are incidental to the context in which they are stated elsewhere, they may be viewed as lending support to the Revelation. Therefore, the Revelation will be the superstructure upon which this study will be built. Other Scriptures finding correlation in the Revelation will be cited in the appropriate places.

There will be no spiritualizing or allegorizing of any Scripture that speaks plainly. We will not concern ourselves with conjectured meanings of those things that are symbolic other than to offer possibilities from which the reader may draw his own conclusions. For example, whether the locusts released from the bottomless pit in chapter nine are "helicopters" is irrelevant. These attempts at guesswork only serve to cloud the issue. The important thing is the sequence of events and whether those events have already transpired or will transpire in the future. We will skip over the first three chapters since they do not offer anything specific about the chronology of events leading up to Jesus' Second Coming.

CHAPTER 4

We see a heavenly scene: the throne of God; the twenty-four elders, the seven lamps of fire before the throne, which are the seven Spirits of God; the sea of glass before the throne; the four living creatures around the throne (the lion, calf, man, flying eagle), all having six wings, and being full of eyes. All are worshipping before the throne of God (vss. 1-11).

It is often said by pretribulationists that the twenty-four elders represent the Church that has been raptured. But this is speculation. There is no clear understanding of this from Scripture. They more likely are the twelve patriarchs of Israel, and the twelve apostles who walked with Jesus. But, again, Scripture does not identify conclusively who they are, except that they are redeemed men (5:9-10). This serves as an example of how human reasoning often impacts theological concepts. While certain Scriptures are symbolical in nature, unless that is clearly evident, we must take them as literal.

CHAPTER 5

The Lamb of God is alone worthy to open the book with seven seals, and He is worshipped by every creature (vss. 1-14).

CHAPTER 6

The Lamb of God begins to open the seals. From this point on we will see a series of events that transpire in chronological order. Except where the sequence is clearly broken we must assume that it continues in that order, just as we would in reading any portion of Scripture. To do otherwise would leave the Scriptures open to the wildest conjectures.

The First Seal:

And I saw, and behold a white horse: and he that sat on him had a bow; and a crown was given unto him: and he went forth conquering, and to conquer (vss. 1-2).

The Second Seal:

And there went out another horse that was red: and power was given to him that sat thereon to take peace from the earth, and that they should kill one another: and there was given unto him a great sword (vss. 3-4).

The Third Seal:

And when he had opened the third seal, I heard the third beast say, Come and see. And I beheld, and lo a black horse; and he that sat on him had a pair of balances in his hand.

And I heard a voice in the midst of the four beasts say, A measure of wheat for a penny, and three measures of barley for a penny; and see thou hurt not the oil and wine (vss. 5-6).

The Fourth Seal:

And I looked, and behold a pale horse: and his name that sat on him was Death, and Hell followed with him. And power was given unto them over the fourth part of the earth, to kill with sword, and with hunger, and with death, and with the beasts of the earth (vss. 7-8).

It is commonly believed that the first horse represents the anti-Christ, the second, warfare, the third, famine, and the fourth, pestilence. Except for the first, these descriptions are clear. The first horseman does have a bow and a crown, which would suggest a king or mighty ruler over much if not all the land.

The four horses are described in much the same manner in Zechariah 6:1-4. In Zechariah 6:5, the angel tells him that they are the "four spirits of the heavens, which go forth from standing before the Lord of all the earth."

We can at least understand, then, that these destructive elements come from the throne of God to judge the earth.

The Fifth Seal:

John sees those who are martyred for the word of God and for their testimonies, crying out to God for vengeance.

There is no indication that these are "tribulation saints" distinct from saints allegedly raptured before the tribulation. That they are tribulation saints is clear; but that there is a rapture before this is not evidenced. To try to separate chapters one through five and say that, since the church is not mentioned past chapter three, it must have been raptured, is speculation.

Chapters one through three were specific messages to the seven churches in Asia which existed during the time the book was written. That they represent the condition of the Church throughout the ages, is likewise speculation. There is no historical evidence that the Church went through periods described in these messages to the seven churches in Asia.

The Church in Laodicea is said to be today's Church. But that is an American application. The Church throughout other portions of the earth is in various stages of maturity and apostasy. It has been this way since the beginning, with the exception that the Roman Catholic Church had about fifteen hundred years of preeminence until the Reformation took root. But even the Reformation churches have fallen into apostasy today.

Even if the seven churches in Revelation do represent the condition of the Church throughout different historical periods, that doesn't conclusively prove a pretribulational rapture.

So the only thing that is clear from Scripture is that there is to be a series of future events that will bring persecution to the Church and God's judgment upon the earth. The persecution began in the first century and has continued throughout history. There have been many anti-Christs from Nero onward.

The question is, do the seven seals represent events during the first century, or are they specific to the last years before Jesus returns? The answer lies in the next two seals:

The Sixth Seal:

> *And I beheld when he had opened the sixth seal, and, lo, there was a great earthquake; and the sun became black as sackcloth of hair, and the moon became as blood;*
>
> *And the stars of heaven fell unto the earth, even as a fig tree casteth her untimely figs, when she is shaken of a mighty wind.*
>
> *And the heaven departed as a scroll when it is rolled together; and every mountain and island were moved out of their places.*
>
> *And the kings of the earth, and the great men, and the rich men, and the chief captains, and the mighty men, and every bondman, and every free man, hid themselves in the dens and in the rocks of the mountains;*
>
> *And said to the mountains and rocks, Fall on us, and hide us from the face of him that sitteth on the throne, and from the wrath of the Lamb:*
>
> *For the great day of his wrath is come; and who shall be able to stand?* (Revelation 6:12-17)

It is clear that the people of the earth know that Jesus is about to pour out His wrath upon them. At what stage does this take place? Is this the beginning of the Great Tribulation, or after the Great Tribulation? For the answer we must go to Matthew 24, Mark 13, and Daniel 12, which describe these same events:

Matthew 24:29-31:

> *Immediately after the tribulation of those days shall the sun be darkened, and the moon shall not give her light, and the stars shall fall from heaven, and the powers of the heavens shall be shaken:*
>
> *And then shall appear the sign of the Son of man in heaven: and then shall all the tribes of the earth mourn, and they shall see the Son of man coming in the clouds of heaven with power and great glory.*
>
> *And he shall send his angels with a great sound of a trumpet, and they shall gather together his elect from the four winds, from one end of heaven to the other.*

Mark 13:24-27:

> *But in those days, after that tribulation, the sun shall be darkened, and the moon shall not give her light,*

And the stars of heaven shall fall, and the powers that are in heaven shall be shaken.

And then shall they see the Son of man coming in the clouds with great power and glory.

And then shall he send his angels, and shall gather together his elect from the four winds, from the uttermost part of the earth to the uttermost part of heaven.

Daniel 12:1-2:

And at that time shall Michael stand up, the great prince which standeth for the children of thy people: and there shall be a time of trouble, such as never was since there was a nation even to that same time: and at that time thy people shall be delivered, every one that shall be found written in the book.

And many of them that sleep in the dust of the earth shall awake, some to everlasting life, and some to shame and everlasting contempt.

All these verses refer to the resurrection after the tribulation of the last days. We see, also, that the resurrection and the rapture will not be secret events. The idea that all of a sudden millions of people will disappear, cars will go out of control, planes will crash because pilots will have been raptured, and so on, is not supported by Scripture. The people of the earth will *see* the Lord Jesus come in the clouds to gather His saints out of the earth. And they will realize that they are about to experience His wrath for having persecuted His saints and for refusing to repent of their sins.

Daniel's reference to the resurrection of both the justified and the unjustified relates to the resurrection in general. It neither speaks of the resurrection at the time of the rapture, nor at the end of the Millennium. It merely says that some will wake to everlasting life, and some to everlasting shame. We cannot use it to prove two resurrections; nor can we use it to prove only one. It can only be used to prove the truth of the resurrection in general. That there would be more than one resurrection since the day of Daniel is evidenced by the resurrection that took place after Jesus rose (Matthew 27:52).

We do know, however, that the resurrection that will be concurrent with the rapture is "immediately *after* the tribulation of those days."

The entire account of events (wars, rumors of wars, the beginnings of sorrows, etc.) in Matthew 24 and Mark 13 can be seen to relate to the last days just prior to and subsequent to the Great Tribulation. The idea that the Great Tribulation took place in A.D. 70 when Titus sacked Jerusalem and defiled the temple is inconsistent with the facts of history. There have been far worse tribulations upon Israel since that time. Besides, Jesus indicates that the tribulation will be upon the elect, which would include both Jewish and Gentile believers. Continuing to Revelation, chapter 7, we see the chronology of events unfold:

> After the Church is taken out of the earth, there is a period of calm. During that time the one hundred and forty-four thousand of all the tribes of the children of Israel are sealed (vss. 1-8).

> The Church is seen in heaven: "After this I beheld, and lo, a great multitude, which no man could number, of all nations, and kindreds, and people, and tongues, stood before the throne, and before the Lamb, clothed with white robes, and holding palms in their hands" (vs. 9).

> Having come out of all nations, and kindreds, and people, and tongues, we see that this is not Israel, but the Church. One of the elders tells John that, "These are they which came out of great tribulation, and have washed their robes, and made them white in the blood of the Lamb" (vss. 13-17).

Thus far the sequence of events is as follows: 1) great tribulation upon God's people, as well as wars, famines, and pestilences upon the earth; 2) after the tribulation there will be signs in the heavens affecting the sun, the moon, and the stars (whether literally or not isn't germane to the discussion; if these are allegorical references, the fact remains that something dramatic happens before Jesus appears in the heavens and gathers together His elect; 3) the saints from all the nations (the Church) are in heaven. At that point, we proceed to the next series of events in Revelation:

The Seventh Seal:

> The last seal heralds the wrath of God through the trumpet judgments and vials. The Church is in heaven, the 144,000—a remnant of natural Israelites (those who looked upon Him and mourned when He came for His elect) have been sealed for protection against God's wrath which is about to be poured out upon an unrepentant humanity.

The seventh seal carries us from chapter eight through chapter eighteen, wherein we see the rise of the anti-Christ, the false prophet, the hatred of the nations toward God because of their afflictions, Mystery Babylon destroyed, the nations of the earth prepared for destruction and the Lord's return to the earth.

CHAPTER 19

The Lord returns and the armies of the earth gather to fight Him, only to be destroyed. This great battle will be fought at Armageddon. It is not a battle between the nations, as has been taught by many. It is the battle between anti-Christ's armies and Jesus when He returns.

But how would the armies of the earth gather to fight the Lord unless they realized that He was the source of their troubles? They had already seen Him gather His saints and knew those troubles were about to come upon them. But they are deceived to believe that they can fight Him because they will have placed their trust in the anti-Christ and the False Prophet. The False Prophet will have gained the confidence of the nations and the churches to believe that the anti-Christ is the true Christ, and that Jesus is their enemy. He will have accomplished this by the performing of miraculous signs and wonders, even calling fire to fall down on the earth from out of the heavens (Revelation 13:13). Man's super technology will no doubt play a part in this deception.

CHAPTER 20

The Millennial reign of Christ is revealed. It clearly establishes a second resurrection after the Millennium (vs. 5), in addition to the resurrection which occurs just after the Great Tribulation and prior to the wrath of God being poured out on the earth.

Satan is loosed to deceive the nations again. This will be the final testing of men—those living and born during the Millennium—to determine who will be faithful to the King.

After all evil is put down, there will be a final resurrection of all men who will stand before the Great White Throne. Satan and all who are not found in the book of life will be cast into the lake of fire. There will be a new heaven and a new earth, wherein will dwell righteousness forever. The bride of Christ, New Jerusalem, will come down to the earth from heaven, and God will establish His throne on the earth for eternity.

A SUMMARY OF EVENTS

In summary we see the sequence of events as follows:

- There will be wars and rumors of wars on the earth;
- There will follow great calamities: earthquakes, famines, and pestilences;
- There will be great tribulation upon God's people;

- The Lord will appear in the skies;
- The resurrection of the saints asleep in Jesus will occur, followed by the translation into immortality of those who are alive;
- Jesus will gather His resurrected and transformed saints to be with Him in heaven while He pours out His wrath upon the earth;
- The 144,000 from every tribe of Israel will be sealed for protection against God's wrath;
- God will pour out his wrath upon the earth;
- The anti-Christ will gather the nations to fight against Jesus when He comes back with His saints;
- Jesus will destroy the armies of the nations;
- The anti-Christ and the False Prophet will be cast into the lake of fire;
- Satan will be bound for one-thousand years so he cannot deceive the nations;
- The Lord will establish a one-thousand-year reign on the earth (the Millennium) and will rule the nations with a rod of iron (Rev. 19:15);
- After the Millennium Satan will be released to again test those who have lived under the Lord's rule;
- Satan will gather the armies of the nations to again fight against Christ;
- The Lord will destroy all rebellion once and for all;
- The final resurrection of all the dead, both the righteous in Christ and the unrighteous, will take place;
- The Great White Throne Judgment will occur;
- All whose names are not found in the Book of Life will be cast into the lake of fire;
- The heavens and the earth will be renovated for the last time;
- New Jerusalem will come down out of heaven to the earth;

- God will make His abode among men on the earth;
- The redeemed of all the ages will dwell in His company on the new earth for eternity.

STUDY TO SHOW YOURSELF APPROVED

This, admittedly, is a sparse rendering of a biblical eschatology. It would take several books to properly address the subject. Many have been written; most are inadequate. I urge the reader to undertake his own diligent study, putting aside all other teachings relative to it (even this one).

An honest heart desirous of knowing God's truth in order that it may follow that truth will be rewarded by God. The Holy Spirit will give understanding to those who approach the Word of God without preconceived notions and attempts to validate a pre-disposed position.

By all means take advantage of available scholarship, but only after having first sought the truth on your own. The greatest safeguard against deception is knowledge of God's Word. It is the sword of truth by which we demolish all arguments against the Faith. By properly applying the Word of Truth to those situations in which we find ourselves engaged in spiritual warfare, we overcome the enemy of our souls.

Those who say that doctrine is not important, or is secondary to the Spirit, are in essence telling us that the Word of God is subject to personal interpretation. Yet it is the work of the Spirit to validate the truth of the Word in order that we may receive the direction we need to be victorious in our warfare for Christ Jesus.

While doctrine itself has no power to sanctify, it is only by knowing and applying sound doctrine to our lives that we can be sanctified. The Law and the Spirit work together to conform us to the image of Christ. Without the Spirit we fall into legalism and bondage; without the Law we fall into mysticism and unbridled searchings, never able to come to a knowledge of the truth.

Let us live as Christ would have us live: in humility before God and men; in boldness to speak the truth regardless of the consequences; in love to manifest the presence of God in our lives.

The Church is on the threshold of its greatest day since the first century. It will be put to the test as never before. I am convinced that, in spite of the persecution that faces us, those who are truly of God will endure to the end.

Those who are the spots and blemishes will cast us out of the churches as we speak the truth in love. They will think that they are doing God a service; they will think they are purifying the

Church in order that it may achieve unity to reign triumphant over the nations before Jesus returns. The truth is that they will indeed be purifying the true Church of their own presence, but they will not triumph over the nations; they will become part of Mystery Babylon out of which came their damnable heresies of pride and self-exaltation.

The true Church, which will come from out of all the churches— will seem defeated. It will be the laughing stock of the nations and of the apostate churches. But it will know in its heart that the secret to triumph lies not it its own strength, but in the might of the Lord, as Zechariah 4:6 says:

> *Not by might, nor by power, but by my spirit, saith the Lord of hosts.*

By His might, by His power, by His Spirit will the Church, at the Lord's return, be acknowledged by all principalities and powers, both in heaven and in the earth, as worthy to take dominion. Then, and only then, can we say, "Vengeance Is Ours."

Notes
PART I - PARADISE LOST

Chapter 3

1. G. de Purucker, *The Esoteric Tradition*, 2 Vols. (Point Loma, CA: Theosophical University Press, 1935), p. 24.
2. Ibid., p. 29.

Chapter 4

1. John H. Dewey, *Christian Theosophy* (New York: J.H. Dewey Publishing Company, 1888), p. vi.
2. Ibid., p. ix.
3. Ibid.
4. Ibid., p. xi.
5. Randy Shankle, "Praise the Lord" program, Trinity Broadcasting Network, c. August, 1986.
6. "Praise the Lord" program, TBN, video tape, c. Spring, 1986.
7. Earl Paulk, *Thrust in the Sickle and Reap* (Atlanta: K Dimension Publishers, 1986), p. 132.
8. *Christian Theosophy*, pp. xi-xii.
9. Earl Paulk, *The Wounded Body of Christ* (Atlanta: K Dimension Publishers, 1985), pp. 124-125.
10. James Robison, "The Miracle of Christmas - Christ Is Formed in You," *Days of Restoration*, November/December, 1986 (Fort Worth: James Robison Evangelistic Association), p. 4.
11. Ibid., p. 5.
12. Ibid., p. 3.
13. *The Esoteric Tradition*, pp. 1104-1105.
14. Ibid., pp. 513-514.
15. *Christian Theosophy*, pp. 28-30.
16. Ibid., p. 291.
17. Ibid., p. 135.
18. Kenneth Copeland, "Praise the Lord" program, TBN, video tape c. September, 1985.
19. *The Esoteric Tradition*, pp. 788-791.
20. Earl Paulk, TBN, video tape of church service, c. October, 1986.

Chapter 5

1. Abraham Friesen, "Wimber, Word and Spirit," *Wonders and the Word: An Examination of Issues Raised by John Wimber and the Vineyard Movement*, James R. Coggins & Paul G. Hiebert, ed. (Winnipeg, MB: Kindred Press, 1989), p. 37.
2. George N. Shuster, *The Confessions of St. Augustine* (New York: The Heritage Press, ©1963 The George Macy Companies, Inc.), pp. viii-ix.
3. Ibid., pp. xii-xiii.
4. *Wonders and the Word*, pp. 38-39.
5. "Praise the Lord," program, TBN, September 17, 1989.
6. *Time*, May 28, 1990, p. 13.
7. Robert Schuller, speech at West Coast Conference on the Holy Spirit and Christian Unity, March 2-4, Theme: "One Body, One Bread," telecast on Trinity Broadcasting Network.
8. *London Times*, October 1, 1989, p. 7.
9. Charles Dickson, Ph.D., "A Pope for All Christians: What Will it Take?," *Catholic Twin Circle*, February 11, 1990, p. 6.

PART II - CHARISMATIC DOMINIONISM

Chapter 1

1. Franklin Hall, *Miracle Word* (Phoenix, AZ: Hall Deliverance Foundation, Summer, 1985), p.10.
2. Ibid.
3. Ibid.
4. Ibid.
5. Ibid., p. 9.
6. Ibid.
7. Franklin Hall, *Atomic Power With God Through Fasting and Prayer*, 5th Edition (Phoenix: Hall Deliverance Foundation, 1975), p. 19.
8. Ibid., p. 9.
9. Franklin Hall, Catalogue of Publications (Phoenix, AZ: Hall Deliverance Foundation, 1986).
10. Franklin Hall, *The Return of Immortality* (Phoenix, AZ: Hall Deliverance Foundation, 1976), pp. 2-3).
11. Ibid., p. 3.
12. Ibid., Inside Front Cover.
13. Ibid., p. 10.
14. Ibid., p. 11.
15. Ibid., p. 60.
16. Ibid., p. 48.
17. Ibid., p. 20.
18. *Atomic Power With God Through Fasting and Prayer*, pp. 29-31.
19. Ibid., p. 7.
20. Ibid., p. 53.
21. Ibid., p. 55.
22. Catalogue of Publications
23. Stanley M. Burgess and Gary B. McGee, *Dictionary of Pentecostal and Charismatic Movements* (Grand Rapids, MI: Zondervan Publishing House, Regency Reference Library, 1989), s.v., "Hall, Franklin."
24. William M. Branham, *Adoption* (Jeffersonville, IN: Spoken Word Publications, 1960), p. 21.
25. William M. Branham, *The Serpent's Seed*, taped sermon, undated.
26. *Adoption*, pp. 31, 104.
27. David E. Harrell, Jr., *All Things Are Possible* (Bloomington, IN: Indiana University Press, 1976), p. 162.
28. William M. Branham, *My Life Story* (Jeffersonville, IN: Spoken Word Publications, undated), p. 19.
29. *The Serpent's Seed*.
30. *All Things Are Possible*, p. 162.
31. *Brother Branham* (Jeffersonville, IN: Spoken Word Publications, undated), p. 19.
32. *My Life Story*, p. 21.
33. Ibid., p. 24.
34. Kurt Koch, *Occult Bondage and Deliverance* (Grand Rapids: Kregel, 1972), p. 50.
35. Ibid.
36. James Randi, *The Faith Healers* (Buffalo, NY: Prometheus Books, 1987).
37. *All Things Are Possible*, p. 161.
38. Ibid.
39. Ibid.
40. Ibid., p. 164.
41. Richard Riss, *The Latter Rain Movement of 1948 and the Mid-twentieth Century Evangelical Awakening* (Thesis), p. 79.

42. Ibid., pp. 80-81.
43. Ibid., pp. 83-84.
44. Ibid., p. 86.
45. Ibid., p. 89.
46. Ibid., pp. 89-90.
47. Ibid., p. 101.
48. Ibid., p. 102.
49. Ibid., p. 154.
50. Ibid., p. 108.
51. Ibid., p. 116.
52. Ibid., p. 104.
53. Ibid.
54. Ibid.
55. George Warnock, *The Feast of Tabernacles* (Cranbrook, B.C.: George Warnock, 1951), pp. 14-20.
56. Ibid., p. 22.
57. *Dictionary of Pentecotal and Charismatic Movements*, s.v. "Roberts, Granville Oral."
58. Ibid.

Chapter 2

1. Curtis Clair Ewing, "For the Benefit of Our Pentecostal and Charismatic Brethren!," (Waynesville, NC: New Beginnings,   undated tract), p. 1.
2. *Time*, October 20, 1986, p. 74.
3. Ibid.
4. Orange County (California) *Register*, October 30, 1986, p. A23.
5. *Time*, October 20, 1986, p. 74.
6. Curtis Clair Ewing, p. 1.
7. Gary North, *Unholy Spirits* (Forth Worth: Dominion Press, 1986), pp. 374-375.
8. Russ Bellant, "Word of God network wants to 'save the world'," *National Catholic Reporter*, November 18, 1988.
9. Ibid.
10. Ibid.
11. Ibid.
12. Ibid.
13. Ibid.
14. Richard Quebedeaux, *The New Charismatics II: How A Christian Renewal Movement Became Part of the American Religious Mainstream* (San Francisco: Harper & Row, 1983), p. 78
15. Minutes from Meeting of the Council, December 17-19, 1975, p. 1.
16. Minutes from Meeting of the Council, January 3-7, 1977, p. 2.
17. Minutes from Meeting of the Council, May/June, 1977, pp. 2-3.
18. Ibid., p. 3.
19. Minutes from Meeting of the Council, August 8-10, 1977, p. 5.

Chapter 3

1. *Harvest Time* (Atlanta: Chapel Hill Harvester Church, December, 1984), p. 15.
2. Earl Paulk, *Held in the Heavens Until. . .* (Atlanta: K Dimension Publishers, 1985), p. 234.
3. Ibid., p. 235.
4. Earl Paulk, *Thrust in the Sickle and Reap* (Atlanta: K Dimension Publishers, 1986), p. 73.
5. Earl Paulk, *Form With Power* (Atlanta: K Dimension Publishers, undated), p. 5.

6. Ibid., p. 4.
7. Earl Paulk, *The Great Escape Theory* (Atlanta: K Dimension Publishers, undated), p. 14.
8. Pat Robertson, video tape of speech at Dallas '84, on TBN.
9. Ibid.
10. *Christianity Today*, "Tracking America's Soul," An interview with Geroge Gallup, Jr., November 17, 1989.
11. Pat Robertson, speech at Dallas '84.
12. Ibid.
13. Pat Robertson, *Answers to 200 of Life's Most Probing Questions* (Nashville, TN: Thomas Nelson, 1984), pp. 145-146.
14. Pat Robertson, speech at Dallas '84.
15. Gary North, *Paradise Restored*, p. 328.
16. Ibid., p. 329.
17. Franklin Hall, *Subdue The Earth, Rule The Nations* (Phoenix, AZ: Franklin Hall Ministries, 1966), p. 11.
18. Ibid., p. 57.
19. Royal Cronquist, ad for speaking engagements, Love Ministries, p. 2.
20. *Your Daily Cross Is Giving Up The Throne Of Self*, p. 4.
21. Royal Cronquist, *Why the Feast of Tabernacles?* (Spokane, WA: Love Ministries Newsletter, August, 1984).
22. *Thrust in the Sickle and Reap*, pp. 103, 104.
23. Dean Gross, "Melchisedec Order Decree" (Chattnooga, TN: Word by Word Association).
24. Sam Fife, *One Corporate Man* (Miami: The Body of Christ), p. 22.
25. Paul Cain, "Joel's Army," cited in *Documentation of the Aberrant Practices and Teachings of Kansas City Fellowship* (Shawnee, KS: Full Faith Church of Love, 1990), p. 218.
26. Ibid.
27. Earl Paulk, *The Proper Function of the Church* (Atlanta: K Dimension Publishers, undated), p. 13.
28. Earl Paulk, *Harvest Time*, July, 1984.
29. Earl Paulk, Video tape of sermon at Chapel Hill Harvester Church, Atlanta, on PTL Network, undated.
30. Earl Paulk, *Held in the Heavens Until. . .*, pp. 21, 22.
31. Ibid., p. 82.
32. Ibid., p. 83.
33. Earl Paulk, "Praise the Lord" program, TBN, March 4, 1986.
34. Earl Paulk, *The Betrothed* (Atlanta: K Dimension Publishers, 1985), p. 7.
35. Earl Paulk, *The Wounded Body of Christ* (Atlanta: K Dimension Pub.), p. 43.
36. Royal Cronquist, *Your Daily Cross Is Giving Up the Throne Of Self* (Spokane, WA: Love Ministries), p. 3.
37. Ibid., p. 4.
38. Ibid., p. 7.
39. Ibid., p. 6.
40. Ibid., p. 4.

Chapter 4

1. Ad for Charismatic Bible Ministries, *Charisma*, May, 1987, p. 53.
2. Mike Bickle, *The Prophetic History of Grace Ministries*, audio tape (Kansas City, MO: Grace Ministries).
3. Ibid.
4. Michael Sullivant, "What Is Grace Ministries?" *Grace City Report*, Special Ed. (Kansas City, MO: Grace Ministries, Fall, 1989), p. 9.
5. Ibid.
6. Ibid.

7. Letter from Mike Bickle to Al Dager
8. Michael Sullivant, "What Is Grace Ministries?" p. 9.
9. Ibid., p. 16.
10. Steve Lambert, "Shiloh: A Prophetic Sanctuary," *Grace City Report*, Special Edition, Fall, 1989, p. 11.
11. Ibid.
12. Interview, Al Dager with Mike Bickle.
13. *Documentation of the Aberrant Practices and Teachings of the Kansas City Fellowship*, p. 63.
14. Terri Sullivant, "Paul Cain: A Personal Profile," *Grace City Report*, Special Edition, Fall, 1989, p. 2.
15. Ibid.
16. Paul Cain, *The New Breed*, audio tape (Kansas City, MO: Grace Ministries, undated).
17. Terri Sullivant, "Paul Cain: A Personal Profile," *Grace City Report*, p. 13.
18. Bob Jones, *Visions and Revelations*, 1988, audio tape, interview with Mike Bickle (Kansas City, MO: Grace Ministries).
19. Paul Cain, *The New Breed*.
20. Terri Sullivant, "Paul Cain: A Personal Profile," *Grace City Report*, p. 16.
21. Terri Sullivant, "Paul Cain's Ministry: Recent Manifestations of the Holy Spirit," *Grace City Report*, Special Edition, Fall, 1989, p. 17.
22. Ibid., p. 5.
23. Ibid.
24. Pamela King, "Bob Jones: A Personal Profile," *Grace City Report*, Special Edition, Fall, 1989, p. 6.
25. Mike Bickle, *Visions and Revelations*, 1988.
26. Bob Jones, Ibid.
27. Bob Jones, *Visions and Revelations*, 1989, audio tape, inteview with Mike Bickle (Kansas City, MO: Grace Ministries).
28. Alice Bailey, *The Externalisation of the Hierarchy* (New York: Lucius Publishing Co., 1957), p. 508.
29. Bob Jones, *Visions and Revelations*, 1988.
30. Rick Joyner, "The Unfolding of a Prophet," *Fulness Magazine* (Fort Worth: Fulness House, Inc., Jan.-Feb., 1990), p. 13.
31. *Documentation of the Aberrant Practices and Teachings of Kansas City Fellowship*, p. 206.
32. Ibid., p. 209.
33. Ibid., p. 211.
34. Ibid., p. 203.
35. Rick Joyner, "1990," *Morning Star Prophetic Newsletter* (Charlotte, NC: Morning Star Publications, Inc., Vol. II, No. V, Oct.-Nov., 1989), p. 4.
36. Mike Bickle, "The Necessity of Judging Prophets," *Grace City Report*, Special Edition, Fall, 1989, p. 20.
37. Ibid.
38. Mike Bickle, *The Prophetic History of Grace Ministries*.
39. Paul Cain, *The New Breed*.
40. Ibid.
41. Bob Jones, *Visions and Revelations*, 1988.
42. Ibid.
43. Bob Jones, *Visions and Revelations*, 1989.
44. Bob Jones, *Visions and Revelations*, 1988.
45. Ibid.
46. Linda Bonville, video tape of small group meeting in a hotel room, March 10, 1990, untitled.
47. Ibid.
48. Paul Cain, "The Prophet," *Christ For The Nations* (Dallas: Christ For The Nations, September, 1989), p. 5.

49. David Minor, "Turn Your Face into the Wind," *He Will Tell You Things to Come* (Fort Lauderdale, FL: Derek Prince Ministries-International, August, 1988), p. 12.
50. Rick Joyner, "A Vision of the Harvest," Ibid., p. 14.
51. Rick Joyner, "1990," Ibid., p. 5.
52. Rick Joyner, "The Prophetic Ministry, Part III - True Spiritual Authority Versus Witchcraft," *Morning Star Prophetic Newsletter*, Vol. III, No. I, January-February, 1990, p. 4.
53. Bob Jones, *Visions and Revelations*, 1988.
54. *Documentation of the Aberrant Practices and Teachings*, p. 209.
55. Ibid., p. 210.
56. *Charisma and Christian Life*, July, 1990, p. 34.
57. James R. Coggins, Paul G. Hiebert, *Wonders and the Word*, p. 16.
58. Ibid., p. 7.
59. Ibid., p. 21.
60. Abraham Friesen, Ibid., p. 41.
61. Ibid., p. 40.
62. Ibid.
63. John Wimber, *Unpacking Your Bags*, audio tape, undated.
64. Ibid.
65. Ibid.
66. Ibid.
67. Ibid.
68. Paul Thigpen, "How Is God Speaking Today?" *Charisma*, Sept. 1989, p. 55.
69. Mike Bickle, *The Prophetic History of Grace Ministries*.

PART III - RECONSTRUCTION

Chapter 1

1. William B. Tucker, *Theonomic Application for a Sociology of Justification by Faith: Weaknesses in the Social Criticisms of Rousas John Rushdoony as Revealed in the Doctrine of Sanctification by Law*, Thesis requirement for Master of Arts in Theological Studies with an emphasis on Church History, Gordon Conwell Theological Seminary, June 1984, unpublished paper, p. 31.
2. R.J. Rushdoony, "Power from Below," *The Journal of Christian Reconstruction* 1:2 (winter, 1974), pp. 9-10, quoted by William B. Tucker, p. 47.
3. R.J. Rushdoony, *Institutes of Biblical Law*, Vol. I (Vallecito, CA: Ross House Books), p. 652, quoted by William B. Tucker, p. 43.
4. "Power from Below."

Chapter 2

1. R.E. McMaster, Jr., "Evolution and New Age Globalism," *Chalcedon Report*, No. 294, January, 1990, p. 7.
2. Ibid., p. 8.
3. R.J. Rushdoony, *Law and Society: Volume II of the Institutes of Biblical Law* (Vallecito, CA: Ross House Books, 1986), p. 180.
4. R.J. Rushdoony, "Inferences and Commandments," *Chalcedon Report*, No. 285, April, 1989, pp. 16-17.
5. Gary North, *Unholy Spirits* (Fort Worth: Dominion Press, 1986), p. 394.
6. Gary North, *Paradise Restored* (Fort Worth: Dominion Press, 1985), p. 339.
7. Ibid., p. 331.
8. David Chilton, *Paradise Restored*, p. 12.
9. Ibid., p. 213.
10. Ibid., p. 214.
11. Ibid., p. 10.
12. Ibid., p. 53.

13. David Chilton, *The Days Of Vengeance: An Exposition of the Book of Revelation* (Fort Worth: Dominion Press, 1987), p. 232.
14. Ray Sutton, *That You May Prosper: Dominion by Covenant* (Tyler, TX: Institute for Christian Economics [ICE], 1987), p. 189.

Chapter 3

1. Ibid., p. 202.
2. Ibid.
3. Gary Crampton, *Journey* (Lynchburg, VA: Grace Orthodox Presbyterian Church, Nov.-Dec., 1986), p. 18.
4. Greg Bahnsen, "An Interview With Dr. Greg Bahnsen," Ibid., p. 10.
5. Ibid.
6. *That You May Prosper*, p. 184.
7. Ibid.
8. Gary North, "The Theonomy Debate," *Journey*, p. 16.
9. *That You May Prosper*, pp. 188-189.
10. Ibid., p. 191.

Chapter 4

1. Coalition on Revival, "The Essentials of a Christian Worldview of the Coalition on Revival," Article 38 (Mountain View, CA: COR).
2. Gary North in "Publisher's Preface," Ray Sutton, *That You May Prosper: Dominion by Covenant* (Tyler, TX: ICE, 1987) p. xii.
3. Ibid., p. xi.
4. Ibid., p. xiii.
5. Ibid., p. xiv.
6. Ray Sutton, Ibid., p. 7.
7. Ibid., p. 18.
8. Ibid., p. 72.
9. Ibid., p. 7.
10. R.J. Rushdoony, Institutes of Biblical Law, p. 99, cited by W.B. Tucker, p. 56.
11. *Thay You May Prosper*, p. 172.
12. Ibid., p. 181.
13. Ibid., p. 70.
14. Ibid., p. 71.
15. Ibid., p. 204.
16. Ibid., p. 210.
17. Lester Sumrall, *World Harvest*, October, 1986, p. 15.
18. COR sphere document, "The Christian World View of Pastoral Renewal," Article 15.
19. Ibid., Specific Actions 6.

Chapter 5

1. A Manifesto for the Christian Church, Declaration and Covenant, July 5, 1986 (Mountain View, CA: Coalition on Revival), p. 18.
2. Gary North, *Unholy Spirits* (Fort Worth: Dominion Press, 1986), p. 394.
3. Kingdom College brochure
4. Ibid.
5. Ibid.
6. Ibid.

PART IV - ESCHATOLOGY

Chapter 1

1. David Chilton, *Paradise Restored:*, p. 221.

WHAT IS MEDIA SPOTLIGHT?

When Media Spotlight began in 1977, we were the first ministry on a national scale to specifically address the problems prevalent in the media, particularly in movies, television, toys, games, heresies in the church, and myriad other problems that have contributed to Christians living no differently from the rest of the world.

Through the mass media the world has evangelized the Church to a far greater extent than the Church has evangelized the world. Many Christians have become so dependent upon the media that they aren't aware of how lukewarm they have become. We have many testimonies from readers who tell us that because of Media Spotlight they no longer compromise their love for God with the need to be entertained. They have become aware of the effect the media have on their thinking, and are now more selective in their choices.

One of our major concerns is the religious media. There are in the Church many who teach contrary to God's Word. We address teachings, customs, traditions, and other aspects of the modern Church's influence upon the believer.

What has escaped the understanding of Christians in general is that what they believe is more often shaped by the teachings of men than by the Word of God. This is true even of "fundamental" and "evangelical" Christians who think they have a lock on truth because of the banner under which they display their Christianity.

The wisdom of the world is no substitute for God's Word, even if offered from the pulpits of conservative churches.

Jesus warns us in Matthew 24:21 that in the last days the love of many toward Him would grow cold because of the increase of evil in the world. There is little time to waste in the short span of human life granted us by God. We must choose today whom we will serve.

Media Spotlight is published by Media Spotlight Ministries, a Christian non-profit organization incorporated under the laws of California and operating in the state of Washington.

Proverbs 23:23 says, "Buy the truth, and sell it not." For this reason we do not sell our publications. They are sent to whomever desires to receive them, and we rely on the freewill gifts of those who believe in this ministry to the Body of Christ.

For those who would like to know, our cost to maintain one name on our mailing list is about $20 per year. This includes the costs for our magazine, which is produced four to six times per year, plus all of our special reports. Expenses for our radio and book publishing ministry are met through additional gifts.

We wish to stress that there is no obligation to receive Media Spotlight's publications. However, if you care to send any gifts now or in the future, we ask that you not send cash through the mail as we've had some problems in the past. A check or money order payable to Media Spotlight is best.

We hope you'll make Media Spotlight your ministry through your input of ideas, prayer, and regular financial support.

SPECIAL REPORTS

PLEASE MARK QUANTITY DESIRED

A SAMPLE PACKET INCLUDING OUR MAGAZINE WILL BE SENT WITH ALL ORDERS

___ **ACUPUNCTURE:** Magic Or Medical Science?

___ **ANGELS ON ASSIGNMENT** - Or Demons Of Deception?

___ **ARE YOU IN A CULT?** Questions To Answer

___ **C.S. LEWIS:** The Man And His Myths

___ **CARE BEARS:** Not Your Ordinary Yogi Bear

___ **COALITION ON REVIVAL:** A Biblical Analysis (included in the book, *Vengeance Is Ours*)

___ **DRAGONRAID:** Can Fantasy Role-playing Games Be "Christianized?"

___ **DUNGEONS & DRAGONS:** A Look at Fantasy Role-playing Games

___ **E.T.:** Space-Age Messiah

___ **FACTS & FALLACIES OF THE RESURRECTION:** Did Jesus Really Die On Friday And Rise On Sunday?

___ **THE FORCE BEHIND THE FORCE:** Star Wars Theology Examined

___ **THE GOSPEL IN THE ZODIAC:** A Biblical Analysis

___ **GANDHI:** The Movie, The Man

___ **HALLOWE'EN:** Should Christians Be Apart?

___ **INNER HEALING:** A Biblical Analysis (80-page booklet)

___ **JEHOVAH'S WITNESSES:** Comparing Their Teachings With Scripture

___ **LATTER-DAY PROPHETS:** The Kansas City Connection

___ **MARTIAL ARTS AND THE CHRISTIAN**

___ **A MASONIC HISTORY OF AMERICA**

___ **ORAL ROBERTS:** An Open Letter Regarding False Prophecies

___ **THE ORIGINS OF CHRISTMAS TRADITIONS**

___ **OUT ON A LIMB:** New Age Evangelism And The Church

___ **PSYCHIC COUNSELING:** Astrology, Palmistry, Tarot

___ **PSYCHOLOGY:** Science Or Religion?

___ **REBECCA & ELAINE:** Can Christians Be Demon-Possessed?

___ **SIX ROMAN CATHOLIC DOCTRINES THAT NULLIFY SALVATION BY GRACE** (46-page booklet)

___ **GARY SMALLEY:** The Psychology Of Matriarchy

___ **STIGMATA:** Is Lucy Rael For Real?

___ **THIS PRESENT DARKNESS:** Spiritual Warfare - Fact Or Fantasy?

___ **THE UNICORN:** Fabled Beast Of Myth And Magic

PLEASE PRINT CLEARLY

Name _____

Address _____

City _____ State ____ Zip _____

Enclosed is my gift to the ministry: $_____

Please send _____ copies of your book, *Vengeance Is Ours* (requested donation $8.95 ea.)

MEDIA SPOTLIGHT • P.O. BOX 290 • REDMOND, WA 98073-0290